MALTA

PREHISTORY AND TEMPLES

MALTA

PREHISTORY AND TEMPLES

DAVID H. TRUMP

PHOTOGRAPHY
DANIEL CILIA

MIDSEA BOOKS

TEMPLE GRAPHICS CODE:

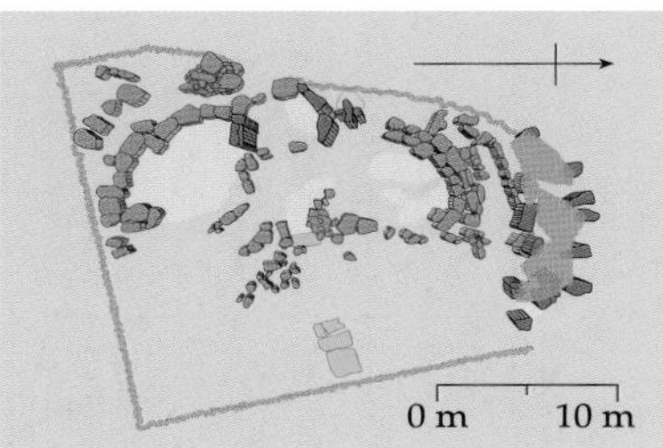

Ground (rock, soil, etc...)

Upright Megaliths

Small Upright Megaliths

Capstones

Ground Flagstones

Torba

Stone Fill

Altars, Statues, etc...

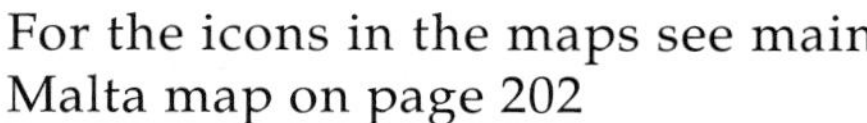
For the icons in the maps see main Malta map on page 202

Images on previous pages:
Page 1: Illustration of an image on a sherd found in the terrace retaining wall at Ġgantija.
Pages 2-3: Back wall of the Ġgantija Temples.
Page 6: Watercolour by Charles Brochtorff of the Ġgantija complex, c.1820.

PROLOGUE

The archaeological monuments surviving on the Maltese islands attracted interest from a very early date, and many people visited, wondered at, and speculated about them. Today most of the answers then suggested seem quaint, to say the least, but without those questions being asked, we would have known much less than we do. It is salutary to wonder how many current beliefs and interpretations will be replaced, or ridiculed, in the years to come.

We may, I think, leave aside the earliest, popular attribution of the prehistoric temples to giants – not unreasonable given the size of their building-blocks and the state of knowledge at the time. In the sixteenth century, Quintinus Haeduus mentioned ruins near Marsaxlokk, which are rather more likely to have been the Phoenician temple at Tas-Silġ than the Bronze Age defensive wall at Borġ in-Nadur. Commendatore G.F. Abela certainly referred to the prehistoric sites in his *Della Descrittione di Malta* (1647), though it was another 250 years before anyone realized that they were indeed prehistoric.

His descriptions were expanded and republished by Count G.A. Ciantar in 1772. Thereafter, interest increased sharply. A number of visitors to the islands recorded what they had seen. The most useful of these was the engraver to Louis XVI, Jean Houel who, in *Voyages pittoresque des isles de Sicile, de Malte, et de Lipari* (1787), published not only descriptions but a number of plans and views, still useful to us in showing how the sites appeared in his day, before any clearance or excavation had been done. Later, in

1819, the English antiquary Sir Richard Colt Hoare was among many other interested visitors, though neither he nor they added much useful information.

By the 1820s, clearance of some of the sites had begun – one can hardly call it excavation. Otto Bayer dug into the Xagħra Circle in 1826 and emptied the Ġgantija nearby in 1827. In 1839 Col. J.G. Vance did the same at Ħaġar Qim, and the following year at Mnajdra. Neither finds nor records were kept, and publication was sketchy in the extreme, if attempted at all.

Again the most helpful records were from artists, particularly Charles Brochtorff, who left drawings and watercolours of Bayer's sites. Although no further digging took place until A.A Caruana investigated Borġ in-Nadur in 1881 and Kordin in 1892, knowledge of the temples gained some wider recognition, though most writers, including Caruana himself, still regarded them as Phoenician.

This guess, though still wide of the mark, is again understandable. Like the Gauls and the ancient Britons in their respective homelands, the Phoenicians were the earliest known people in the islands. As early as 1819, Christian Thomsen in Denmark had propounded the revolutionary idea which became embodied in the so-called Three Age System. He realized that not only was Europe inhabited long before the classical writers first named their occupants, but that the occupation covered an immensely long period which could be subdivided according to whether stone, bronze, or iron was in use for tools and weapons. In view of the casual approach to excavation, the absence of metal in the Maltese temples had probably not even been noticed, let alone its significance realized. To most people, the temples were still 'Phoenician'.

In 1901 the German scholar Albert Mayr in *Die vorgeschichtlichen Denkmäler vom Malta* at last brought the evidence from the sites together, and realized that they were far older than the Phoenicians, and strangely different from anything else known through the Mediterranean.

By then, excavation techniques were beginning to improve too. Father E. Magri dug a temple site at Xewkija in 1900 and published it. Unfortunately, if he kept notes and finds from the much more important site of Ħal Saflieni, 1902-06, they could not be found after he left for missionary work abroad, where he died in 1907. Dr Thomas Ashby of the British School at Rome worked with T.E. Peet from 1908 to 1911 on a number of sites, including Ħaġar Qim, Mnajdra, Kordin III, Santa Verna, and Baħrija, and again published them at least to the standards of the day.

Most importantly of all, Dr, later Sir, Themistocles Zammit, Director of the Malta Museum from 1904, took over work at the Hypogeum of Ħal Saflieni in 1910, and made the best of a bad job in rescuing information from the deposits not cleared by Magri.

The real breakthrough came when he began work at the newly-discovered temple at Tarxien in 1915. At last a clear stratigraphy showed that the amorphous mass of prehistoric pottery could be divided into a Neolithic, lacking any metal, and a Bronze Age, though it took a Zammit to dig, record, and interpret carefully enough to demonstrate this.

Further subdivision, however, had to wait another 35 years. During that time, many more sites were investigated and much new material recovered, from temples at Xrobb il-Għaġin, Borġ in-Nadur, Mġarr, Tal-Qadi, and Buġibba, by Ashby, Dr Margaret Murray, and Zammit himself. Three things were needed before a coherent story could emerge from all this. Firstly, a fresh look was required by someone not bogged down in the details of a particular site. Secondly, knowledge of the advances being made in other parts of the Mediterranean, particularly Sicily, was required. That in turn went some way towards the third requirement, a means of establishing a chronology, of putting dates on the Maltese periods.

In the early 1950s, a survey of the islands' antiquities was commissioned, backed by the Royal University of Malta and the National Museum, with funds provided by the Inter-University Council for Higher Education in the Colonies. John D. Evans, later Dr Evans and later still Prof Evans, director of the Institute of Archaeology, London University, was entrusted with the task, and brought to it those necessary skills.

Evans first produced a typological sequence of the local pottery, backed by a wide-ranging comparative study of pottery styles elsewhere, not previously attempted. Then, in key-hole excavations on a number of sites, he confirmed the validity of at least the greater part of that sequence. Furthermore, he clearly demonstrated its value by tying the development of the temples into it. His masterly publication of the sequence in the *Proceedings of the Prehistoric Society* in 1953, expanded in 1959 and 1971 (see bibliography), provided the foundation for all subsequent work on Maltese prehistory.

His chronology, however, again suffered from the climate of opinion prevailing at the time. In the absence of objective evidence, it was the fashion in the 1950s for all dates to be reduced to the bare minimum. He suggested 'the first colonization of Malta probably during the last centuries of the third millennium BC' (PPS 1953, p.93), while he quoted 'evidence compelling us to date Period Ic [Tarxien] in Malta at least in part to the sixteenth century BC' (PPS 1953, p.82), with the Tarxien Cemetery following by about 1500 BC. Zammit's estimates, perhaps guestimates would describe them better, had been 3000 and 2000 BC.

Further progress came between 1958 and 1963 when, as curator of archaeology at the National Museum, I was able to excavate further at Borġ in-Nadur, Baħrija and, most significantly, at Skorba.

There the whole Neolithic (this term will shortly need qualification) sequence was present in stratigraphic order, switching two of the Evans phases and adding two new ones. Furthermore, by that time, the new technique of radiocarbon dating had become available (see p. 309), and was employed with the following results: first colonization by 5,000 BC, the temples began about 3,500 and fell, to be replaced by the Tarxien Cemetery Bronze Age about 2500. It will be noted that Zammit's guesswork can only be described as inspired. Equally valuable were traces of underlying huts, the long-sought-after settlement site, and the footings of a much earlier sanctuary.

Just as unexpected were the discoveries in the 1970s of a temple and Bronze Age occupation by the Italian team excavating the Punic temple site at Tas-Silġ and a rich Borġ in-Nadur deposit at Għar Mirdum, below Dingli Cliffs. The next major advance came with the investigation of the mysterious Xagħra Circle between 1987 and 1994, where a second hypogeum was found whose contents are still under study at the time of writing. This already goes far to make up for the information lost at Ħal Saflieni.

Another unencumbered settlement site recently discovered at Taċ-Ċawla, Victoria, should illuminate another very dark area in our understanding, the nature of the Temple Period settlements. Meanwhile, there are also new questions being asked, on population estimates, social organisation, and religious practices. Prof Lord Renfrew, Drs S. Stoddart and C. Malone, and Prof A. Bonanno have contributed usefully here. The future too looks bright as new techniques of analysis are developed. In particular, the application of DNA studies to the human remains could soon prove to be highly informative. It is through advances like this that we may shortly have to revise our story drastically.

It has to be acknowledged that in many of the matters treated here there is ample scope for differences of interpretation, even controversy. I have tried to indicate where such differences exist, but to attempt to give equal coverage to all of them would be neither warranted by their merits nor justified within the set limits. I have at least attempted to quote fairly the evidence currently available, for and against, on which I have based my own, or which seem to me to be preferred to those advanced by others.

Images on the next pages, from left to right: Top: Għar Dalam, Skorba figurine, Tarxien Temples, Ta' Ċenc dolmen, Baħrija lamp, Roman mosaic

Bottom: Bryn Celli Ddu: Anglesey, UK, Jemdet Nasr Tablet: Iraq; Saqqara Pyramid: Egypt; Stonehenge: UK; Gold Mask: Mycenae; The Parthenon: Greece

The succession of cultures followed each other in Malta over a span o
five thousand years, with one hiccup at 2500 BC. The chart is necessaril
much simplified for presentation in this form.
For example, the first temples appeared only about 3500 BC. Othe
parts of the world each followed their own trajectories, with ever

THE NEOLITHIC — TEMPLE PERIOD

5000 BC | 4500 BC | 4000 BC | 3500 BC | 3000 BC

GĦAR DALAM

GREY SKORBA

RED SKORBA

ŻEBBUĠ

MĠARR

ĠGANTIJA

SAFLIENI

TARXIEN

5000 BC | 4000 BC | 3000 BC

COLONIZATION
IMPRESSED WARE
WEST EUROPE MEGALITHS

WRITING MESOPOTAMIA
EGYPT

COPPER I
INDUS CI

greater simplification on the chart. As pointed out in the text, the irst of Egypt's pyramids was raised only after the fall of Malta's emples.

A closer comparison of dates between Malta and the rest of the world s made in the box on Worldwide Contemporaries, p.241.

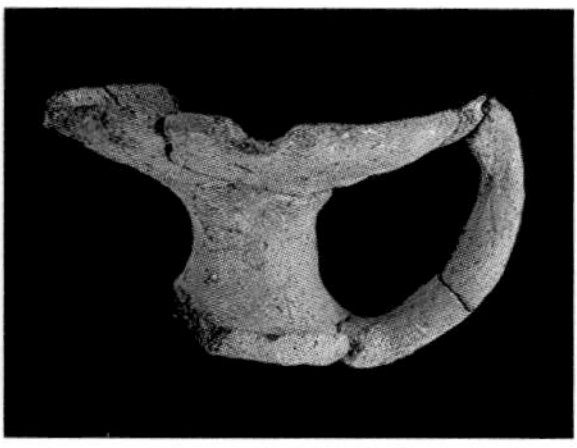

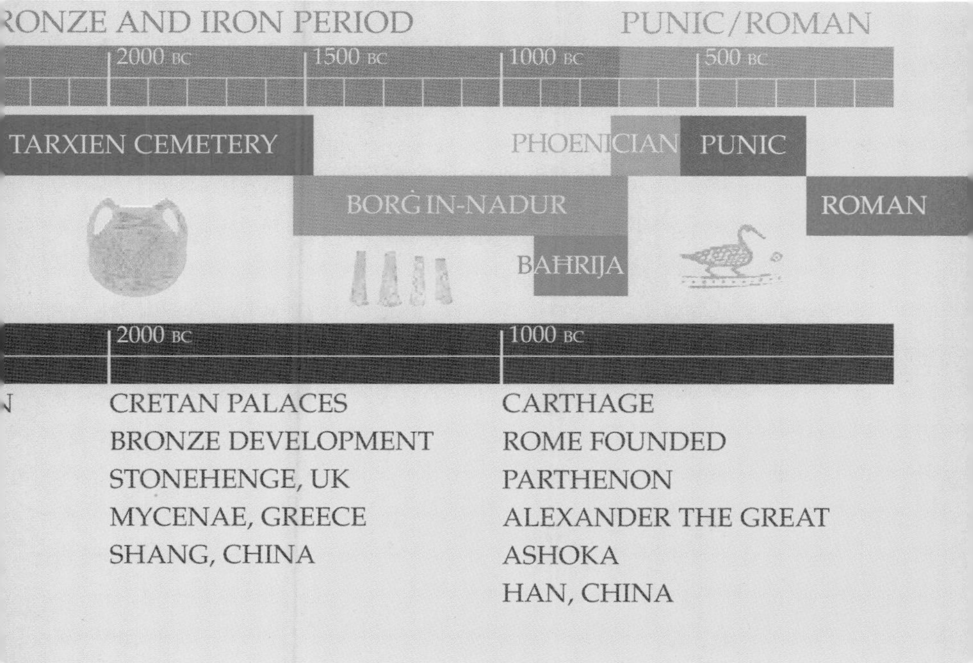

RONZE AND IRON PERIOD

PUNIC/ROMAN

2000 BC | 1500 BC | 1000 BC | 500 BC

TARXIEN CEMETERY

PHOENICIAN

PUNIC

BORĠ IN-NADUR

ROMAN

BAHRIJA

2000 BC | 1000 BC

N

CRETAN PALACES
BRONZE DEVELOPMENT
STONEHENGE, UK
MYCENAE, GREECE
SHANG, CHINA

CARTHAGE
ROME FOUNDED
PARTHENON
ALEXANDER THE GREAT
ASHOKA
HAN, CHINA

Malta and Gozo are small islands set well out in the Mediterranean Sea. To understand the development of human societies on the islands, we have to look first at their nature and position. These do not dictate, but certainly influence, what their inhabitants were and were not able to do. The fascinating interaction of society and environment will be explored in later chapters.

CHAPTER 1

THE ISLANDS IN PREHISTORY

From the time fully human settlers began spreading round the Mediterranean coasts, the over-all geography of the Maltese islands has hardly changed. A little land has been lost by cliff erosion in the south and west, and a little more through a small rise in sea level – or subsidence of the land – in the north and east. The islands' general shape, altitude, and distance from Sicily were then much as they are now.

A recent claim that remains of a temple have been recognized at a considerable depth off the north coast of Malta should be treated with caution. So far beneath the surface, the site could hardly have been dry land at any time since the ocean breached the barrier now marked by the Straits of Gibraltar, at a period in geological time since the water of the world's oceans was locked up in the arctic ice sheets during the last

The rocky islet of Filfla off their south coast effectively symbolizes the islands' remoteness between the wide expanses of sea and sky.

Ice Age, 15,000 or more years ago. Without going so far as to say that the claim is impossible, before being taken seriously it would require far stronger evidence than has yet been offered that the features observed were indeed of human construction, as opposed to the work of mermaids.

Wied Ħanzira below Xewkija cuts into the limestone. It protects a fragment of natural vegetation while, on the slopes above, farmers have terraced the thin soils for cultivation.

However, there have been three major changes in surface details. One is the transfer of great quantities of soil by erosion from what are now bare rocky uplands to low-lying alluvial plains, notably the Marsa at the head of Grand Harbour and Burmarrad inland from Salina Bay. At both, the sea once extended much farther inland, as shown by Roman harbour works along Stables Street beside the Marsa, for example, a kilometre from the present water front. This additional surface area probably balances the losses mentioned above, leaving the total, then and now, at or very close to 314 square kilometres (121 square miles). Secondly, there is every reason to suppose that before it was cleared to make way for fields and grazing, much of the land surface would have been covered with trees, presumably mainly pine and evergreen oak. These had almost completely vanished by the Bronze Age, as shown by pollen samples from cisterns at Tal-Mejtin, Luqa.

Thirdly there are the houses, churches, roads, field walls, and all

hose other constructional works of nan. They are obviously the result of human interference, but the other wo are also. It was by stripping the ree cover and breaking up the surace for growing their crops that the armers exposed the soil to erosion. The only places in Malta or Gozo today where we can get any idea of their appearance in prehistoric times are probably in the rock tumble of the *irdum* slopes below the western cliffs.

The human geography, as opposed to the topography, has changed in another and less obvious way. As already mentioned, Malta's position in the Mediterranean has not altered, 80 km south of Sicily, 290 east of Tunisia, 355 north of Libya, and 815 west of Crete, but the significance of that position has, and drastically so. Since the Phoenicians mastered the art of open-sea, day-and-night, navigation around 1000 BC, Malta has been the meeting place of busy shipping routes.

Given also its magnificent harbours, its strategic importance to the military and commercial fleets of Phoenicia, Carthage, Rome, the medieval dynasties, the Order of St John, the French, the British, and the present need no spelling out. Earlier sailors did not dare the open seas but clung to the coasts, mooring or hauling their boats ashore every night. In those circumstances, shipping routes had perforce to follow the shores. The crossing from Cape Passero in Sicily to the north coast of Malta and Gozo could be achieved in a day, but not that from Malta to Libya, still less to Crete or the Levant. Any longer voyage would start with a return to Sicily, thence to follow its shores east or west, hopping by intermediate islands to Tunisia and Africa or to Greece, Turkey, and Asia.

At an earlier stage still, there were no sailors at all, since there were as yet no sea-going boats. Inhabitants of Sicily might have noticed that cloud cap off to the south, or even on exceptionally clear

Although winter rains produce lush green vegetation and even some standing water, as here in Marsalforn valley, Gozo, summer heat soon evaporates the latter and scorches the former to brown. Yet within the terraced fields, rich seasonal crops can be raised.

days seen land beneath it, but would have been quite unable to reach it.

Since we are here interested in the prehistoric period, only that second stage concerns us, with the Maltese islands a *cul de sac* or back-water, accessible but remote.

That proves to be the main key to understanding the extraordinary developments it witnessed.

The basic structure of the islands, with all its consequences for human exploitation, has changed even less than their shape. Leaving the superficial deposits aside, five superimposed layers can be clearly recognized all laid down beneath the se which covered the area in th Miocene era, between 27 and million years ago, a period lon enough for substantial changes o conditions.

The lowest and highest layers both of Coralline Limestone, wer built up, as their name suggests by corals in warm, clear, shal low seas. The result is a hard an durable rock, almost impossibl to shape until the introductio of efficient metal tools. It could however, be split, producing slab of strongly weather-resistant ston for building. Over time, though a a very slow rate, it is dissolved by rainwater, leaving a characteristi bright red fertile soil, the ħamr-ija. Further dissolution resulted in the formation of caves as sur-

Bare limestone plateaux break down over slopes of Blue Clay to an even bluer sea along the northwest coast of Malta. Here Ġnejna and Għajn Tuffieħa bays are in the foreground with the wide sweep of Gozo in the distance.

The soft yellow Globigerina Limestone of Malta was laid down on ocean beds several million years ago. Here in a quarry at Qrendi it can be seen how readily it splits into very convenient blocks for building. Where less cracked, it can still be easily cut. The nature of the stone itself encouraged both megalithic architecture and the delicate carving so characteristic of the temples, as well as of much later periods. While it can support tree cover, like the dark carobs in the background here, its surface can be, and for long has been, broken up to produce fertile fields. By contrast, the local Coralline Limestone is resistant to both tools and weather.

face water found cracks to drain through and enlarge.

The land surface then sank, allowing a deep sea ooze consisting of the skeletons of myriads of minute creatures living in it, predominantly the Globigerina Foraminifera. This also hardened into limestone over succeeding millions of years, though of a very different kind. It is homogeneous, a rich golden colour, and much easier to cut, making a very convenient building stone, though more liable to weathering. It also produces a soil more rapidly than the Coralline Limestone, since the process of soil formation can be speeded up by breaking up the surface of the rock and, by repeated cultivation, pulverizing it. In addition, in places chert formed within it, only slightly inferior to flint for flaking into tools.

The land then rose again, though still below sea level. However, a continental landmass had emerged at no great distance, from which debris washed into the sea as mud, to accumulate as Blue Clay. This had two main uses to the later human inhabitants. It provided the raw material for pottery and other clay products and, even more significantly, water falling as rain on the Upper Coralline was trapped by this impermeable layer, to break out as prolific life-giving springs around the slopes. Above this, a thin layer of Greensand, a rather misleading term, being neither green nor sand, has little significance, either economically or scenically.

The cliffs on the north side of Ras ir-Raħeb are the face of the Great Fault, on the right of the photo.
The displacement of the strata is clearly visible in the scarp at the head of Fomm ir-Riħ bay.

The Upper Coralline Limestone, barely distinguishable by eye from the lower, forms the high plateaux of western Malta and the characteristic flat-topped hills of Gozo.

The slopes of Blue Clay are most noticeable on the west side of Malta between the upper and lower cliffs, their soft consistency undermining the former and explaining the tumble of rocks forming the *irdum* slopes. Most of central and eastern Malta, and the main central plateau of Gozo, are of Globigerina, and it is in these areas, at Mqabba, Naxxar, Sannat, and San Lawrenz particularly, that the enormous building stone quarries are found. The Lower Coralline is exposed mainly near sea level, though it extends to enormous depths beneath it as was shown by boreholes seeking oil. In two areas it outcrops at much higher levels. These are around Naxxar and again at Ta' Ċenċ, where pressures on major fault lines have pushed blocks of Lower Coralline way above neighbouring Globigerina.

Faulting is indeed a major feature of Maltese scenery, explaining the alternating ridges and valleys across the north of Malta, and particularly the scarp crowned by the Victoria Lines, the Great Fault. This is most noticeable at the head of Fomm ir-Riħ at its western end, where the actual thrust of the fault

s clearly visible, continuing the ine of the Ras ir-Raħeb cliffs. Farher east the upper lip has tended o crumble, partly obscuring the still impressive scarp.

The second complication is that he five major deposits listed above are of far from uniform thickness. The Blue Clay, for example, which forms spectacular slopes many metres high west of Mġarr is much less apparent on the eastern side of the high ground or in Gozo, though still sufficient to produce those important springs.

The importance of those last is increased by the nature of Malta's climate. Typically Mediterranean, the rainfall, averaging 55 cm though very variable from year to year, is largely confined to the winter months, the summer being marked by drought. Already in the Neolithic, methods of water catchment and storage were devised, as shown by cisterns of the period, one within the Ħal Saflieni complex, others at Misqa, the hilltop above Mnajdra. Simpler bell-shaped ones are found on many Bronze Age sites. Those springs would still have been of vital importance, providing the island's main water supply, as they continue to do today, though now having to be supplemented by desalination plants. As with rainfall, so it is with temperature, again typically Mediterranean summers are hot but not unbearably so, while winters are comparatively mild and frost virtually unknown. Strong winds can be a feature at all seasons, which could interfere with trade and fishing, though rarely for more than a few days at a time.

Malta and Gozo were then as now well suited to human habitation, providing soils, water, chert for tools, seafood. There were, however, omissions. Timber, though present, was limited, and probably increasingly inadequate to meet rising demands.

As with many islands of restricted size, game was almost non-existent. Flint was lacking and even the Coralline Limestone

The Blue Clay weathers into bare slopes, where it is readily accessible for making mud bricks or pottery. This example is near Għasri, Gozo.

was nowhere near hard enough for ground-stone tools. Later and more seriously, there were no local metal ores. Only overseas trade could supply these needs.

'Suitable for human habitation' is obviously a very general expression. How many people are we talking about? Population figures before the days of accurate censuses are notoriously difficult to obtain, depending as they do on so many different factors. We have looked at area, accessibility, and climate. At least as important as any or all of these is economy, how that population obtains its subsistence, and this has changed far more than any of the others.

There is little level land and elaborate terracing is necessary to keep the thin soils from washing off slopes, like this one below in-Nuffara, Gozo.

Streams like this at Fiddien, beyond Rabat, are rare on the islands, and very few flow all year round.

Today, Malta is built into a world economy; exports, services, and the remittances from emigrants support a population well over 350,000. Under the Order and the British, funds poured into the islands for strategic reasons, distorting the economy. In Roman times there was a flourishing export of high quality textiles. Before that, with the population's subsistence depending on its own productivity and with agricultural methods much less advanced than today's, numbers would have been far lower. Figures based on the few and unreliable medieval statistics and on estimates of the 'carrying capacity', based on

areas with similar environments, resources, and simple agricultural technology, like the Aegean islands, naturally vary, but cluster around a figure of 10,000 people.

Advances in agriculture since the prehistoric period were few, and could probably be balanced out against the reduction in soil cover as discussed above. 10,000 then is as close an estimate as we are likely to get for the maximum number of people the island could support in prehistoric times, but it has to be remembered that this is only a very rough estimate.

Malta's superb natural harbours have been of great historical importance, and have attracted the densest settlement around them. Above is Marsamxett, with Valletta, Manoel Island, and Gżira.

On the other side of Grand Harbour, below, are the Dockyard, the tightly packed promontories of Senglea and Vittoriosa, with Bighi and Fort Ricasoli beyond.

The first settlers found empty islands, which they tamed and cultivated, building up their population and culture steadily over two and a half thousand years.

CHAPTER 2

BEFORE THE TEMPLES

The earliest concrete evidence for human occupation of the islands goes back to the early Neolithic period, by which time the human population had adopted farming, in the broadest sense, allowing them to settle in permanent villages, though still using stone for their main tools. More specifically, thanks to radiocarbon, we can set a date on this.

First published as 4190+160BC (see p.309), with the correction available through tree-ring dates, we would now place this at 5266-4846 BC, or around 5000 BC in round figures. The dated sample came from a deposit at Skorba alongside a substantial wall. That does not look like the work of pioneer colonists but of a well-established farming community. How much earlier the first settlement might have occurred is a matter of pure guesswork. It has been known since the 1960s that men were

Għar Dalam, an impressive cave near Marsaxlokk Bay (see p.56) was hollowed out by percolating water over millions of years. Later, the bones of numerous Pleistocene animals accumulated on its floor. Long after this, it attracted early human occupation.

In the Għar Dalam Museum are displaye a sample of the enormous number of bone of hippopotamus and other animals long extinct in these islands.

sailing the Mediterranean by 8000 BC, well before farming had been introduced to the area. The proof comes from the discovery of obsidian, a highly-prized volcanic glass which will be discussed later (see p. 66), in levels of that date in the cave of Franchthi on the south-eastern tip of the Peloponnese. There is no obsidian on the mainland of Greece, so it had to have been brought by boat from the island of Melos, 60 km out into the Aegean. The distance from Sicily to Malta is not much greater, and Palaeolithic and Mesolithic material is well-known from many Sicilian sites, from Messina in the east to the Egadi islands in the far west, most notably at the Grotta del Uzzo near Palermo. Thus an earlier colonization of our islands was by no means impossible.

There is one small clue whic may or may not be relevant. Bac in the Pleistocene, Malta had a faun including strange creatures lik pygmy elephants and hippopotamuses, giant swans, and dormice represented by their bones in Għa Dalam and other caves and fissures None of these occurs in deposit containing human cultural material. Why did they become extinct It is now well documented tha many aberrant isolated faunas, fron Majorca to New Zealand and Patagonia, survived down to the arriva of the first human settlers, but die

out immediately afterwards. With some cases it is proven, in virtually all of them highly probable, that this was no coincidence, that the new arrivals in a short space of time hunted to extinction the ill-prepared native animals and birds – a little antelope in Majorca, the giant ostrich-like moa in New Zealand, the ground sloth in Patagonia, and many others.

It may be, then, that the Pleistocene animals failed to survive into later times because man had wiped them out. Even if this was the case in Malta, however, we have no close date on the disappearance of the one and their replacement by the other.

More recently, and much more startlingly, vastly earlier flintwork of Lower to Middle Palaeolithic type, and so dating to before 100,000 years ago, has now been confirmed from Sardinia, an island which, although at that time attached to Corsica, has never been separated from continental Italy by less than 20 km of open sea, even with sea levels at their lowest. That early date was even before the appearance of modern man, so boats must have been available to our forebears, *Homo erectus*. The fact remains, however, that despite early claims of 'Neanderthal' teeth from Għar Dalam, claims recently revived, and of Palaeolithic cave art in Għar Ħassan, and Clactonian and microlithic flints from various much later sites, there is no secure evidence yet for human settlement before the end of the sixth millennium BC, much though we should welcome it. We can begin our story safely only with the early farmers. If they had predecessors here, they would have been wandering hunters and food gatherers, and of these no traces have yet come to light. In view of the absence of suitable river gravel and nil returns so far from the Maltese caves, it is on the whole very unlikely that they will be found now, even if they had once existed.

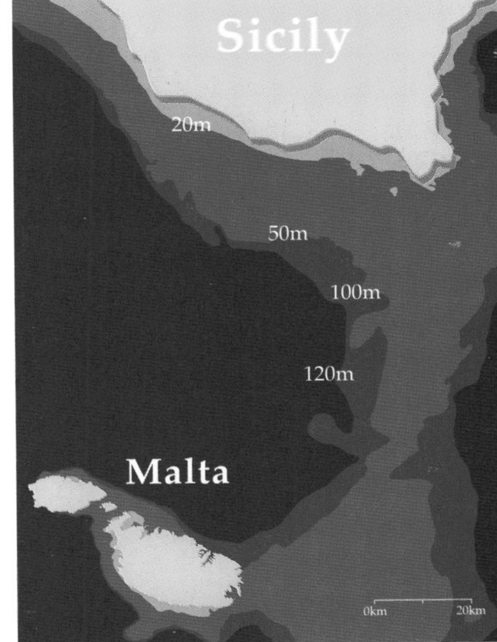

If the Mediterranean sea level were to drop by 100 m, as it did at the peak of the Ice Ages, Malta would be joined to Sicily by a long curving isthmus.

By 5000 BC, sea crossings, though always hazardous, were no barrier to settlers. As good farming land was taken up, and populations in the new colonies rose, boatloads of pioneers pushed on along the coasts, and across any straits which threatened to limit their expansion. The coastwise distribution of sites gives ample confirmation of this picture, reinforced once more by the evidence of the obsidian. In the western basin of the Mediterranean it is found naturally on only four islands, Lipari off the north coast of Sicily, Pantelleria between it and Tunisia, Palmarola off the bay of Naples, and Monte Arci in western Sardinia. Yet from before 5000 BC fragments of it have been recovered from cultural deposits of a great many sites, not only on those islands but widely on Sicily and the mainlands of southern Europe and North Africa. Malta, for example was receiving obsidian from both Lipari and Pantelleria.

This leads on to a number of questions which we cannot yet answer. We have guessed at the driving force which pushed colonists on to settle ever more distant shores, and the nature of the obsidian and other trade will be reviewed later. Where we have to admit almost total ignorance is on the question of what sort of boats were used for those sea-crossings.

The sea must always have been important to the Maltese. The first inhabitants arrived across it and continued to import exotic raw materials. It was also a source for fish and an influence on the climate.

Ve come closest to the early Maltese when e contemplate their mortal remains, ut dry bones are still depressingly npersonal. Progress is being made, owever, in methods for reconstructing he living appearance of long dead persons nd on studying their diseases and ijuries. Though work is in progress on he latter, particularly with the skeletons ecovered from the hypogeum beneath the Xagħra Circle, the former has not yet been ttempted here.
'he skull illustrated is one of the few reserved ones from Ħal Saflieni.

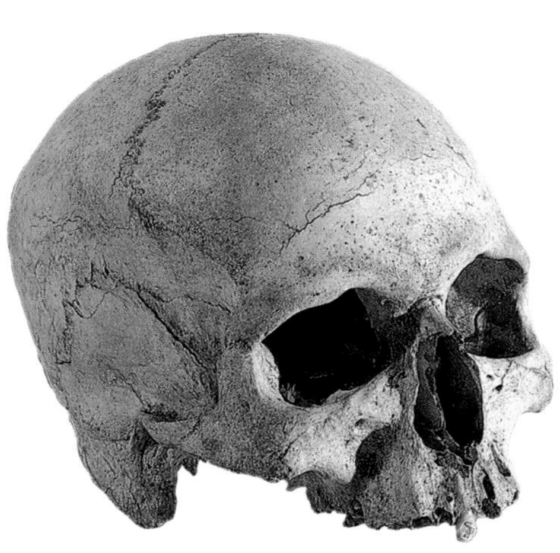

The oldest sea-going vessel of which we have surviving remains, found under Dover in England, dates only from the second millennium BC, while we want to know about those of three to four thousand years before that. We have earlier vessels, found buried beside the pyramids of Egypt and going back to 2500, but these were river craft rather than sea-going vessels. From the same country, pictures of boats on pots go back a thousand years earlier, but again river boats, and not very clearly depicted either. Much earlier dugout canoes have been recovered from peat bogs or river clays in northwest Europe, but they would be quite unsuitable for any but quiet inland waters, the rivers, and lakes by which they were found. All that we know about the seafarers between Sicily and Malta at this early period is that they managed it somehow.

Although now largely discredited, the evidence of skull shapes (see box, p. 29) tended to confirm that the first Maltese were an offshoot of the long-headed race widely distributed round the Mediterranean, as is only to be expected.

While detailed measurements of the numerous skulls recovered from the Xagħra Hypogeum have not been taken, such is the current scepticism of their significance, it can be said as a generalisation that almost all from that site fall within the long to middle range. The exercise might become much more worthwhile in the unlikely event of a group from the Bronze Age becoming available for study and comparison.

The story must begin at Għar Dalam (p. 56), a cave in the side of a rocky valley running down to Marsaxlokk Bay. This had trapped the bones of that extraordinary range of Pleistocene animals, washed off the surrounding hills. As has been said, though, so far there is nothing to suggest that there were men and women about at the time.

Evidence of habitation came only from the topmost, disturbed, layer. Amongst the mixed material it contained, Evans recognized sherds of

This column of deposit in Għar Dalam was left by the excavators to demonstrate the succession of deposits within the cave.

A delicately decorated and highly polished sherd of an Għar Dalam bowl from Skorba is typical of the local Impressed Ware.

pottery virtually identical to that from Stentinello on the Sicilian coast, a local version of the widespread family of Impressed Wares found from Dalmatia to Spain.

Throughout that range, they were produced by the first farmers in the area, and he judged the same to be true of Malta. Accordingly he made Għar Dalam, the only site where this type of pottery was then known on these islands, the type site for his first phase. This despite the fact that there was no great quantity of it, and that it was mixed with sherds of obviously much later type. Since then it has appeared in several other places, from a cave at Għajn Abdul and as a surface scatter on Ta' Kuljat,

his seven-thousand-year-old length of all of the Għar Dalam phase was found neath the temples at Skorba.

both in western Gozo, and more importantly in an intact deposit at Taċ-Ċawla, Victoria, though this has yet to be investigated properly.

By far the clearest picture yet comes from Skorba, since it is the only one so far to give more than a scatter of pottery. What is clear is that the newcomers spread rapidly to establish a viable population over both islands.

A rich deposit of Għar Dalam domestic material was found beside a substantial stone wall beneath, but fortunately not completely masked by, the South Temple on that site, giving useful evidence on architecture, economy, and pottery, each of which will be examined in more detail in due course. Suffice it to say here that it confirms the presence of a farming community with its

KULLS

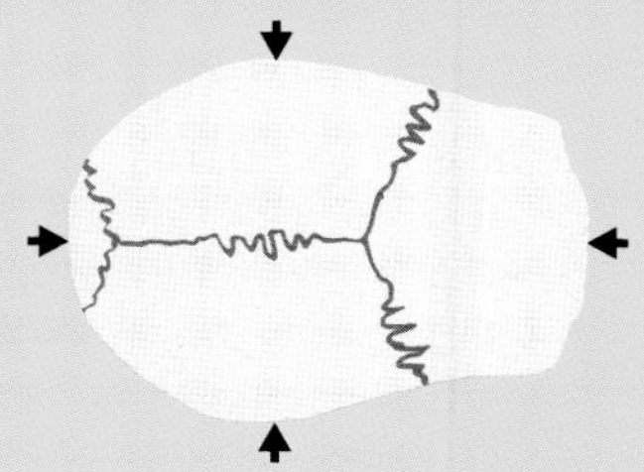

:ulls have for long been subject of particular udy, and obviously ill are for the origins man, an issue not ising in Malta. owever, we now ubt several of the nclusions we thought could draw from em, on their use for identifying races by comparison of their length and breadth, and their giving accurate estimates of their age at death from the closure of their sutures for example.

They can still give information on cause of death, particularly violent death, on some diseases, and on the sex of the individual (though here the pelvis is more reliable).

An exciting new development is of techniques for reconstructing the features of long deceased persons.

antecedents back in Sicily but now well established in Malta. Here its culture began to diverge.

Associated with a hut under the field east of the temples, the pottery could be seen to be evolving away from the ancestral Impressed Ware, into a purely local version, Grey Skorba. Although no transitional deposit between Grey and Red Skorba was identified, the similarities are so marked, particularly the continuation of the characteristic speckled fabric and evolution of the handle shapes, that continuity between these two phases is absolutely secure. The sudden appearance of red slip, perhaps also of the trumpet lugs, the two most distinctive features of this next phase, show that there were at least contacts, and resulting cultural influence, from Sicily

A beautifully slipped and polished jar of the Red Skorba phase has trumpet lugs set vertically on its wall. These are more usually placed horizontally.

at this time, where the same tw features are notably present in th Late Neolithic Diana Ware.

That being so, we are in mor of a quandary over the next phas in the Maltese sequence. Żebbu pottery has very little in commo in fabric, shape, or decoration wit Red Skorba, yet shows a stron resemblance to that of Copper Ag southeast Sicily, a complex of rela ed styles including San Cono, Pian Notaro, and Grotta Zubbia. Th problem lies in deciding whethe these similarities are close enoug and the preceding break marke

nough, to imply a new immigration of people across the straits, or only strengthening of commercial and ultural links. This must at present emain an open question until more vidence can be found. Unlike the imilar problem at the end of the 'emple Period, we cannot even ope for DNA tests to solve it for is, since so far we have found no uman skeletal remains from any of those first three phases. In the Żebbuġ phase we find the earliest Maltese rock-cut tombs, demonstrating the introduction of a new burial rite, and this strengthens the argument for new peoples, while alling far short of proving it.

Although there is little in the Żebbuġ material to suggest coninuity, it will be argued shortly hat certain elements occurring in he Red Skorba phase reappear in he Temple Period, which would mply survival of a cultural tradition. They include architecture and the figurines, to be described below. Whether or not the Żebbuġ phase represents a new wave of colonists, thereafter there is overwhelming evidence that there was no cultural break for the next millennium-and-a-half, through to the end of the Temple Period. Instead, Malta was left to follow its own local development of both pottery and, more remarkably, architecture, without further external stimuli, though the import of certain raw materials and a very few artefacts continued. The achievements of these people will provide the core of our story in the following pages, the climax of Maltese prehistory.

Not a great deal can be said about dwellings and settlements in the earliest period of the occupation of Malta.

Natural caves were certainly used on occasion, as at Għar Dalam itself and Għajn Abdul on Gozo. In the field to the east of the Skorba temples was found a hut of this period, or rather, the transition between the first two phases, Għar Dalam and Grey Skorba. All but the

Għar Dalam was not the only cave occupied. Early material was also recovered from others around Għajn Abdul, Santa Luċija, Gozo. Għar Mixta is the best of these caves to survive quarrying in the area.

lowest few centimetres had been ploughed away, though its clay floor did at the very least give us a plan for the building, an oval hut something over 6 metres long. Apart from some stones marking its line, all walls and superstructure had gone. In fact, the most important new evidence that this hut gave us was that, as guessed, Grey Skorba pottery had indeed evolved locally out of Għar Dalam. The pottery story will be reviewed shortly.

This hut is the only one from the earlier phases yet to come to light in its entirety. Others of the Żebbu and Mġarr phases were located i the deep trenches behind the we temple at the same site, but wer not fully exposed. Though othe sites are known, represented b surface scatters of pottery, in th absence of excavation we can onl suppose, though not prove, sim lar oval clay floors and stone wa footings, probably supporting mu brick walls. Even excavation migh not tell us more. Within the Xagħr Circle thin layers of deposit wit numerous Żebbuġ sherds atteste domestic occupation on the site, bu no structures had survived the late intensive cultivation of the shallo soil. Only the tomb (p. 60) cut dow into the protective rock was pre served.

So far this suggests a very sim ple society and architecture, bu

Only the floor and scanty traces of the wall survive of this hut at Skorba. But it is remarkable that anything is left from so long ago under such thin soil cover.

he field wall behind in the photograph corporates the outer wall of Skorba's ast Temple but there was no sign of the rlier structures alongside before their ccavation in 1963.
he irregular bedrock floor can be seen this, the southern of the two possible rines of the Red Skorba phase. The one footings survive, but the upper alls of mudbrick had crumbled into a rey sludge, which covered many exciting nds.

wo more structures found at Skorba show that that is not the whole picture.

Underlying the West Temple, and as a result only partly available or investigation, was an 11-metre length of straight wall. It was 1 m wide and survived for a height of 45cm. Though the deposit banked against it was of pure Għar Dalam domestic refuse, it did not itself look like a domestic structure. For example, there was no laid floor on either side of it, nor any sign in the area cleared of a return wall. Perhaps it formed part of some sort of enclosure. Only by the unacceptable sacrifice of the temple could it have been pursued further. We can only hope for a comparable structure to turn up on a less encumbered site.

Much clearer was a substantial building under the east field. Two adjacent chambers, 8.40 x 5.40 and 5.60 x 3.20 m stood side by side within solid masonry – a style of building we shall meet again in the later temples. Cobbled surfaces lay to east and west but the chambers had only the bare rock, often quite irregular, to serve as floors. The walls varied from 1 to 1.90 or more metres thick and stood 70 cm high. There was very little stone rubble and instead, both chambers were filled with blue-grey clay, in the lower levels of which nodules could be recognized. Clearly, the stone walls are much as they were built, having been continued upwards in mudbrick made of the Maltese Blue Clay, imported to the site for

This roughly carved stone, barely recognizable as a female human figure, was found with the more obvious ones on p.42 on the floor of the Red Skorba shrine.

the purpose. Roofing, of course, can only be guessed at. The irregularity of the floor, absence of hearths or even, in the case of the south room, a doorway, and the nature of the contents, including figurines and goat skulls to be discussed below, suggested that this building should be interpreted as a shrine, and so a precursor to the later temples.

To date, Skorba is still the only site to give detailed evidence on the economy of the earlier phases of Maltese prehistory. The deposit alongside the Għar Dalam wall was particularly informative. From it we recovered, grain by grain, nearly 50 cc of carbonized cereals in 1962. Only later were flotation techniques developed which, by separating organic matter from soil by wet sieving with detergent, would have done the job far more expeditiously. Forty c were of barley, but too distorte by the burning for the variety – 6 row or 2-row, to be determined though paradoxically had it no been burned it would not have sur vived at all. Another 3.5 cc wer identified as mostly *Triticum dicoc cum*, emmer wheat. Two or thre grains were of a naked wheat probably *T. compactum*, clu wheat. Five seeds were of a primi tive lentil, similar to specimen from Neolithic Anatolia. A coupl of weed seeds, madder (*Sherardia* and caterpillar (*Scorpiurus*), wer

lso noticed. Though only a small ample, it showed that at least hree cereals, and the lentils, had een introduced to Malta at this arly stage.

Indirect evidence, though none he less significant for that, is pro- ided by the number of querns and ccasional flints showing the charac- eristic gloss left by their having been sed for cutting straw. Both attest o the harvesting and processing of rain crops. Domestic animals were ven better represented. Sheep and oats were together the common- st, though expert analysis would be eeded to separate the two, a noto- iously difficult task. Cattle were lso frequent, of distinctly large size, heir numbers tending to decrease omewhat in later levels. A small log was also present.

It is noticeable, though perhaps ot surprising in view of the size of the islands and their distance rom other land, that no wild ani- nals were represented. The red leer recorded from late Pleistocene leposits had apparently been hunted out. One antler from a Tarxien phase leposit seems insufficient on its own o prove the red deer's survival to hat date since it might have been mported from Sicily. The bone sam- ple size was very much larger than for the grain.

The evidence, then, strongly suggests an economy based on mixed farming. No fish bones were noted, though the same flotation methods might have produced them too. Skorba, however, is well away from the coast. It would be surprising indeed if marine resources were not exploited from seashore sites.

While we lack human skeletons from the first three phases, those studied from the Żebbuġ tomb within the Xagħra Circle suggested that this economy was an efficient one since they showed an exceptionally healthy population. While the low incidence of bone fractures can hardly be attributed to a satisfactory diet, the absence of signs of malnutrition and low level of tooth decay provide more reliable evidence. The

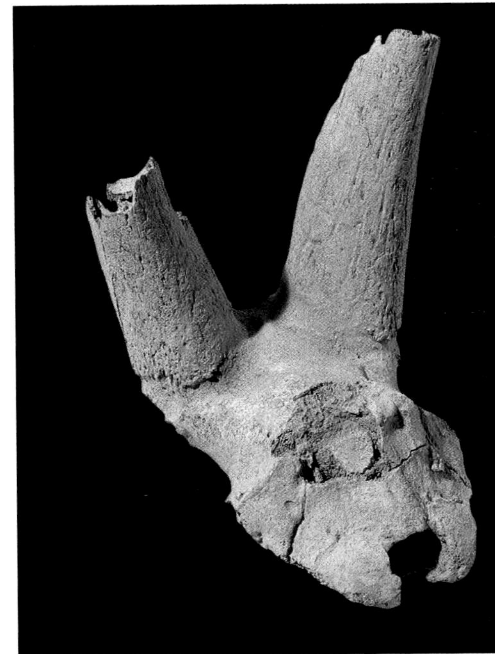

Goats were among the domestic animals of the early settlers. This fine skull with horns was found with others in the Red Skorba shrine, presumably a votive sacrifice.

earliest Maltese lived well, at least in comparison with later ones and their contemporaries elsewhere.

We have talked about food production as a general, and of course very necessary, activity, but not how it was organized, if at all. By and large at this stage it is highly likely that it was at a purely subsistence level, each family producing and consuming its own supplies from its own crops and stock. Doubtless there was co-operation between neighbours with tasks like house building where a larger labour force woul have had distinct advantages even more so for the constructio of a community building as th Skorba shrine presumably was Otherwise, cultivation and stoc raising were surely carried out a the household level, with surplu production required only for stor age against future shortage, t support social activities, or fo a limited amount of trade, to b considered shortly.

Securing an adequate supply c food was, of course, not the onl aspect of economics. The mai industry, if it can be called that, wa the manufacture of pottery. The rav materials were generally availabl equipment and expertise minima yet the need universal. Though ther could already have been specialis craftsmen, or -women, to suppl

Some sheep still graze the Maltese countryside, as they have done since the Early Neolithic.
These are Barbary sheep, not hybrids with goats as their goat-like heads might suggest.

Though cloth does not survive, spindle whorls show that yarn was regularly being spun, and presumably then woven. Loomweights would prove it, but these do not appear until the Borġ in-Nadur phase, when they become common.
This particularly fine whorl, unusual for both its decoration and its large size, 6.5 cm diameter, was found at Skorba in a Red Skorba level.
It is not known whether the fibres to be spun were from sheep's wool or from some vegetable source, both of which were certainly readily available.

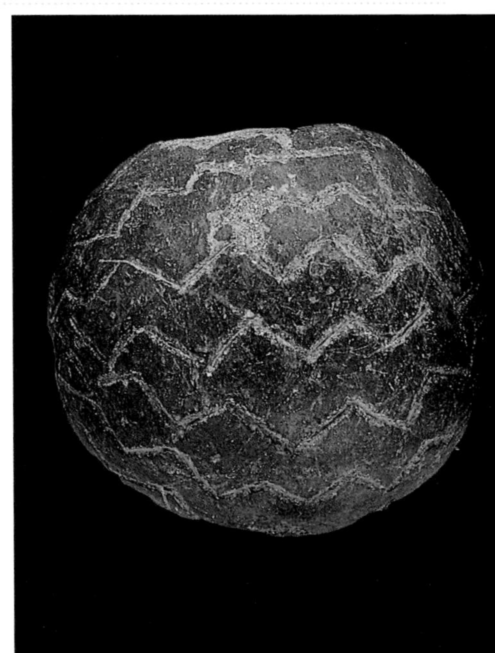

that need, there is at this stage no evidence that it was other than a household chore, each family making its own. The same applies, even more forcibly perhaps, to the manufacture of stone and bone tools. The products of all these will be described later.

All these survive well in the archaeological record, but there must have been many others of organic materials which do not. A clear example of this is textiles. Spindle whorls, appearing at least by Red Skorba times, demonstrate unequivocally the spinning of yarn, though not the nature of the fibres employed. Sheep bones show that wool would have been available though at this early period it was probably still very coarse, and there may well have been vegetable fibres like linen from flax. And if they had yarn, it is highly probable that it was being woven into cloth, though we have to guess at the techniques employed to produce it. Weights for use with upright looms do not appear until the later Bronze Age, but their are several other methods of weaving which would leave no trace.

Quite apart from simple probabilities, a stronger clue to the production of cloth is offered by the V-perforated buttons from Żebbuġ tombs. Although it is just possible that they were attached by thongs to garments of skins, that seems highly unlikely, given those spindle whorls.

Trade is another special aspect of economics which requires separate consideration. It has been suggested that some of the changes in local pottery styles, notably the distinctive slip of Red Skorba and the Żebbuġ scratched and painted decoration, were the result of influences from Sicily. It can be clearly demonstrated that more or less regular contacts were maintained after the initial Għar Dalam colonization, most obviously from the frequent presence of raw materials not naturally available in the islands.

The most significant of these are geological, since as well as surviving in archaeological deposits, they have clearly defined distributions.

Obsidian (see p.66) is the best example. Malta, consisting entirely of sedimentary deposits, had none, so that the quite considerable quantity found in prehistoric contexts there must have come from outside, from Pantelleria and Lipari as chemical analyses have shown. But obsidian is by no means the only imported material. Pumice, useful for grinding and polishing, comes from similar sources, particularly Lipari, but its presence is less significant since it contains air bubbles which make it light enough to float. In consequence, though also originating from Lipari, it could possibly have been picked up on a Maltese beach. Malta has a distinctive chert in several parts of the islands and flakes of it are found commonly in the archaeological deposits. However, tools with secondary working are nearly always of true flint, which was obviously preferred.

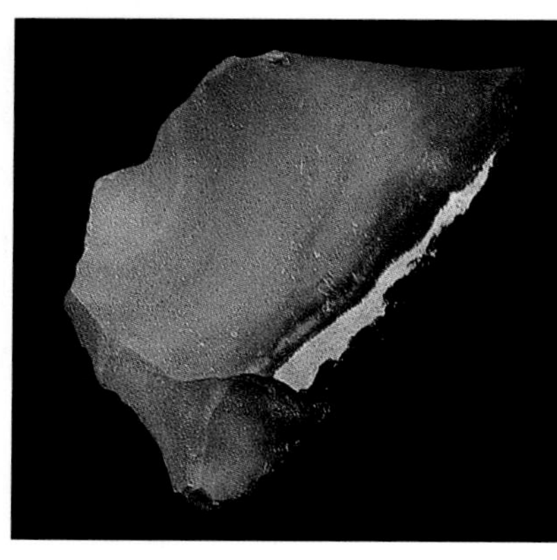

This large knife blade, one of a group of four found in the Xagħra Circle, was made of imported flint.

This cannot be obtained locally, the nearest source being the Monti Iblei, inland from Syracuse in Sicily. Similarly, for manufacturing ground stone axes, even the local Coralline Limestone was neither hard enough nor sufficiently homogeneous.

Few such axes have turned up in Malta (see box on page 41) and they, or at least the raw material from which they were made, must have come from a nearest the northeast corner of Sicily, the mountains behind Messina. Miniature axes found in the Żebbuġ phase tomb at Xagħra can only have come from the same area or even further off.

The Sila massif in Calabria in particular has outcrops of the serpentine and other rocks represented.

In a rather different category, red ochre, a natural oxide of iron, does not occur in Malta's geology

ut has been found in archaeological contexts there, particularly o accompany burials (see p.61) nd to decorate pots. Deposits in he Agrigento area are the likeliest source.

Finally, archaeological rather han geological, two sherds from Santa Verna in Gozo and five from Skorba, all from layers with local Grey Skorba or Żebbuġ sherds, annot be matched in the Maltese sequence but are identical vith others known from Sicily or beyond. One from Skorba is typical of Sicilian Late Neolithic Diana Ware in shape and red slip, while standard Red Skorba, though howing marked similarities, is not identical.

Another from Skorba is equally characteristic of Serra d'Alto Ware, a buff fabric with dark purple paint and a distinctive form of handle. Serra d'Alto is more widely distributed, from Sicily up into peninsular taly. The other five sherds are of open bowls with finely scratched cross-hatched triangles on their nner surfaces, indistinguishable from examples from Trefontane, a Neolithic site on the slopes of Mount Etna.

These are all certainly imports and one is tempted to quote them as examples of trade. This should only be accepted if the word 'trade' is used rather more loosely than is generally the case. The pottery in particular is unlikely to have had any commercial value, Malta producing all it needed locally. And the open bowls could hardly have served as containers for some tradable commodity.

It looks more casual than that, as a by-product of more meaningful exchanges or even merely 'souvenirs from our holiday abroad'. The quantities of stone being brought into the island are stronger evidence of trade, but still with reservations. Whereas barter has a very long history, much early trade was probably more within the framework of gift exchange, a complex social rather than economic mechanism, as has been

These four sherds from deep levels at Skorba were all imported from Sicily. The red-slipped one is Diana Ware, the two with cross-hatched triangles Trefontane, the lug with purple paint Serra d'Alto.

recorded still taking place in the southwest Pacific, for example. In this you do not take your surplus goods to your trading contact and ask what he will give in exchange. Instead, you throw a party, invite him along, and in the course of it give him those surplus goods unasked – though you almost certainly have a very good idea of what he would find acceptable. Before very long he has to reciprocate with another party, when he gives you something in return of equal, or preferably higher, value. This is where it differs most markedly from more strictly commercial transactions. If his return gift is o lower value, he loses face and yo gain it. The main object, then, is no economic gain but social status, th exchange of goods being almos coincidental, though in purel practical terms more useful.

This sort of arrangement seem more likely at this early perio than that the Maltese sailed of to Sicily to collect their own ra materials or to 'buy' them from th locals; that the Sicilians, Liparian or Pantellerians sailed to Malta t hawk their products; or yet agai that Sicilian middlemen controlle the distribution, making a profi in the process. A further seriou question is what the Maltese wer producing acceptable to thei

This extraordinary stone head came from tomb 5 at Żebbuġ, though a similar one was found later in the Xagħra Circle.

The best preserved of the figurines from Skorba was found in three pieces. The head belonged to a second specimen.

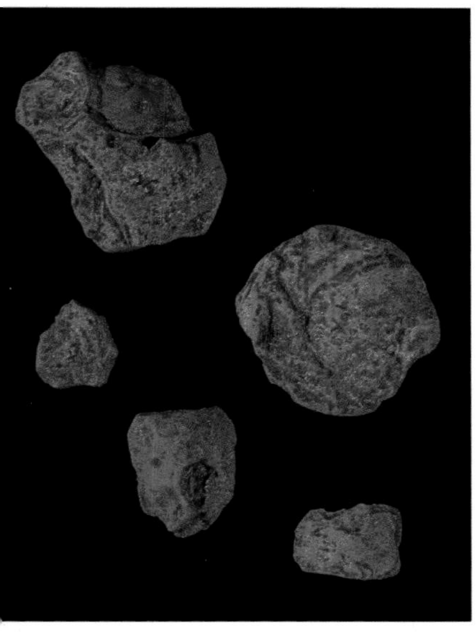

ed ochre was imported for a variety of urposes. It would have been ground to owder for use.

trading partners to fulfil their side of the exchange, however organized. To this we have no answer, but since organic goods will not have survived, their absence from the archaeological record need not make us abandon the picture drawn above. Stone certainly came into Malta by some means or another, and those who produced it must surely have expected something by way of recompense. And finally, as we noted some while back, we have no evidence of any kind on the appearance of the boats without which those exchanges could not have taken place.

Evidence on beliefs and death is plentiful, almost embarrassingly so, for the Temple Period, but extremely scanty before then. We do, however, have one small observation hole on

TONE AXES

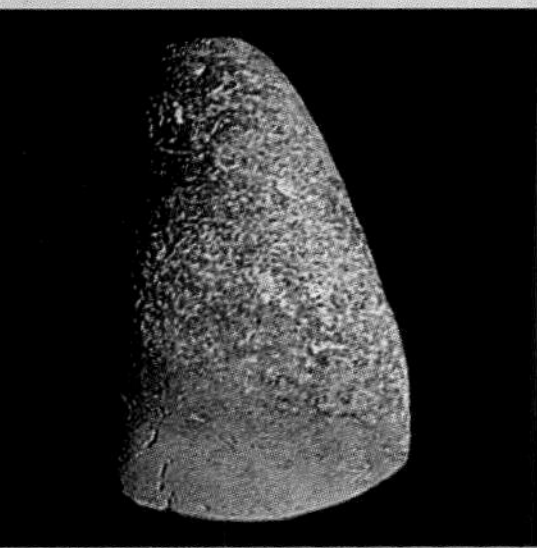

unctional ground stone xes are remarkably few om prehistoric Malta, aving one to wonder ow they carried out heir carpentry. wo were found at korba in Żebbuġ hase levels, two less losely dated from Ħal Saflieni, and recently an undatable one was recovered in a field at Mistra (top right). That they were widely known is shown by miniature examples, as little as 3 cm long, from the Żebbuġ tomb in the Xagħra Circle, and others from the Xemxija tombs and Saflieni (see p.213). These seem too small to have had a practical use, and the fact that many are perforated through their narrower ends strongly suggests that they were carried, or even worn, as amulets. No raw material suitable for their manufacture occurs in Malta, so it had to be imported from foreign sources, often from long distances.

Most unexpected in the excavations at Skorba was a series of fragmentary female figurines, schematic but clearly recognizable.

each which, it is worth noting, is more than we have for many prehistoric societies. The Red Skorba 'shrine' to the east of the Skorba temples has been described for its architecture, but more can be said on its function. Most significant are the figurines, of which five came from the north room. Four were of terracotta, in typical Red Skorba ware, and though none was complete, between them they allowed the full reconstruction of a standing female figure some 9 cm high, very schematically rendered. The face is represented by a backward tilted triangle with a knob for nose at the top edge and a small circular pit for the mouth. The breasts appear as diagonal bosses. The most notable features are the exaggerated thighs combined with even more exaggerated buttocks and female triangle, a marked case of what is known technically as steatopygia. In contrast, neither arms nor lower limbs are represented at all. Clothing, if such it can be called, is limited to an applied cordon forming a girdle round the waist and pairs of incised lines, straight on the front, curved on the back, presumably a necklace. The fifth piece from the north room was carved from stone and, though of the same general form, is even simpler. One other chest fragment was found in a Red Skorba level in one of the deep trenches, the other three, chest, leg

nd head, of similar form and idencal ware, from later mixed levels. further and substantially larger ragment was then recognized mongst material recovered from ne Mġarr temple in 1925. Although has been pointed out that female gurines do not necessarily imply, till less prove, the worship of a Mother Goddess, this remains the nost economical explanation of hese intriguing objects. Their find pot, with some risk of circularity f argument, could be quoted in upport, as can other finds from he same rooms.

Another fragment of terracotta ppears to show one leg, and the eginnings of a second, of a table r bed. Its upper surface bears a scar vhere some additional element had roken away. One is reminded forcibly of the 'Sleeping Lady' from Ħal Saflieni. On the rock floor of hat same north room lay side by ide two goat skulls complete with heir horns though with the facial ones broken off, and others were cattered through both rooms. The uantities of other animal bones and ottery were remarkable considerng that the deposit was mainly of vall decay rather than domestic rubbish. They would seem to suggest otive offerings. Other bones are puzzling if even less informative. Of numerous cow toe bones, no less than twenty had their proximal faces ground smooth. This must have been deliberate, probably to allow them to stand upright. Why? They would have made good gaming pieces, such as halma men or chess pawns, but this is hardly likely at that remote period. Perhaps it is not too fanciful to attribute to them a phallic significance. Certainly that would fit the context where they were found, and there are more explicit examples from the temples later. They would thus support the idea of a fertility cult.

As regards burials and associated religious beliefs, the tombs at Żebbuġ itself (Ta' Trapna iż-Żgħira, Żebbuġ, Malta – there is a second

From Skorba's early shrine were recovered a number of cow toe bones. The top one is unaltered but the second has its base ground smooth to stand upright.

village of the same name in Gozo) were too ruined to tell much, apart from demonstrating collective burial (see p.62). That found within the Xagħra Circle (see p.60) was much more informative.

Here successive collective burial was most evident as the chambers could not have contained the 65 bodies represented had they been inserted intact. Early depositions were pushed to the back or ejected to make room for later ones. This seems to indicate the widely-held view that personality remained with the bodies only so long as they were clothed in flesh. Once
reduced to dry bones, they com
monly received scant respect.

Burials were accompanie
by decorated pots. All but tw
small cups were found broke
but whether deliberately so a
the time of burial or only as th
result of subsequent disturbanc
or clearance is uncertain. Persona
ornaments were added too, par
ticularly a variety of beads, sma
discs, longer tubes and intermedi
ate forms, also a few V-perforate
buttons, strange vaguely anthropo
morphic pendants (the excavator
referred to them as 'jelly babies'
these all of fossil shell or bone
Miniature axes, some of them als
perforated for suspension, wer
of imported stone as noted above
Fresh shell was also employed fo
pendants or, in the case of a larg
Tonna galea shell, a sort of conch

The Żebbuġ tomb in the Xagħra Circle had two chambers opening off its shaft. The roof of that on the left was broken open by a recent vine-planting trench.

his enigmatic head was found, as if on uard, just inside one of the chambers hen the stones sealing the entrances ere removed. A very similar one came om one of the tombs at Ta' Trapna, ebbuġ.
he chambers inside were packed with uman bone and pottery. At least 65 odies in all had been interred here. learly the shaft had been emptied any times to insert later burials. See lustration on p.60.

ossibly as a musical instrument. Hinting strongly at religious beliefs, the bones were freely sprinkled with imported red ochre. This was used almost world-wide symbolically for blood, and so life. It s very probable that it was used n the living too, though even as cosmetic it could have had both nagical and social significance. Finally, the crudely-carved stone ead placed at the entrance of one hamber, remarkably like the one ecovered from one of the tombs at Żebbuġ, seems to have been placed s a guardian over the spirits, or at east the bodies, of the deceased. Though we can never recover the whole pattern of beliefs from the listant past, we get many intriguing hints.

POTTERY STYLES

It will already be apparent that the yardstick by which Maltese prehistory is ordered is provided by the development over time of the pottery, as Evans was the first to demonstrate in the early 1950s. This was not a matter of technical improvement but purely of fashion – what shapes and decorations were considered acceptable at any one moment, as opposed to those which had dropped out of favour earlier, or had not yet been devised.

This is not the place to follow these changes in minute detail, but a general outline would be helpful, especially where it can throw light on connections through time and space.

Għar Dalam sherds from Għajn Abdul show some of the Impressed Ware techniques. Note the white inlay in the first and the comb impressions on the fourth.

GĦAR DALAM

It has already been mentioned that the earliest pottery on Malta is a member of the Impressed Ware family, widely distributed around the central and western Mediterranean. Not surprisingly, it is closest to the Stentinello ware of southeast Sicily, with its type site on the coast 8 km north of Syracuse. A finer ware is thin, polished, usually grey to black. Roughly half the sherds are decorated with a row of impressions (demonstrating its external affinities) following the rim or the base of the neck or, more frequently, narrow cut-out lines, close spaced, as bands or chevrons. Some certainly, originally probably all, were filled with a white paste. Curved-wall bowls and globular jars with necks were standard forms and round bases were th norm as sherds of flat ones wer very rare. A few fragments of pec estals were also recovered. Handl were very varied: pierced lug vertical strap handles (one mark edly angled and saddled), vertic and horizontal tunnel handles, i descending order of frequency, ar reported. Two from Għar Dala and one from Skorba were moc elled into animal heads, bearin characteristic decoration.

A rather thicker ware was mor variable in colour and shape, les finely polished and, if decorate

ıerely with haphazard incisions r finger-tip pinchings. Shapes in ıis heavier ware are more diffi-ult to determine, given the small ıze of the sherds. In one trench at korba, a second Għar Dalam ıyer overlying the first had a ›wer proportion of decorated herds, a diminution noticed ıroughout the wide distribution f Impressed Ware. More of the oarser fabric appeared here too nd there were more white grits ı the paste. These characteristics ppear to foreshadow the Grey korba ware which follows, and learly develops out of it.

;REY SKORBA

'he two Skorba wares are imme-iately distinguished from earlier nd later ones by a very distinc-.ve fine white speckle in the fabric, rom the nature of the tempering .sed in the clay. They are separat-d from each other by a number of eatures. As the name implies, Grey korba has a grey surface, polished nd almost invariably undecorated. 'he commonest shapes are round-ottomed dippers and open bowls vith various roughly S-profile .ecks. Short pedestals occur not ıfrequently, and otherwise bases an be round or flat. By far the most frequent handle is a horizon-tal lug, somewhat splayed, either pierced, imperforate, or dimpled at the ends to suggest a perforation. A particularly interesting handle form shows development through-out the phase. The angled Għar Dalam handle mentioned above becomes higher and more deeply saddled, particularly on the ladles. But then, while the inner face becomes steadily longer and the saddle more exaggerated, the outer strap appears to shrink until it is a mere perforated lug on the back of an indented projection of the vessel rim. In fact, of course, the handles do not themselves go through these motions. It is the potters' changing fancies which produced the succes-sive alterations. The coarser ware

'he top and bottom sherds here are f bowls with typical Grey Skorba nperforated splayed lugs. The right and entre sherds are successive stages in the evelopment of the Red Skorba handles see p.49).

also continues from Għar Dalam, now with the characteristic Skorba grits, and often with a poorly-polished pinkish surface, though not yet with any trace of red slip.

RED SKORBA

Again, as the name implies, it is the brilliant red slip which most clearly distinguishes this ware. Admittedly, reducing conditions occasionally turned it black in the firing.

While influence from the contemporary red slip widely distributed in Sicily and Italy at this time is highly probable, a number of differences in detail from the Diana ware in shape and decoration make it certain that the slip is in every sense of the term a superficial addition to what remains basically a local ware, developing directly from Grey Skorba.

A fine Red Skorba carinated bowl, with its typical slip, has here been reconstructed from surviving sherds.

In the case of abraded sherds where the surface no longer survives, the two cannot be told apart, showing the same characteristic speckled white grits. But differences between the two there are. Red Skorba went in for larger and more distinctly carinated bowls. The nearly-straight lip above the carination can slope in or out. These bowls are now regularly if not invariably flat based, or mo remarkably stand on longer pede tals which uniquely slope in rath than out. A variety of more or le globular jars was found, some wit prominent necks.

The most distinctive vessel is ladle with a broad forked tongu rising from the lip by way of ha dle, deeply notched at the ti and thickened on its outer fac at the base of th V Sherds of thes were most pu zling until on was found com plete. They ar the final stage the developme which bega with the saddle strap handl back in Għa Dalam. On th other hand, th splayed lugs the Grey Skorb phase are fewe and much mo exaggerated, tru 'trumpet' lugs. In contrast t those of Diana ware, they coul be placed vertically. Vertica tunnel handles continue an variously pierced ribs or co dons make their appearanc Decoration is restrained an not infrequent, usually base on deeply-scratched Cs, var ously combined into crescent Ss, loops, or even, in one cas a spiral. These motifs stand o or below the carination.

ıese attractive objects of Red Skorba ıre served as ladles, as wear on their lips ows.

agments of the forked handles greatly ızzled the excavators until a complete ·e was found. Later, others showed e development of the form over the eceding Għar Dalam and Grey Skorba ıases (see examples on p.47). It did not, wever, continue into the Żebbuġ phase.

.EBBUĠ

Iere we have a strong contrast in lmost every respect, deriving from very different, foreign, tradition. or a start, the fabric no longer has ne small white grits and is usu-lly markedly less well fired and o softer, often tending to a brown-ıh black. New also is a thinner and ıore friable yellow ware.

Except on small cups, round ases have disappeared, as have all edestals. Jars show a wide range f variation, the most notable hav-ng a distinct shoulder and, after a reak in angle, a bulging neck and verted lip. However, this profile ecomes progressively slacker, lead-ng imperceptibly through to the ther extreme, a simple ovoid jar r even a deep bowl, depending on its proportions. Interestingly, the decoration, to be described next, still usually bears witness to the former neck-body distinction.

The more typical jars have two opposed vertical handles on their shoulders and four smaller pierced lugs equispaced high on the neck. Vertical strap handles on rim or shoulder occur on the more cup-like forms. They sometimes have a pair of dimples either side of their lower root recalling the openings of the pierced lugs, and the same can be found on imperforate lugs.

Decoration was scratched into the leather-hard surface before fir-ing, leaving a fairly-broad groove which was certainly on occasion white-filled. Lines are untidily, not to say casually, drawn and designs

As well as the buff and grey wares, the Żebbuġ phase potters covered some of their pots with a creamy slip, which they then painted in bright red with similar designs.

correspondingly irregular. Almost universal is a horizontal line or pair of lines round the base of the 'neck'. The inverted commas are required since, as just noted, this 'neck' often runs smoothly into the body without any break in angle. The vessel above and below this line is quartered vertically, resulting panels frequently containing single or multiple standing arcs or chevrons. Incorporated into this decor are often short crossed diagonals with shorter verticals depending from their tips like flails. Rather more elaborate ones, as Evans showed, were clearly meant to be seen as little men. Other plain lines, continuous or interrupted, often run round inside the vessel's lip. Lines can occasionally be wavy rather than straight, fringed on one or both sides with excised triangles, or bordered on both sides with rows of dashe
At Xagħra, apparently rather lat
in the phase than either Skorba
Ta' Trapna, a certain amount
cross-hatching was incorporate
Decoration frequently runs over th
handles. The whole effect is exube
ant, far from the restraint of Re
Skorba, but casual, if not downrig
incompetent.

Identical in its motifs though i
a quite different technique, a se
ond ware found on domestic site
but very rarely in the tombs, wa
given a thick creamy or yellow sli
and then decorated with lines

ed paint. Different yet again is an ncommon thinner ware, undecoated other than with its thin red ip, still easily distinguished from ed Skorba and not even necessary derived from the latter. Finally, finer hard grey ware, found only ccasionally at Skorba and Santa erna in the earliest Żebbuġ layrs, was used for tronco-conic bowls ith decoration both inside and out. onfluent broad hatched or excised iangles inside the rim remind one f those imported Trefontane sherds, hereas zigzags, dash-bordered, nd triangle-fringed lines clearly oreshadow standard Żebbuġ decoation.

An additional feature which was resumably considered decorative as to notch the rim lightly with a row of closely-spaced dimples. The same can sometimes be found along the edges of handles.

Whereas the pottery is distinctly Maltese throughout, artefacts in stone and bone, much less versatile materials, are simpler and more generalized. Bone was apparently used only for awls, burnishers, and the occasional pendant, ground from animal long bones, doubtless after their meat had been consumed. One piece of pumice with a deep groove across its surface shows how they were finished off. Shells perforated as pendants were probably picked up on the shore already empty. Others were more elaborately shaped, and are described in the section on the Xagħra Circle tomb (p.60).

ŻEBBUĠ ANTHROPOMORPHS

here can be little oubt that the design cratched onto the sherd n the left was intended o represent a human gure, with head, arms, nd legs, albeit very chematic. That on he next sherd is more sketchy, but surely with a similar significance. The use of roughly scratched lines is typical of Żebbuġ phase pottery decoration.
By the time we come to the third illustration, it is most unlikely that the human form would have been recognized if the more explicit ones to the left had not come to light also. Other good examples can be made out on the complete pot pictured on the next page.

Stonework falls into two major categories. On the one hand, some objects were shaped by grinding. Saddle querns for reducing their grain to flour were shaped from the local Coralline Limestone, though this must have been barely hard enough for the purpose. That being so, the teeth recovered from Żebbuġ tombs are not as worn down by excessive grit in the flour as one might have expected. A few sherds of carved stone bowls were found in a Red Skorba level. More intriguing are a collection of biconical objects. It is difficult to see what else they could have been other than

Żebbuġ pots often have simple, indeed rather clumsy, shapes, as here. The fring of chipped triangles are common.

Carefully carved stone objects like these, average 5 cm long, may have served as ammunition for slings.

sling-stones. They were carefull carved from Globigerina Limeston and recovered from a Grey Skorb layer. Associated rounded beac pebbles were probably collecte for the same purpose, though wh they were used on, considering th absence of game on the islands, i indeed puzzling. At an average c 65 gm apiece, they would have bee formidable missiles. If used agains human enemies, they would provid the only evidence for warfare befor the Bronze Age. Polished stone axe are in a different category (p.41).

Secondly, there are many item flaked from stone, whether obsid ian, flint, both imports, or the loca chert. The last was very common i Red Skorba contexts, used for simpl

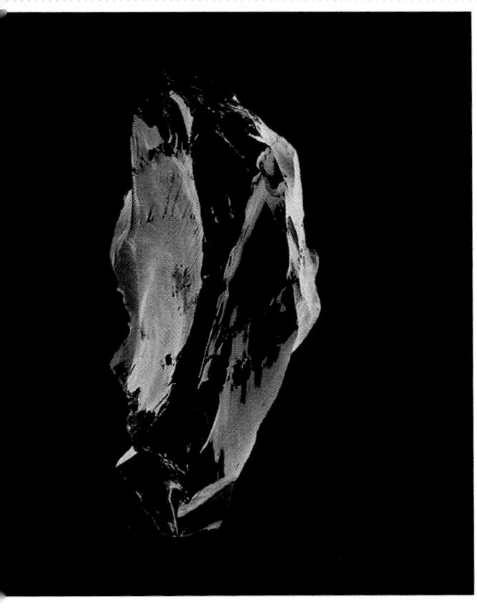

hiny black obsidian was imported from olcanic sources outside Malta (see p.66). ike flint, it was flaked into remarkably harp knife blades.

flakes or blades, rarely showing signs of secondary working and little even of use. The obsidian, as already noted, nearly always turns up as tiny flakes, probably rejected as no longer large enough for practical use. The cores from Skorba, however, show that fine blades up to 8 cm long were produced and presumably then put to use. Also flint had intermediate value, being employed directly as blades, or retouched to form backed knives, scrapers, or awls. Sickle gloss on some of the blades shows what at least those particular ones were used for. All these are again of the most generalized types.

What could conveniently be mentioned here are spindle whorls of terracotta, appearing first in Red Skorba deposits. Some were

'LINT FLAKING

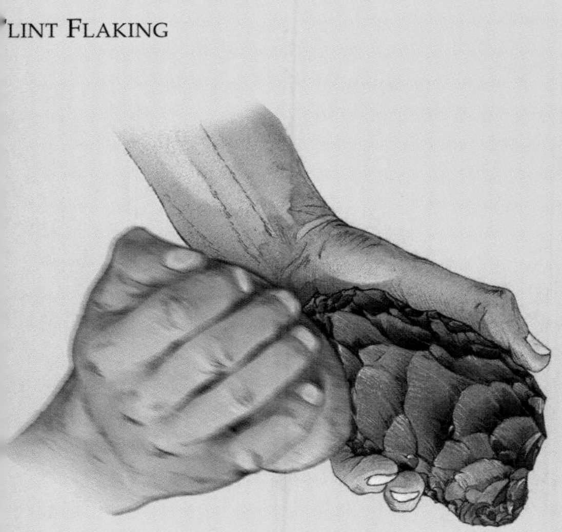

To flake into a useful tool, a stone has to be hard, brittle, and without grain or marked cleavage planes. Obsidian, flint, and chert were the best available to the Maltese, although only the last is found in these islands. To get the stone to break in the desired way, thus controlling the shape of the resulting flake, requires considerable skill and practice.

Flakes would then need delicate retouching to turn them into working tools – backed knives, scrapers for cleaning hides, arrowheads, or whatever.

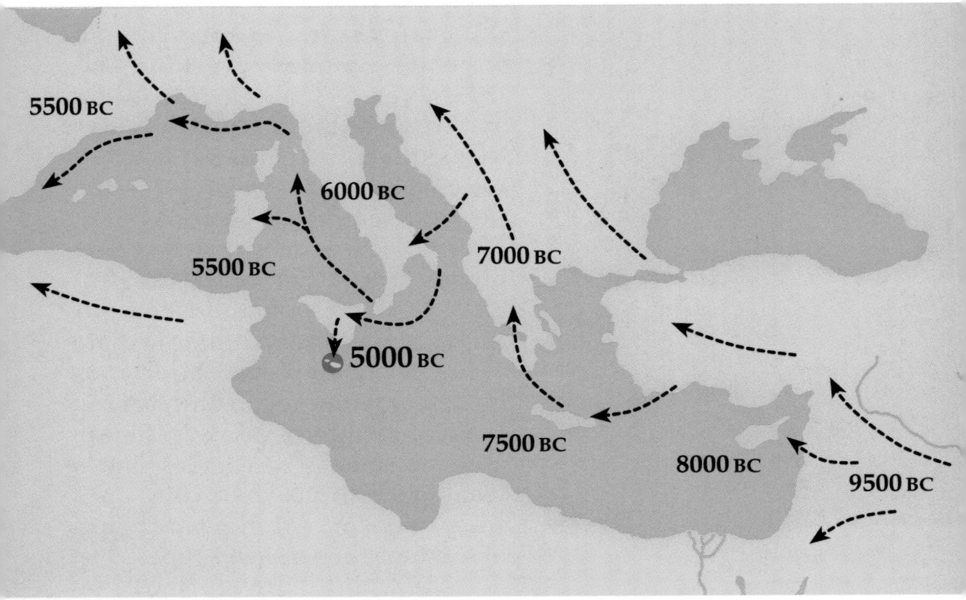

From its origins in the Near East, the knowledge of farming spread steadily through Europe, by land through Anatolia, the Balkans and the Danube valley, by sea round the Mediterranean, reaching Malta comparatively late.

modelled directly from the clay before baking, spherical, conical, or discoid. Others were chipped and ground to shape from potsherds. They attest yarn production at this period, and so presumably textiles.

To get the fullest value from our sequence, we need to be able to put dates on the successive phases, not only to compare progress here with that abroad but also to recover the duration of these periods, and so to assist in their interpretation. Earlier attempts to do so by means of parallels with other, often only marginally better dated, sequences elsewhere in the Mediterranean met with only limited success. The real breakthrough came with the introduction of radiocarbon dating.

For the start of this perio we have only two carbon date both with rather large standar deviations, somewhat blurrin their significance. They there fore give little more than general indication.

To quote them in their offi cial form, they are BM-37 6148+160 BP (before present and BM-216, 5760+200 BP. Cal bration would put them aroun 5000 and 4600 BC.

On the one hand, since the were taken from wood cha coal, possibly old heartwoo

ıey may well be too early by a ɜntury or so. This applies par- cularly to the first, since the vo came from the same deposit t Skorba. But, as already noted, ıat deposit was banked against very substantial wall, surely ot constructed by pioneers just rrived in a new land.

The first colonization is like- / to have been distinctly before ıis. There are few dates for com- arable material outside Malta to elp, though one from Poggio/ iano Vento, Agrigento, Sicily, is lmost identical with the earlier f our two. Until more analy- es are carried out, we can only uggest that these first farmers rrived in the islands around 000 BC, though it could have een appreciably before that. A ingle sample from Red Skorba t 5175+150 BP (roughly 4000 BC alibrated) falls neatly between ıis and the next group, though ʼith no great precision.

The end of the first cycle is ıuch more securely placed. We ave no less than six samples ɾom Żebbuġ contexts at Skorba nd the Xagħra Circle in close greement with each other, span- ing after calibration 4300 to 3600 ı round figures, with a seventh ather later, down to 3100.

Only two are available from Sicily within this same bracket. A terminal date for Żebbuġ at around 3500 BC or a little later looks reasonable then. Two other samples gave very similar dates and were probably mistakenly attributed to later phases. This is easily done if deposits were disturbed, some pieces of charcoal being brought up from an earlier level, as sherds certainly were on occasion.

adiocarbon allows us to put at least ɒproximate dates on the prehistoric hases. The technique is explained on .309.

'he last three, historic, periods are dated ʼom the records rather than from C14.

Maltese Chronology

NEOLITHIC	
Għar Dalam	5,000-4,300 BC
Grey Skorba	4,500-4,400 BC
Red Skorba	4,400-4,100 BC
TEMPLE PERIOD	
Żebbuġ	4,100-3,700 BC
Mġarr	3,800-3,600 BC
Ġgantija	3,600-3,200 BC
Saflieni	3,300-3,000 BC
Tarxien	3,150-2,500 BC
BRONZE AGE	
Tarxien Cemetery	2,400-1,500 BC
Borġ in-Nadur	1,500- 700 BC
Baħrija	900- 700 BC
PHOENICIAN	
Phoenician	700-550 BC
Punic	550-218 BC
Roman	218 BC-330 BC

GĦAR DALAM
BIRŻEBBUĠA

Going towards Birżebbuġa down the main roa Triq iż-Żejtun, the Għar Dalam Visitor Centre easily visible on the right side of the road after tl bus stop. A parking area is available.

Today the cave is an impressive passage varying considerably in height and width which runs horizontally north-eastwards from Wied Dalam, some 6 m above its bed and 550 m inland from the head of St George's Bay, an arm of Marsaxlokk Bay. Eighty metres of it are lit by electricity and open to the public, another 137 m are of difficult, not to say dangerous, access. After that it is blocked with inwashed silt, so how much further it runs into the hillside is unknown.

Originally cut by water percolating through and dissolving the Lower Coralline Limestone, its deposits contain three layers of interest. In the lowest, vast numbers of animal bones accumulated during the Pleistocen era. They represented a strang fauna, though not unique since was found in other Mediterranea islands like Cyprus. It include three species of dwarf elephant, th smallest, *Elephas falconeri*, no large than a St Bernard dog. Even com moner were dwarf hippopotamu

y contrast, the fauna included oth swans and dormice of gigantic ize. It is thought that the ances- ors of all these may have reached he islands overland in the distant ast, and developed their unusual haracteristics after the rising sea evels had cut their populations ff from the continent. Alterna- ively, they may have hitched lifts n flood debris, with similar sub- equent local specialization. There s nothing to suggest that men and vomen followed either of these ourses. They had to make their wn way, much later.

In the second layer, all these pecies had vanished, to be eplaced by a population of red leer, *Cervus elaphus*. The date s now probably in the early Holocene, after the end of the ce Ages, some 10,000 years ago. Though no human remains have been found, (the strange teeth of Neanderthal form once claimed are now known to be of more recent date, though this has recently been disputed), there is a possibility that it was men who both exterminated the earlier fauna and introduced the deer to be 'cropped' for their meat.

Above this again, a comparatively thin and badly-disturbed layer contained mixed cultural material from the Early Neolithic, named after this site, right down to recent times.

Excavations of varying efficiency took place sporadically over many years, from 1865 to 1937, concentrating almost exclusively on the lower bone level. A pillar of deposit was left as a testimony, and can be seen on the right of the path. Some of the lowest bone layer is visible in position also.

Għar Dalam (left), the 'Cave of Darkness', s now equipped with walkway, balustrade and electric light for the convenience of visitors.

Above: the excavators left the pillar of deposit to illustrate the succession of layers.

The amusing head of a cow once decorated the rim of a bowl of the Għar Dalam phase. It was found in this site, though in a mixed level.

SKORBA
(BEFORE THE TEMPLES)
MĠARR

A quite unexpected discovery of the excavations at Skorba in 1961-63 was that the site had been occupied continuously for a very long period before the temples were built (see p.156). The major result of the work was the succession of layers to a depth of 2 m showing the development of pottery over the period of their accumulation, from the Għar Dalam to Ġgantija phase, including two, Grey and Red Skorba, not previously recognized. Samples of charcoal were dated by the radiocarbon technique (see p.309), giving the sequence a time span of some 1500 years from 5000 BC. Hut walls and floors were identified in several phases and trenches, but only four were cleared to give anything like a meaningful plan. To the Għar Dalam phase belonged a straight wall of which an 11 m length was exposed. The nature of the building to which it belonged is not known since most of it was inaccessible beneath the West Temple. More huts were

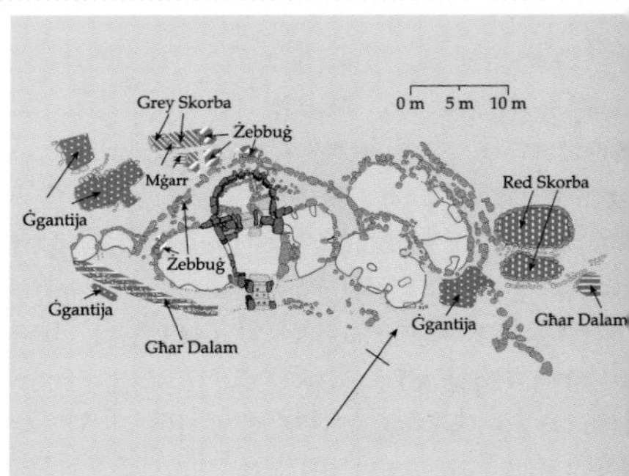

Some of the structures of an earlier village were found beside, behind, and beneath the two temples at Skorba.

Trenches behind the temple revealed 2 m of deposit, almost incredible for Malta, where soil erosion has been so active.

Even more remarkable, its layers were undisturbed, preserving an unbroken sequence of the islands' earliest cultural phases.

Within them were found fragments of the huts which had preceded the building of the temple, some of them by many centuries.

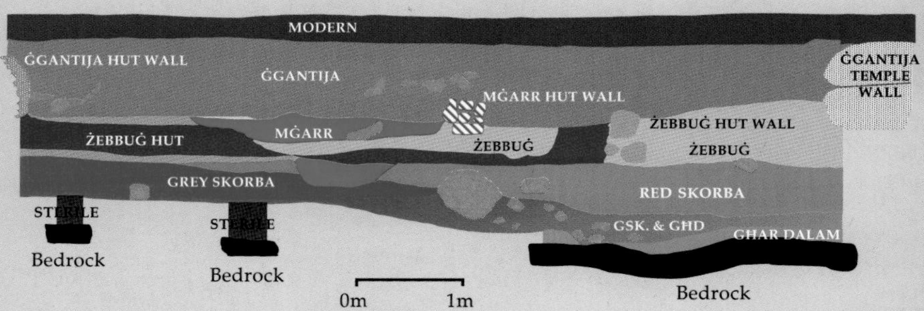

lmost certainly cut away when ıe temples were scarped back ıto the earlier village deposits. races survived under the now ıissing walls of the East Temle.

In the field to the east, a hut oor was fully opened, dating to ıe transition between the Għar 'alam and Grey Skorba phases, ut the deposits above it were educed by recent ploughing to nly a few centimetres.

Far more importantly, in this ame field were found the subtantial remains of two adjoining ooms. They had massive stone otings and were filled with grey lay, disintegrated mud brick rom their upper walls. With ough bedrock as floor, no hearth r entrance, and goat skulls and ottery figurines among the finds, ıese were interpreted as some form of shrine. They yielded considerable quantities of the previously unrecognized Red Skorba pottery. These are of particular interest for two reasons. Firstly, the evidence for the use of mud brick in an island where stone is so prolific was a considerable surprise. Indeed, its colour shows that it was made of blue clay, brought to the site from at least a kilometre away. Secondly, these shrines could be regarded as ancestral, in both architecture and function, to the later temples.

Finally, another hut, of slighter construction though of the same materials, was exposed to the northwest of the temples, and dated to the Ġgantija phase by its contents. Amongst these were several restorable bowls and eleven querns of Coralline Limestone for grinding corn to flour.

he south wall of the Red Skorba shrine is een as first discovered, with only half the ıamber cleared. An earlier hut appears in e corner of the trench behind.

The hut of the Ġgantija phase was abandoned at the time the West Temple was built, with querns and pottery still lying on its floor.

XAGĦRA CIRCLE
(ŻEBBUĠ TOMB)
XAGĦRA, GOZO

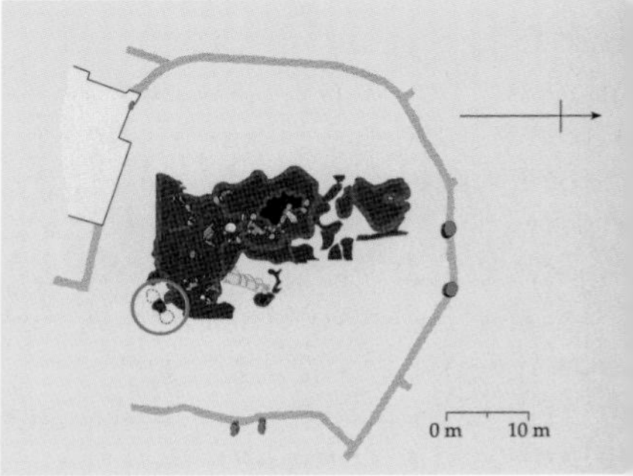

Within the Xagħra Circle, a much earlier chambered tomb, ringed in red, was discovered and excavated.

The discovery in 1988 of an intact tomb within the Xagħra Circle, though dating to a much earlier period, indeed, the earliest rock-cut tomb yet found in the islands, allowed a more detailed study of the Żebbuġ phase. Two oval chambers had been cut from the rock, opening off the bottom of a 70 cm deep vertical shaft, their entrances closed with stone slabs.

The bones represented a minimum of 65 individuals, this being the number of left knee-caps found, 54 adults and 11 children, all exceptionally healthy for prehistoric times. There is no way that that many corpses could have been placed in the chambers since their maximum length was only 2.6 r and height 1.4 m. The procedur was clearly to place the body of th deceased in the tomb, since the las skeletons were largely intact. Bu this was only possible because th now dry and loose bones of earlie ones had been swept to the bac or even, when the accumulatin

ɔne heap took up too much space, ected from the tomb altogether. was noticeable that the smaller ɔnes of the skeleton, like fingers, ›es, and those kneecaps, were ıore numerous than the larger and ıore easily removed ones.

The same story is told by the ɔttery. Only two small cups were •und complete, and of the other 60 : so broken vessels, all had many f their sherds missing, thrown ut like so many of the bones. he burial added in the last reo- ening was accompanied by two gantija phase bowls, all the oth- :s being of Żebbuġ type, a very ıluable group for demonstrating ıe range of shape and decoration : that phase. The deposits in both ıambers included quantities of ·d ochre, assumed to be used, as ı many other cultures, as sym- ɔlic of blood and life. Not being found in Malta, it had had to be imported from Sicily for the purpose. Personal ornaments figured prominently too. There were over 400 beads of fossil shell and 27 pendants, dubbed 'jelly babies' by the excavators because of their resemblance, surely intentional, to schematic human figures. There were also six V-perforated buttons and 16 miniature stone axes, ranging from 86 down to 22 mm in length. Fifty-two sea- shells, including one large *Tonna galea*, possibly used as a musical instrument, were amongst the offerings. Finally, just inside the entrance to one chamber, an enigmatic stone head, remarkably like one found at Żebbuġ itself, had been placed, possibly as a guardian of the tomb, but whether to keep evil influences out or the spirits of the dead in is not clear.

ıis strange carved head, with only es, nose, nostrils and chin, stood in the orway.

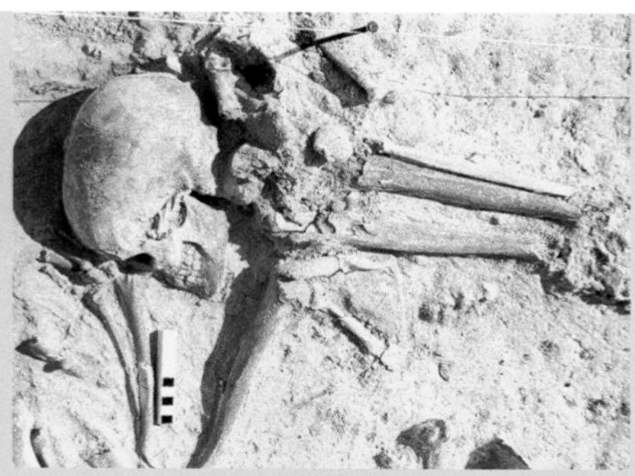

A partially intact crouched skeleton, undisturbed by later burials and so more or less in its correct anatomical position.

. 60 (left):
ıe Żebbuġ tomb was found to hold bones ɔm at least 65 individuals, with many oken pots and ornaments. Though difficult to photograph in the confined space, in the picture opposite, human and sheep jaws can be seen in the jumble of bone.

ROCK CUT TOMBS
VARIOUS LOCATIONS

A burial rite widely spread through the whole of the Mediterranean basin from France and Spain to the Levant and Egypt was that of carving chambers out of the rock to receive the bodies of the dead and any accompanying grave furniture. Such chambers are usually small and of roughly oval shape. Only rarely, as in the royal tombs of Egypt, were they found to hold a single body. Indeed, that seems to explain the thinking behind them. They were indeed communal burials. Though they would require much more effort to excavate than would a simple earth grave, they were much more durable and could be reopened to take later burials, probably of successive members of the family which had carved out the tomb in the first place. Wha is more, if dry and scattered bone were thought to need no furthe preservation – and this seems t have been a common belief – the could be pushed to the back c even thrown out altogether, allowing a single chamber to be re-use indefinitely.

To this end, a few of th chambers were found to have removable stone slab still blocking their doorway; many wer provided with a rebate to hol such a stone, now missing; an it is very probable that all wer once closed in this manner. Th stone which was rolled asid from the tomb of Christ outsid Jerusalem was a late and graphi example of a practice which ha started 4,000 years earlier.

The greatest variation in thes tombs lies in the means of acces

ome were cut directly into a cliff ıce, suggesting that the first nes could have been artificial ubstitutes for natural caves, hich were used from very early mes and virtually worldwide s appropriate resting places for ıe dead. More commonly, they onsist of two elements, a vertical haft and the chamber opening om the foot of it. These could erive from a simple grave pit. or example, the shaft graves f Mycenae had their bottoms onverted into chambers by the ddition of a roof before the shaft as refilled. But they, like nearly ll pit or shaft burials, were for ingle interments. An interme-iate form has a sloping ramp r *dromos* cut into a hillside or evel ground, to create an artifi-ial 'cliff' into which the chamber ould be excavated.

While most chambers were simple oval ones, other shapes came into use later, D-shaped, square or rectangular. A more common variant was for two, or occasionally more, chambers to be cut from the foot of a single shaft, or additional chambers could open off the first – a common practice in Sardinia. As well as having good examples of single and double chambers (see p.162), Malta also some of the most complex of all prehistoric tombs, in the Xagħra Circle and, the most spectacular of all, the Hypogeum of Ħal Saflieni.

It also has numerous examples of rock-cut tombs coming well down into the historic period – Phoenician, Punic, and Roman – leading on to the latest of the complex ones, the catacombs.

he photo above shows the entrance shaft ıd broken chamber roof of tomb 6 at emxija.

ı the photograph opposite, one can see ıe reconstruction of a tomb and its ontents in the National Museum of ırchaeology.

A detail of the interior of tomb 5 at Xemxija showing the cut-out columns holding the ceiling.
These tombs were of the rather later Ġgantija phase (see p.162).

POTTERY MAKING

There are basically four stages in pottery making:

First the clay has to be dug and prepared. Maltese blue clay needs no further cleaning, but like all clays, does require tempering. This adds some refractory material, usually sand or crushed stone, to reduce excessive shrinking as the clay dries.

Secondly the pot is shaped. Before the fast wheel was introduced by the Phoenicians, this was done by hand, the commonest technique, as shown by the way the sherds break, being to roll out a thin sausage of clay, flatten it into a ribbon, then join up lengths of this edge to edge (the coil technique).

Though by no means universal, the most distinctive and attractive feature of pottery is often its decoration, in a bewildering variet of techniques.

The pot surface could be incise before or after firing, pinched, jabbe impressed, gouged out (excised roughened (rusticated), presse out into bosses or in into dimple ribbed or cordoned with applie strips of clay, slipped (dipped int a runny clay of different compos tion), and polished or burnishe Colour could be added to designs b infilling with a red (ochre) or whit (gypsum plaster) paste, or by pain ing on the surface. There is also, c course, almost infinite variation i the designs executed in these variou techniques.

Finally, to turn the result into useful product, it has to be bake at 700°C or more or it will reve to its original soft clay on wettin

Coils of clay were smoothed into each other to build up the walls of pots. These often broke along the lines of the joins.

Part of the surface of these Tarxien phase vessels was gouged out, to be filled with an ochreous clay baking to red, contrasting in colour with the yellow of the pots' walls.
Note the tunnel handle on the left, and th nose-bridge handle on the right.

imple air drying is not enough. lotchy colours imply that wood or harcoal was heaped over the pots nd ignited, clearly for a long time ne standard practice.

However, from a quite early eriod a few pots of uniform colur imply that proper closed kilns, hich allow the supply of air to be ontrolled, were already occasionlly used. If plentiful air is admitted nto the kiln, the iron oxides will roduce reds and yellows, but if ne oxygen is restricted or excluded, nose oxides will be reduced to give reys and blacks. Pots were often aked in reducing conditions, air dmitted towards the end of the firng, resulting in an apparent 'sandrich', a yellow or buff ware with a lack core. Examples of different abrics, shaping, decoration, and ring will be noted appropriately n the text.

Apart from functional effects, such as availability of clays, technical skills of the potters and the intended use of the vessel, pottery varies mainly as the result of fashion. While that possible variation is virtually unlimited, a single society at any one period of its history will normally employ a very restricted range of pottery techniques, shapes and decoration. Any departure from this narrow range will be unacceptable. It is this restriction which, together with its commonness, fragility (making it frequently discarded) and durability (if only in fragments) makes pottery so valuable to archaeologists studying the past.

ome Tarxien phase pots were decorated ith pellets of clay, probably once ppearing as dark circles against a white aste background. This is a detail of the owl on p.226.

While all pots before the Temple Period were baked in open bonfires, some, like the fine ones on the opposite page, must have been fired in a simple kiln.
The illustration above is of a structure of intermediate type.

OBSIDIAN

This shiny black volcanic glass was highly prized in antiquity for several reasons. Quite apart from its attractive appearance, it had excellent flaking qualities, superior to those of flint or any other natural stone. Furthermore, it is found only in restricted and scattered sources, giving it rarity value also, so it is not surprising that it was traded widely from very early times. The obsidian found in the cave of Franchthi on mainland Greece in levels of 8000 BC and imported from the island of Melos out in the Aegean was only the first of many reported cases.

In the central Mediterranean, the only sources are on Sardinia, Lipari, and Pantelleria, with a little on Palmarola, an islet west of Naples. Obsidian differs slightly from source to source, so that an sample can be attributed secur ly to its place of origin by ey or, more securely, by chemic analysis. Obsidian was reachin Malta from Pantelleria, 240 km t the west in a direct line, and fro Lipari, 300 km to the north.

Two substantial cores, weighin 1700 gm and 400 gm, one from eac of those sources, were found in Grey Skorba level at Skorba, bu it usually turns up in small flak or chips, as if it could not be di carded until reduced to unusab tiny fragments. This makes thos two cores the more remarkable an puzzling. They do, however, sho the form in which it was importe as blocks ready for blades to b struck from them, as well as th skill of the knappers who wer striking off regular blades 8 c long. At Skorba, Pantelleria

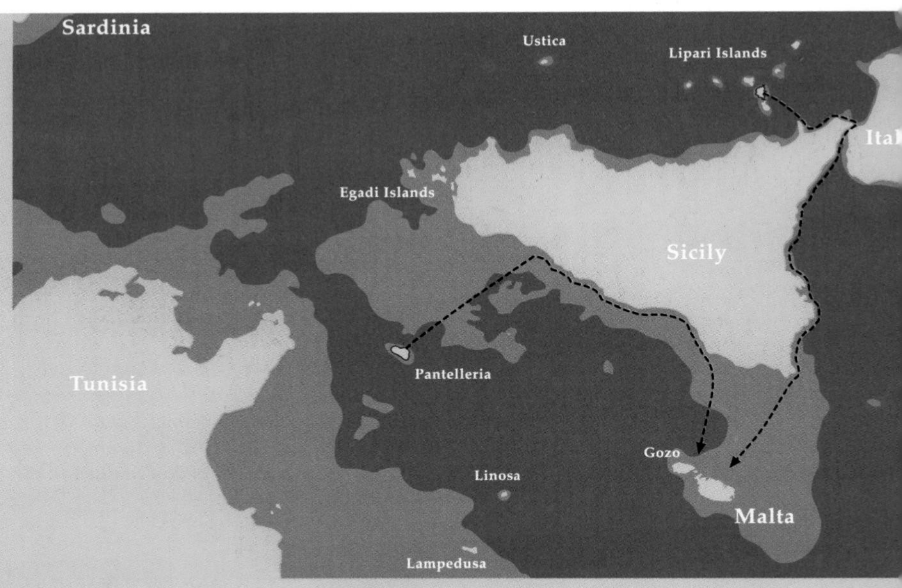

f these two obsidian cores found at korba, the smaller one had been imported sea from Lipari, the larger from antelleria.

obsidian was the more frequent in early levels, whereas the Liparian overtook it by the full Temple Period. At Xagħra, however, Pantellerian remained the commoner of the two throughout. How these facts should be interpreted remains obscure.

Elsewhere in the world, a major source on Melos supplied most of the Aegean area, as has already been mentioned. Two others in eastern Turkey supplied obsidian which was traded over enormous distances in the Near and Middle East. Another was exploited in Hungary but one in Iceland was not discovered until long after iron had come into full use. Further afield, there are occurrences in East Africa, exploited from a very early date, in Mexico, there used more for polished mirrors than for tools, Japan, New Zealand, etc.

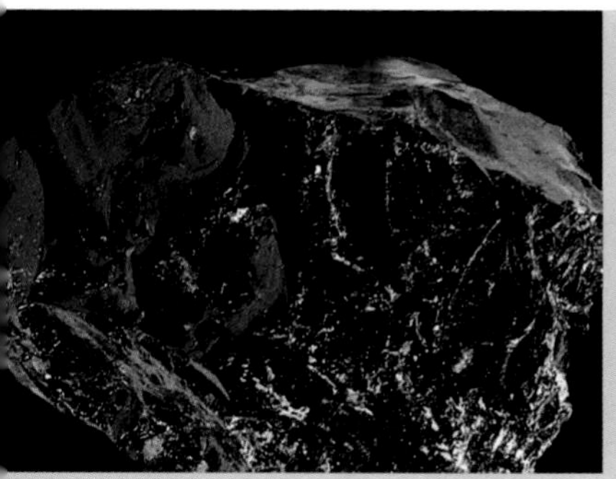

detail of one of the cores above shows here flakes have been detached. Although ese are the only two cores yet found Malta, probably all the obsidian was ported in this form, subsequent flaking ing carried out in the islands.

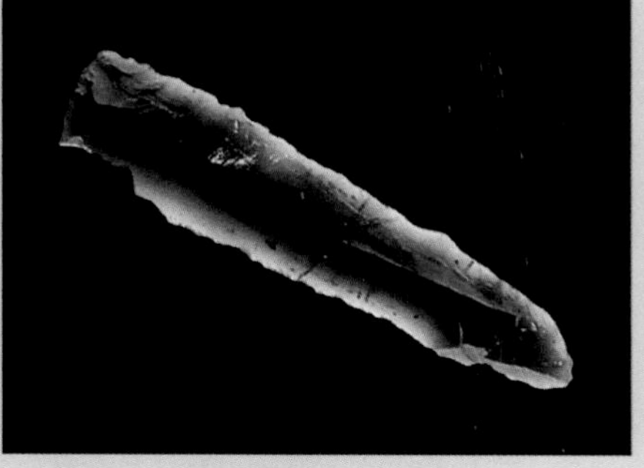

This fine blade of Lipari obsidian would have required great skill on the part of the knapper.
The transparency of its cutting edges emphasizes just how sharp they could be.

The Maltese temples were the climax of the islands' prehistoric development. As well as honouring the local gods, they may have been deliberately elaborated to emphasize the islands' cultural independence.

CHAPTER 3

THE TEMPLES

Up to this point, our story has differed little from that of any other Neolithic society around the Mediterranean. This was all about to change. From 3500 to 2500 BC the islands of Malta and Gozo made the most extraordinary advances with their art and architecture, a truly unique achievement which we have come nowhere near explaining.

Most readers will already be familiar with the Maltese temples, and individual descriptions and illustrations will be found in the boxes here. We have to stand back and try to draw a general picture, to see the wood as well as the trees.

One of the first things we have to appreciate is that their sophisticated architecture is extraordinarily precocious. At the time they were being built, beginning around 3500 BC, no-one else was raising free-standing buildings in stone anywhere else in the world.

An overhead view of Ħagar Qim makes manifest the skill and sophistication of Maltese temple architecture, as also the beauty of the local stone. Its anomalous plan is discussed on p.142.

The façade of the Ġgantija temples, though damaged, is still impressive. The left hand corner still stands 7m high after 5,500 years.

The pyramids of Egypt were long claimed to be the world's first stone architecture, but they date to very nearly a millennium later. While the use of huge blocks of stone, perhaps the most obtrusive feature of the temples, was shared by much of western Europe, outside Malta, with the sole exception of Stonehenge in Britain, megaliths were used as found or quarried. The carefully-dressed stone in our temples puts them in a class of their own. Nor can their plans be matched convincingly in any other monuments. When we come to seek their origins, we shall get no help from abroad.

The typical temple consists of a number of elements. It is approached across an oval space, levelled up by terracing if the ground slopes, and possibly bounded on the outer edge by a setting of stones. This forecourt i overlooked by the temple façad which faces the south or south east and is composed of a row o large stone slabs on end, techni cally known as orthostats, wit their faces in the line of the wal Where surviving, the corner ston at either end of the façade is talle than the rest. Above the first ro of orthostats, the wall is contin ued upwards in smaller block either irregular or neatly-squared depending on whether the wall i constructed in the hard Corallin Limestone which could not b

haped or the softer, more easily vorked, Globigerina. Beyond these orner stones, the concave curve of he façade could be continued as free-standing wall of orthostats nly.

The side and rear walls are again uilt of orthostats, often much arger than those of the façade, surnounted by horizontal courses. The rthostats differ from those in the açade by being set alternately face ut and edge out, a sort of 'long nd short' work, with the very practical advantage of tying the wall ace securely into the body of the tructure.

The centre of the façade is interupted by the entrance doorway, onsisting of a pair of orthostats acing each other, capped with a nassive lintel slab, the convenient erm 'trilithon', simply meaning hree stones'. Even where the exteral wall was of Coralline blocks, Globigerina had to be imported to he site, from a distance if necesary, to produce the neatly-worked oorway. Further trilithons form passage, which is always paved n stone.

This in turn gives onto an open pace or court, floored with either nore paving or *torba* (see box on .77). This area is rather more ifficult to define since it may be fully open to the internal chambers or, probably as the result of later alteration, separated from them by screening walls. It was, however, roofed over, the evidence for which is discussed in the box on the subject (p.196).

The next element is a pair of D-shaped or ovoid chambers, usually, if somewhat misleadingly, referred to as apses, opening to left and right, though as noted, they could be closed off with cross-walls, each with a central trilithon doorway. These ovoid chambers were planned quite independently of th[illegible]ternal wall, the irre[illegible]e between the tw[illegible] being filled wit[illegible] and earth, the[illegible]

hrough the smoothly carved Globigerina imestone doorway can be seen the ough Coralline walls of the inner apses, urviving to the same height as the gantija façade.

containing cultural debris including sherds, a valuable aid to dating their construction. Apses were nearly always floored with *torba*.

The main variation in the typical temples lies in the number of apses – three, four, five, or six. If three, they open directly from the central court in trefoil fashion, resembling the ace of clubs, though again they were on occasion, particularly the one on the main axis, walled off at a subsequent moment, access being restricted to trilithon doorways. In the cases of more complex temples, a second axial passage of th same trilithon construction as th main entrance leads from the cou between the first pair to the inne ones, another lateral pair, an either a fifth central one or a me niche, giving the five- or four-aps forms. In one case, Tarxien Centra that fifth apse or niche is replace by yet another passage, leading t a final pair of apses, making si in all, still with a central niche In Kordin II, a smaller and rathe more irregular plan also seems t have six apses.

Finally, in several temples space was found between apse an external walls for small subsidi ary chambers, usually approache through further doorways sup plemented by porthole slabs, fla slabs within the trilithon whic would completely block them i

Doorways, as here in a side chamber at Mnajdra, could be cut through orthostats, the so-called portholes. The convexity of all blocks deliberately emphasizes their stability.

t first glance this is just a jumble of ones. It was in fact the outer wall of the outh Temple at Ġgantija, to the left. It as then buried by the infill of the wall of e North Temple on the right when that as later built up against it. was only revealed for the first time hen part of the façade of both temples fell way a few years ago. Another block of the outh Temple can be seen in the wall of e North Temple's inner left apse.

ey had not had rectangular holes ut through them to allow access. eing rectangular rather than circu- r, 'porthole' is another misleading erm, though hallowed by use. It not easy to see how they could e described better by any other ingle word.

With the standard temple plan, f which some 30 are known, there a certain amount of variation both number of apses, as noted, and size, from 6.5 m in overall length Mnajdra East) to 23 m (the six-apse arxien Central). They are often, ndeed usually, found grouped, ith two or three immediately jux- aposed, or at least closely adjacent. t Ġgantija and Skorba, part of the xternal wall of the first temple on e site was demolished to allow a second to be nestled up close to it, partially encroaching on it.

It should not be overlooked, however, that there are a number of other sites which share with these certain characteristics but by no means all. We cannot say how many such sites should be counted since some are too ruinous for their original form to be recovered. For example, Qala, Gozo, or Ta' Lippija, above Ġnejna Bay, consist now of no more than one or two irregular blocks, with only a scatter of sherds of appropriate date around to sug- gest that they may once have been compar-able temples. The same could have been said of Santa Verna, Xagħra, until excavation in 1908 revealed a *torba* floor approaching a typical trefoil plan. Only three blocks of its original walls survived above ground. Sites like Borġ l-Imramma, Ta' Ċenċ, Sannat, or Ħal-Ġinwi, Żejtun, or Qortin l'Mdawwar, (Kunċizzjoni) beyond San Martin tal-Baħrija, have better-preserved plans, but resemble the temples in a general way only, with clusters of ovoid chambers, in no way based on the standard plan. It is not even certain that they were employed in the same way, as temples. However, Ħaġar Qim too has oval chambers tacked on to its four-apse plan, all enclosed within a single external wall, so it is unlikely that they served some entirely different purpose.

An important part of these structures which has nowhere survived is the roofs. These are separately discussed in one of the boxes (p.196).

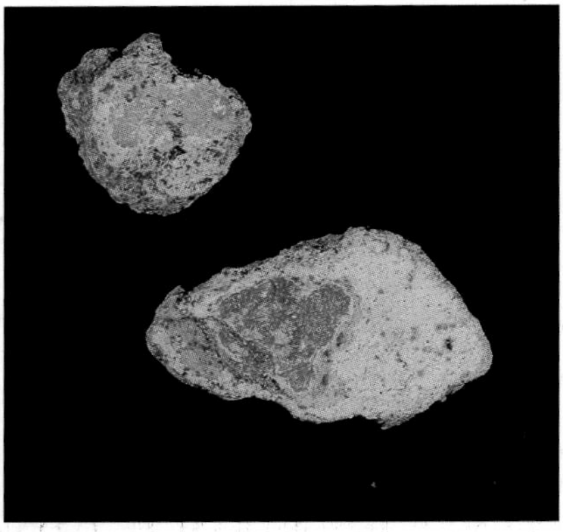

While smoothly cut stone was left exposed, rough rubble was plastered and painted with red ochre, as these fragments from Ġgantija show.

Interior fittings again show a general pattern, with variation from site to site. Circumstances dictated the main treatment of the walls. Those built in neatly-cut Globigerina slabs, like Ħaġar Qim or Tarxien, needed nothing further, unless they received a wash of red ochre. Those of coarse Coralline rubble were probably all smoothed off in plaster and ochred, traces of which survived in the Ġgantija North and Skorba outbuildings. The final result of the two techniques would, then have been very similar.

Most temples, again probably all originally, had structures within them which we interpret as altars usually placed against the innermost wall. Many are simply rectangular blocks of stone, often decorated with pitting or in relief. At Skorba West in the central apse to the right of the doorway one was built of plaster-faced rubble, perhaps as the corner was too cramped for Globigerina blocks to be manoeuvred into it.

A second group is constructed by the same trilithon technique as the entrance doorways and passages though usually but by no means always, on a much smaller scale. The trilithons in the central niche of Mnajdra Central and at the back of the first apse left of Tarxien Central stand 1.8 and 2.4 m high. It is difficult to picture ceremonial activities on top of them. In two cases, second apse left Mnajdra South and third apse left Tarxien Central, double-decker slab altars were installed, the former with central support pillars the latter looking like nothing so much as a small cupboard

ther altars at Mnajdra also ave central supports.

The third variety is completely ifferent. It consists of a small at or slightly concave tray-like pper surface set on a metre-high illar which rises from a broad- base. On one of four at Ħaġar im, the surface has a tray-like m and perforations through the edestal, as if to make the whole ovable, though with some dif- culty considering its weight. he second and third are plainer ut the fourth much more elabo- ate, the tray more like a very iallow bowl or saucer and the illar carved to represent two ilithon structures back to back ecorated with pitting, with etween them on all four faces lower pots' from which sprout rees'. The base is only slightly ider than the pillar, stepped accommodate the trilithons, iving it a near-cruciform plan. hese altars were not placed in articularly prominent positions, vo beside the second left apse- assage, one very discreetly in a nall intra-mural chamber, the nest in an angle to the left of ie centre court.

Block altars were usually and trilithon altars occasionally decorated, as discussed under sculpture. The Ħaġar Qim pillar altar with its pot plants has already been mentioned.

A further feature at Ħaġar Qim looks as if it should be highly significant, though of what is less clear. At the back of the single apse tacked on to the south side of the main four-apse temple stands a prominent cylindrical pillar with rounded top, 1.45 m high. A second, at 2 m rather taller and nearer square in section, is even more prominently displayed in its own shrine in the north-eastern outer wall. In front of it stood a low altar on a wedge-shaped, pitted-decorated, support, though

he triangular block probably supported a orizontal slab within a trilithon shrine. his formed an unusual feature in the cternal wall of Ħaġar Qim.

the horizontal slab is now missing. This seems a better explanation than that it represented the female triangle, associated with the male, phallic, standing stone, even if it leaves the original meaning of the two elements unexplained. Similar objects, known as betyls, were frequent in religious contexts in the Near East, where texts show that they were revered as aniconic, non-representational, images of the deity. Could they be the same here?

A small vertical pillar or betyl stands against the ashlar wall of an inner apse a Ħaġar Qim. Its function is uncertain.

The two V-perforations and larger hole on the right would have held a screen and bar to secure it at Ħaġar Qim.

If there were additional interior fittings or decoration in organic materials, wall hangings or carpetting for example, they have c course not survived. The possibi ity should be borne in mind. Thi is demonstrated by the presence c holes in the door jambs, V-perfora tions clearly intended to hold som sort of door or screen, and large horizontal holes equally clearl designed for bars, although neithe doors, bars, nor screens remain now Several sites have provision for fire within them, small reddened pave areas or low bowls. However, if th temples were indeed close-roofed, i is rather surprising that we find n provision for the artificial lightin which that would have necessi tated.

How were they built? That reall breaks down into three questions

e inner court at Ġgantija South has ircular paved hearth, centre, and two ars, at the right and towards the back.

how they were physically constructed, how they were planned, and how society mobilized the necessary resources of manpower. Construction involved a series of steps. Since all temples were built on level or at most gently sloping ground, site clearance would not have been a serious problem. Quarrying the stone would have required more effort, though not an excessive amount. In many parts of the islands, Coralline Limestone has cracked naturally into removable blocks, and it is probable that many more were available 5,000 years ago than are today. Simple wedging and splitting would provide more, and a certain amount of subdividing and shaping where necessary.

Globigerina Limestone is a different problem as it splits less

)RBA

plaster-like material ıch used in the nples' flooring. It was oduced by crushing obigerina Limestone, en spreading it over a bble foundation. After peated wetting and unding, it set hard d could be polished.

The result can easily be mistaken for bedrock, and in excavations it frequently is.
A similar but less durable plaster was applied to rubble walls, where the pounding process could not of course be applied. Traces of this were recovered between the wall blocks in the Ġgantija North temple, together with fallen fragments preserving their red-painted surface.

Related yet again is deffun. *With this the same processes are applied, but using crushed pottery instead of stone. It was the favoured material for watertight roofs in recent centuries, being less liable to cracking than cement.*
Archaeologically the results were deplorable as prehistoric sherds made a far superior product than later ones, and so were avidly collected for the purpose by local farmers.

adily, but on the other hand it is uch softer, so that more active ıtting was possible. Naturally, hichever of the two major rock 'pes was immediately to hand at .e site would be used as far as pos- ble.

Tarxien and Ħaġar Qim, for ‹ample, are both built entirely the local Globigerina, although eathering of the external walls the latter demonstrates that ere could be disadvantages. For any purposes, however, particu- rly doorways and altars inside e building, where weathering as not a problem but a much eater finish was required, Glo- gerina had to be used, whether not it was available on site. The ost instructive case is Ġgantija, here a large number of blocks of onsiderable size were required. he temples stand on the Upper oralline, and though Globigerina nderlies this at no great depth, it inaccessible there, and the slope front of the temples is too steep r it to have been brought from e nearest outcrop. The likeliest ource is on the valley floor a little ver a kilometre to the west, and early 50 metres nearer sea level. To transport the blocks up a slope for that distance would obviously have been a major undertaking. We can assume the use of rollers, sledges, ropes, and levers, though wheeled vehicles capable of carrying such weights are highly unlikely. The requisite manpower will be dis- cussed shortly.

e grooved trough in Kordin III was ade of Coralline Limestone brought om a kilometre away. It stood across e entrance of an apse, beside the central urt of the temple, and was probably ed by the womenfolk of the community grinding their families' corn.

Globigerina was also imported over greater or lesser distances to Mġarr, Skorba, and Mnajdra. There is one converse case, Kordin III. There, a single flooring slab across the left apse is the only one on the site of Coralline Limestone, out- cropping at the nearest a kilometre to the northeast near Żabbar. This slab, 2.66 m in length, bears seven ground hollows in its surface. Since the block was clearly built into the temple – no-one would have imported it to the site later – and use as a quern would seem the only explanation for wanting exotic Coralline, we must assume that the grooves, with the stone rubber Ashby found lying in one of them, are also contemporary with the use of the temple.

Once more, a functional need, which we shall need to look at again later, forced the moving of a hefty slab to a temple site.

We have referred perhaps rather glibly to rollers, sledges, ropes, and levers, all readily available in antiq- uity. The idea that the Globigerina stone spheres found above all at Tarxien were used to manoeuvre building blocks looks increasing- ly unlikely for two reasons. They could hardly withstand crushing

under the weight of some of the blocks moved, and would need a carefully smoothed and hard surface to roll on. Whatever their real function, we should be unwise to hail them as the world's first ball bearings.

Unlike the other aids, the use of levers is more than supposition. In Tarxien East, many of the uprights have a notch at their base, as does the tallest upright at Ħaġar Qim. The only explanation must be to take the tip of a wooden lever to assist the final adjustment into place. As for raising orthostats into their upright position, although no proof is possible, experimental work has been done on megaliths elsewhere, showing that the best solution was the use of a ramp of earth or rubble, then tipping the block off its end, finally raising it to

Note the notches at the base of the block by which they could be levered into position. These are still visible, despite t severe weathering of these orthostats at Ħaġar Qim.

the vertical with levers and rop helped by the use of A-frames, an of course, a large labour force. T lifting of lintels could be done the same way or by means of a cr of balks of timber. Care would required of course, and a willi and adequate labour force, b no great technical skill. Beams f roofing could be raised by simil means.

Spoil for the ramps and wa packing was probably carried baskets by labourers, as it still in Third World countries whe mechanical equipment is unavail ble. When one block was in positio its ramp could be dismantled a

ıe material moved to assist in the ·ection of the next one. Only after ıe last was in position would the te be cleared and tidied up.

That the final dressing of the one took place after it was in place shown by Tarxien East again, here the rock surface has been cut way slightly after the orthostats ·ere raised, leaving them stand-ıg on a low shelf. At this stage too ıe walls would be plastered and ainted where necessary, and altar locks carved and installed, requir-ıg yet more labour. It can also be ıown that the decoration by pit-ng or relief was added only after locks were in position. The temple ·ould then be ready for business.

But we have sidestepped one nportant issue. Someone had to lan the structure and supervise its rection. Since most ancient archi-ecture follows a long-standing ·adition closely, there is no need ɔ postulate an individual contri-ution to the planning, in a word, n architect, but there are intrigu-ıg hints that it was not as simple s that here. For a start, the first ppearance of the temples seems ɔ have been quite sudden – their rigin will be examined shortly. It ·ould appear probable, though of ourse unprovable, that someone, rather than either a long line of people or a committee, took that first step, and, as we shall show, subsequent ones. The contemporary models described in the box on the subject, and one of them in particular, provide valuable clues. Whereas most of them could be representations of temples already built, the engraving on an orthostat at Mnajdra Central being the most obvious example, some could equally well be models, plans, or elevations prepared in advance, in effect blueprints. The terracotta model from Ħaġar Qim could hardly be anything else. When complete it showed a five-apse temple in plan, its walls represented as low stumps. At no point in time, before, during, or after construction, did it

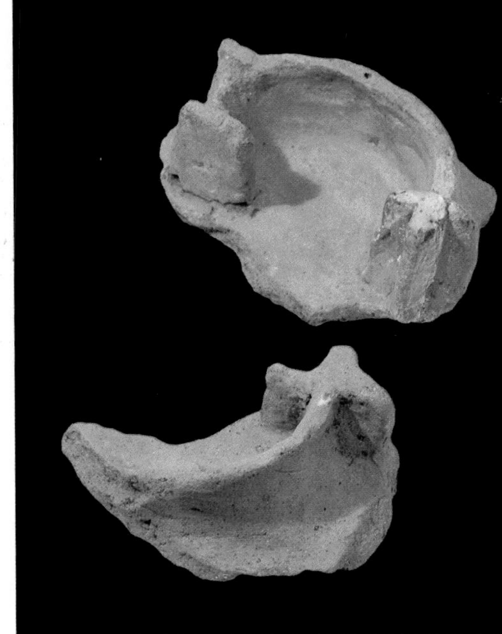

'he two fragments of a ceramic ɜmple model found at Ħaġar Qim re interpreted as an architect's trial iece. Apses, walls and doorways are learly represented.

look remotely like this. It is a purely schematic rendering. While not perhaps the only possible explanation, this would make more sense as a plan, prepared before work began, and the person who could prepare such a plan can only be called an architect. While architecture flourished in the prehistoric past, this is the nearest we come to identifying an architect, albeit a nameless one.

But if the architects and the priests were the officers, it was the ordinary people who provided the rank and file, the labour force which put those ambitious pla
into effect. How many peopl
Calculations have been made f
many ancient monuments, and
admit that no simple answer is po
sible unless one is given a figu
for the duration of the work, whi
of course one never is. We have
equation with two unknowns, tin
and numbers, which is therefo
insoluble. What can be worked ou
if only within a fairly wide marg
of error, is an input measured
man/days. A further proviso is th
women and children would doub
less have made their contributio
also, particularly, but not only,
providing food and support.

Recent research by Daniel Clar
which earned him a well-deserve
Ph.D. from Bristol University, an
to whom I am very grateful for pe
mission to use his figures, tackle

The beautifully cut stonework of the temples is well shown here in Mnajdra Central, a first course of orthostats, face out, with horizontal courses above.

similar arrangement at Ħaġar Qim ows the horizontal courses beginning oversail, to reduce the roof span. The ditional orthostats forming a sort of pen ithin the apse, and the vertical pillar hind, are both exceptional though their spective functions are uncertain. owever, the hole piercing the wall slab the right has parallels at Mnajdra d Tarxien, and may have served as an racle' hole, whatever that may mean. ssibilities are discussed on p.111.

his question with reference to gantija, as the best preserved of ll the temples. Helped by a back-round in engineering, and building n previous work on Mayan tem-les in Guatemala and Sardinian *uraghi* by other scholars, as well s advice from Maltese quarrymen nd stone masons, he estimated ne number of man/days required or each of those steps enumer-ted above separately, then added hem together to reach a total of 0,372 man/days. Recognizing hat this could only be an estimate f course, and that the true figure ould be well above or below that ne, he further calculated lowest nd highest reasonable figures for ach step, which added to 3,702 to 5,294 man/days respectively.

That man/day total must have limits also. Clearly the task could neither have been completed in one day, however many men were put on the job, since too many of them would surely get in each other's way. But nor could one man have raised the Ġgantija single-handed, however many days or years he took to do it. A minimum number of men would be that required to erect the largest of the external wall orthostats, say 50. And enthusiasm for the project might have been difficult to maintain after some five seasons of work. The seasonal factor is important too. The full labour force could not have been kept on the job all year round because of the essential requirements of food production. The numbers of men

vailable would clearly fluctuate idely throughout the year, depend-ıg on the competing demands of griculture and fishing, though it is uite possible that a skeleton staff f specialists was maintained on ıe site all the time.

One other factor is that the two mples and terrace out in front hich make up the Ġgantija were emonstrably constructed suc-ssively, with gaps of unknown uration between them (the north mple and terrace both produced ıly Tarxien phase sherds). Clark timated that the main building, e south temple, took just over half ıe total effort, 15,529 man/days. everal more assumptions have be made before we can proceed ırther.

If, for the sake of argument, we ıppose a building period of three ears, and allow three months of ork in each year, our estimate for e number of men required comes ıt at 131 men. With a population 10,000 suggested for the islands ıck in Chapter 2, and allowing ozo one-sixth of that total, and ıe-fifth of those available to pro-de the workforce, we come to 30 men, two-and-a-half times the number required for Clark's median total, and still quite sufficient for his maximum one. Our figures, though all to a greater or lesser extent speculative, look in no way unreasonable.

The main object of Dr Daniel Clark's research was to test the hypothesis that the demands of temple-building imposed a dangerous stress on contemporary society, and was a major factor in its collapse. His figures clearly do not bear that out.

Some stress there may have been, to be examined further when we look at society at the time, but it should not be exaggerated. It is more likely to have been a cause of the temples than a result of them. The motivation of the workforce was probably religious fervour rather than social coercion.

The building of Europe's medieval cathedrals would be a better parallel than the raising of the pyramids – and, even with them, the major effort was probably more from willing subjects than from Israelite or other slaves. Closer to home, a comparison with the dome of Mġarr's parish church in the background of Ta' Ħaġrat temples would be entirely apposite.

As has been stated, the temples are unique to the Maltese islands, so where did they come from? Leaving aside for the moment the difficult question of motivation, we do have some evidence on their antecedents. Dr John Evans noted that the temples could be sorted into a developmental sequence. This

ıilding the temples was obviously a ıjor undertaking.
ıe reconstructions opposite show some of e necessary steps: quarrying the stone, ınsporting it to the site and raising rights and lintels into position, and ding timbers to support the roof. ıally, all would need dressing, and, in me cases, decoration.

would place rather irregular lobed temples like Mġarr East and Kordin III East at the head of the sequence, followed by the three-apse trefoils, similar, but 'tidied up' to a neater plan. Then another pair of apses was added to the front, presumably as a result of a need for more space inside, without enlarging chambers to a point where they could not be bridged by rafters of the lengths available, giving the five-apse form. It appears that the three inner apses were now felt to provide more space than was required, so the terminal apse was reduced in size to a niche, large enough for an altar only. This then constituted the four-apse plan, or more correctly four-apses-and-a-niche. Finally, yet another pair of apses could be added to give Tarxien Central its six-and-a-niche. These results are summarized in the table (p.202). The question marks are unfortunately necessary where later damage causes uncertainty.

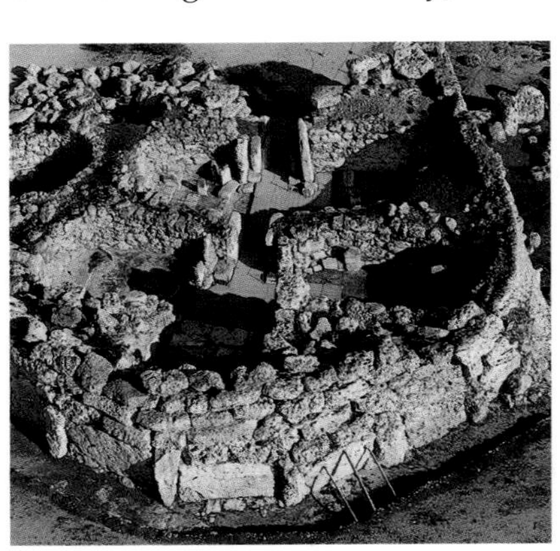

In Ġgantija South, the larger size of the inner apses is clearly apparent in this aerial view.

Ġgantija South is instructive for three reasons. Unlike other five-apse temples, its outer pair are smaller than the inner, as if added as an afterthought, though before the external wall was erected to enclose the whole.

Secondly, its large terminal aps was completely filled with an alta appreciably greater in area tha any other. It is easy to see that it builders would soon realize tha this was far larger than requirec and although too late to make th necessary adjustment here, woul decide to reduce this apse to nich size on future occasions. This, inc dentally, reinforces our view tha architects wer involved, peopl who recognize and solved prob lems of planning a they cropped up.

Thirdly, her there is clear struc tural evidence tha the four-apse pla of Ġgantija Nort is later than th five-apse one c its partner.

This develop mental sequenc of temple plan receives genera support whe correlated with the succession c pottery styles, which is in turn full substantiated by the stratigraphy though there are some minor dis crepancies. As a general rule, lobec three- and five-apse temples fa into the Ġgantija phase, four-an six-apse ones into Tarxien.

The lobed temple of Mġarr Eas which from its plan should stan at the head of the sequence, an therefore Ġgantija or earlier, ha Saflieni sherds beneath its lowe

loor. It might be suggested that hat floor replaced an earlier one, tripped out at least at the point ampled, though this would savour f special pleading. Ħaġar Qim Jorth is in a similar situation, its loors producing Tarxien rather han the Ġgantija expected. From wo four-apse temples, Ġgantija Jorth and Ħaġar Qim Central, the atter already anomalous in having an external doorway in place f its central apse or niche, Evans ecovered only Ġgantija sherds, vhere the later Tarxien ones would ave been appropriate. However, hose sherds give only what archaelogists refer to as a terminus *post uem*. The building could not be arlier than the sherds, but could e any time later, and not necesarily of the Ġgantija phase.

The point is illustrated by the hird apse left of Tarxien Central, eneath the floor of which Evans lso found only Ġgantija sherds. later trench, however, recovred a few of the Tarxien phase, roving that this temple was uilt at that later date despite the reater number of Ġgantija sherds resent.

So far, we have described the volving temple plans, but not tacked the question of where the first ones came form. Evans pointed out the similarity between the plans of the lobed temples and that of the more complex rock-cut tombs, particularly Tomb 5 at Xemxija. This led him to suggest that the first temples were in effect tombs built above ground instead of hollowed out of the rock below, but for ritual use, not for burials. While not capable of proof, this is not unreasonable, remembering the close link between the two classes of monument demonstrated by the hypogea of Ħal Saflieni and the Xagħra Circle. Skorba added another piece to the jigsaw, by showing that the building of substantial structures for religious use began well before

n the inner apse of Tarxien Central, a rench revealed details of its torba *floor, enewed at a higher level (see also p.77).*

the first temples appeared. By combining the two ideas of built shrine and ancestral tomb, it is easy to see where the first lobed temples could have come from. At the very least, no better suggestion has been put forward.

It has several times been suggested that the plan of the temples was modelled on the form of the 'fat lady' statues, assumed to be of the goddess worshipped in them. This is an intriguing idea but hardly borne out by the facts. It is only one of several temple plans, the four-apse one, which is not the earliest, that is compared

The three temples at Mnajdra nestle together, all opening from the oval court on the right of the photograph.

The suggestion that the plan of a 4-apse temple resembles the outline of a seated 'fat lady' is discussed on p.113.

with one of a wide range of re
presentations of the fat lady, t
be considered below, namely th
seated figures from Ħaġar Qin
Admittedly, the terracotta temp
model from that same site show
that the temples could be viewe
as plans, but that model is uniqu
There is undoubtedly a stylist
connection between the two, temp
plans and fat ladies, other than th
obvious link between sanctuary ar
deity, although only in the ove
whelming predilection for curv
over straight lines and right-angl
in this period of Malta's past.

Later developments can all b
explained by increasing techn
cal ability coupled with subtl
changing ritual needs. On the or

he Tarxien temple complex includes a -, two 4-, and one 6-apse temples, in ewildering juxtaposition.

hand, the builders became able to construct bigger and better, on the other, to be examined further below, there is evidence that there was a move towards a stricter separation between 'public' and 'private' areas within them.

One of the most curious features of the temples is the way they cluster. The 24 temple units, if we can call them that, occupy only fourteen sites. While there are singletons like Borġ in-Nadur or Tal-Qadi, there are many pairs, several threes, and one four, Tarxien. It is difficult to see the thinking behind this. In every case, buildings were successive, as shown by either their physical relationship to each other or by the sherds associated with them.

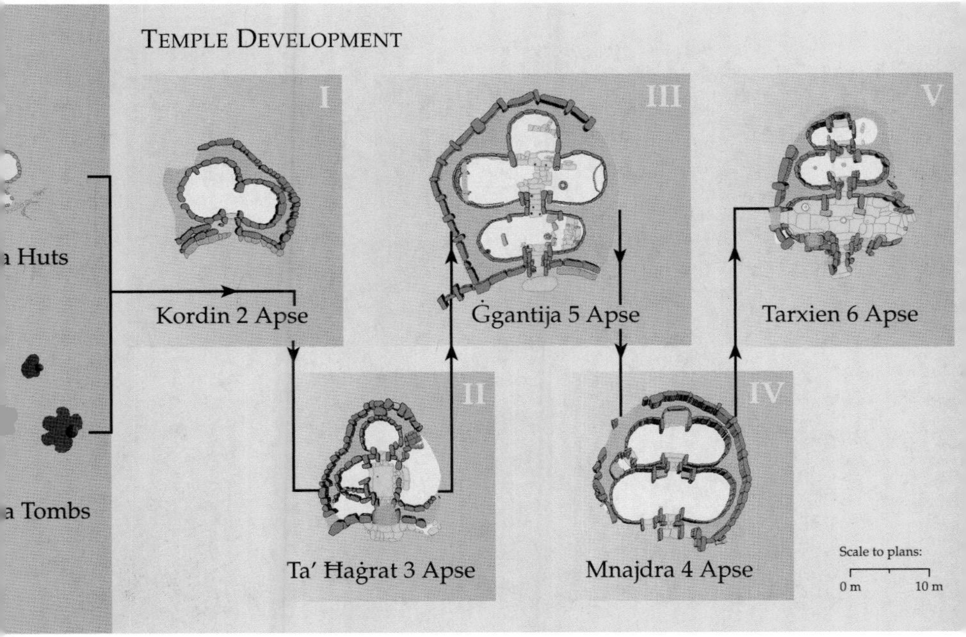

TEMPLE DEVELOPMENT

a Huts

a Tombs

I
Kordin 2 Apse

II
Ta' Ħaġrat 3 Apse

III
Ġgantija 5 Apse

IV
Mnajdra 4 Apse

V
Tarxien 6 Apse

Scale to plans:
0 m 10 m

It seems unlikely that the object was simply to provide enlarged accommodation, as in the addition of aisles to English churches. Similarly, the quantities of material recovered from them suggest that all were fully used, so not built solely as an act of piety, as so many white elephants. While most intriguing, this problem remains at present insoluble.

While still puzzling, more easily explained is the way the groups of temples themselves also cluster. There is an obvious group around the head of Grand Harbour and ot ers around Marsaxlokk and on tl Xagħra plateau in Gozo. Ħaġar Qi and Mnajdra pair off near Qrend Ta' Ħaġrat and Skorba near Mġa and, rather less intimately, Tal-Qa and Buġibba by Salina Bay. It wa Colin Renfrew who first commente on these groupings, suggesting th each in some sense represented territory, occupied by a separa community although sharing common culture and religion. Th implications of this will be explore when we come to look at templ society as a whole.

If there is anything in Maltes prehistory to rival the marvels c the temple architecture, it is th art. This comes in a wide variet of forms, all impressive. The be point to begin would be in the ten ples themselves, since the first grou

With all its surfaces neatly pitted, the side niche in Mnajdra South is a particularly striking feature. Through the porthole within its trilithon frame can be seen altars supported on pillars, the lower one tapering downwards. The flanking orthostats are also wider at the top than at the bottom.

e central altar in Ġgantija South has imitive-looking widely spaced pitting. e scar right of centre is where the wall a libation hole piercing the slab has ked away. Note also the contrast with rough rubble wall behind, though this is almost certainly once smoothed off th plaster.

better described as interior ecoration than art, and leads on irectly from consideration of e buildings. While some walls ere plastered and ochred, as has een noted, and in two cases in al Saflieni painted motifs in the rm of black and white chequers nd a great frieze of red spirals n be seen, altar blocks were also equently decorated. The earlist technique, found only on the ntral altar in Ġgantija South, was idely-spaced pitting, worked in pecking technique and covering e whole surface. Since this block ppears to be integral with the mple which it graces, it must go ack to the same date as that temle, in the Ġgantija phase. Pitting, ow usually produced by drilling as the rotary striations within each pit show, became widely popular, continuing well into the Tarxien phase as is found in temples like Mnajdra which were not built until after the opening of that phase.

Its most dramatic use is in the first apse left at Mnajdra South, where it covers the outer surface of the famous trilithon doorway, the 'back door' to the second apse, and the slightly wedge-shaped orthostats on either side of it. Close inspection of the pits in the angle between jambs and porthole slab shows that the drilling of the pits was executed obliquely after the structure was erected. While not surprising, it shows how even the tiniest detail can provide interesting clues. Here the decoration

continued to the edge of the slabs. More frequently, the surface was cut back slightly before the pitting was added leaving a raised plain border. This same technique continued with all later decoration, which is similarly bordered.

A particularly interesting block is the central altar in Tarxien South. Only when it was lifted out for transfer to safe keeping in the National Museum in 1958, leaving Zammit's modern replica on site, was it realized that there had been successive schemes of decoration. When the stone paving in front of it was added, or raised, it masked a narrow strip of typical pitting-within-border, whereas above that level, the pitting had been cut away to provide a field for running spirals in relief. The two techniques of plain relief spirals and pitting were occasionally used togethe the latter providing a backgroun to set off the former more prom nently. On one fragment found a Skorba, that background had bee ochred to increase the effect, an this may well have been the cas always. It demonstrates also tha the pitting was regarded as deco ration in its own right; it was no simply a key for holding some plas tic infill. The neatness with whic the work was done, notably on th screens across the first pair of apse of Tarxien Central, makes the sam point. These are undoubted mas

The replacement of framed panels of pitting by a design of running spirals with their 'thorns' and 'fishtails' is dramatically clear in this photograph of the central altar in Tarxien South, now housed at the National Museum of Archaeology.

rpieces, each with four spirals, terconnected but in subtly different ways.

Tarxien displays the most varied ɩd exuberant range of relief spills. A pair of them ornament the ɬl-stone of Tarxien Central, the lief rim following only the top ɩge of this. A very similar though ther simpler slab was found in aġar Qim. They could have been eant to suggest eyes, keeping atch over access to this innermost, ost sacred part of the monument. ost, however, decorate the South ɜmple here, including the central tar already mentioned, with 28 terconnected spirals in the main ɩnd, ending in forking 'fishtails' ɩd bearing curved 'thorns'.

Even more famous is the squared ock altar in the first apse right ith its six spirals, these ending in points though with similar orns and fishtail appendages. is possible, though unlikely in ew of its probable derivation om the volutes decorating local ɔttery that a vegetative symbolm was intended for these spirals, ɩd they could be simply abstract otifs. Although they are really ıite similar in appearance to the ell-known ones from the grave ɜlae of Mycenae, the chronology the two categorically rules out ɩy connection. Simpler versions of volutes, even more like those on the pottery and not meriting the name of spirals, occur on smaller blocks around the first apse right. Another fine spiralled block stands in a corresponding position in the left hand apse, where there are also two longer blocks like the central altar. These have 16 and 18 spirals respectively, and more on a curiously-notched step at the back, a feature found also on the temple-façade model, though there it is not spiral-decorated.

The spiralled blocks are outshone by two more which bear friezes of animals instead. On one, two rows of eleven sheep each parade across the face within the usual relief

ɩe design on a side altar at Tarxien ɱple, with less formal symmetry, equally attractive. This looks more ɩe artistic whimsy than an attempt to rtray a thorny tree.

border. On the second there are four sheep, a rather strange ram, if that is what is intended, with opposed horns and a topknot, and an undoubted pig. This block is broken at a V-perforation, so presumably once had more animals on its missing second half. While decidedly unusual, these creatures are not unique on temple reliefs, there being four fish on one from Buġibba, as well as a more usual block with double spirals, and a snake on the narrow edge of an orthostat from Ġgantija.

Ġgantija South also has very similar spiral decorated blocks, clearly shown on Brochtorff's 1828 watercolour but now they have severely eroded by weathering. While on the subject of animals at Tarxien, mention must be made of three in a rather different style on the side slabs of a small chamber within the wall of the Central Temple, opening off its first apse right. On this are portrayed two massive bulls in profile, one of them 1.2 m from muzzle to tail, and a third animal usually, and surely rightly, interpreted as a sow in view of what are clearly meant for piglets at suck, 14 of them. As symbols of female and male fecundity they could hardly be mo obvious, a point to be considere when we come to look at the belie that called forth the art.

The fish in relief at Buġibba, like the rows of animals at Tarxien, offer an amusing contrast to the abstract spirals and pitting elsewhere.

Before turning to the last an most spectacular of Tarxien South art, there is one other strange dec rative technique found only her In both its first apse left and agai in its central niche, a pair of narro orthostats have a slightly projectir surface on the upper halve drawn down the corners rath like sleeves.

The most sig nificant featur however, stand opposite the sa rificial altar in th first apse righ tucked surpri ingly discreet out of view fro the entrance pa sage. It is a huma personage or, i view of its siz more likely deit of extraordinary form. The word are carefully chosen to avoid an implication of sex, which as in th many more complete, if not so ma sive, examples is not only unem phasized but to all appearanc deliberately suppressed. Whi generally referred to as a 'goddes or less respectfully as a 'fat lady those terms are not actually bor out by the evidence. However, the is even less to suggest a male attr bution. Whatever, or whoever,

'hile her monstrous calves and tiny feet ·rdly match modern standards of beauty, e giant statue from Tarxien South is a ıe work of art. It is a great tragedy that survived only from the fringe of the eated skirt down.

ne would have liked to be able to easure that impressive waistline, and ·en more to know its exact original ·ight (it cannot have been much under 3) and the form of its features.

is worth noting, on the evidence of e double statuette from the Xagħra ircle, (p.204), that all these statues may ·iginally have been painted in vivid ·lours.

near-spherical block, for long assumed be another stone roller, has recently ·en tentatively identified as the missing ·ad of this statue.

eing represented, stands, sits, or es at the very heart of the religion f the temples, and will be reconidered in that context shortly.

The giant statue at Tarxien ıows a standing figure, current-· nearly 2-m high though broken ff at the waist, with surviving ·edge slots showing how the pper half was removed, presumbly by local farmers, partly to lear their field of encumbrance, artly simply for use as building tone. Though the figure's proortions are unnatural, perhaps etter supernatural, when complete must have been of the order of .75 m high (see hypotetical illustraon overleaf). The surviving body ·ears a pleated skirt, which recurs ı much of Temple Period statuary, over very generously proportioned waist, buttocks, and thighs. It stops at knee height, leaving exposed a pair of bulging calves and elegant, but severely overburdened, feet.

This is no place to give a detailed catalogue of the other statuettes that were found here, or on other sites, as this can be found elsewhere (Evans 1971) or, indeed better, enjoyed in the showcases of the National Museum of Archaeology. A general summary and a look at some of the more significant pieces, together with some comment, are certainly required. The relief panels and giant statue were clearly, and of necessity, fixtures. One step down from this are a number of statuettes, in their present form

round 20 cm high though again roken off at the waist. Their missing chests and heads might have rought them to around 35 cm but ould probably not have added great deal to their weight. So hile they could be moved at need, ey were presumably intended remain in one position. Three om Tarxien are of familiar 'fat dy' form, skirted, asexual at ast in their surviving form, seatd upright on a backless chair or ool. On two, the stool has smaller gures in relief on their sides, sugesting children gathered round a other figure. A fourth is different being unclothed, making both s corpulence and asexuality that uch more obvious, also seated but a level surface, with feet tucked to one side.

With this group should perhaps e included a standing figure in rracotta from Tarxien, modelled nto a straw core, 60 cm high as stored. Known as 'the priest', the tle is fanciful, the figure probably presenting the same subject as e others. The main differences e that the skirt, with the same ch-topped pleats, is longer, reachg the ground, and the head has survived. A rather chubby face and rolls of hair, rather like a lawyer's wig, still give no clue as to the sex intended and the chest, which might have been indicative, is one of the fragments missing. There are smaller fragments of a very similar figure from the same site, and pieces of another modelled in the same technique were recovered from the temple at Borġ in-Nadur. Many heads of a similar style though in smaller size are known from a number of sites, mainly also in terracotta, their hair more often shown by lines running fore and aft over the crown. The Xagħra hypogeum produced several.

n artist's reconstruction of the setting of e giant diety of Tarxien gives some idea its original appearance. There can be no arantee, of course, that all the details e accurate since we are dealing with a adition which came to an end four-and-half thousand years ago, leaving no ritten record.

Turning to Ħaġar Qim, we find seven stone statuettes identical in stance with the last seated one described from Tarxien, some with the feet tucked up to the left, some to the right. They average 20 cm in height. Two others of a like size have their legs upright, facing forwards. One of them seems to be clothed, and the other wears a long pigtail curving down the back. Most of these figures have sockets surviving in their necks to take separate heads, now missing. Holes in the sides of the sockets served to peg the heads into position, whether rigidly or allowing some movement. They may have been of some material other than stone. If of wood, it would explain why they have not been found. However, heads in Gobigerina of appropriate size have turned up on other sites, two each from the Ġgantija and Ħal Saflieni, for example, which might have come from similar figures. Three more also from Ħaġar Qim, originally 50-75 cm high, are shown standing erect, though with the arms placed in the same way, one across the chest, the other hanging at the side. All appear to have unpleated skirts, though naked to the midriff and again from the thigh down. On the finer of the two, the calves are as gross as those of the giant statue at Tarxien, the feet as small, the toes individually demarcated and the base decorated with two rows of pitting. Again there is a socket to take a separate head, with dowel holes to secure it. Five of these fig ures were found in 1949 in a cach under the step leading into the on apse annexe, apparently secrete for safe-keeping. Both form an findspot strongly imply that w are looking at cult figures.

With them was found a standing figure c its pitted plinth. Like many of the others, the head was made separately, but is now missing.

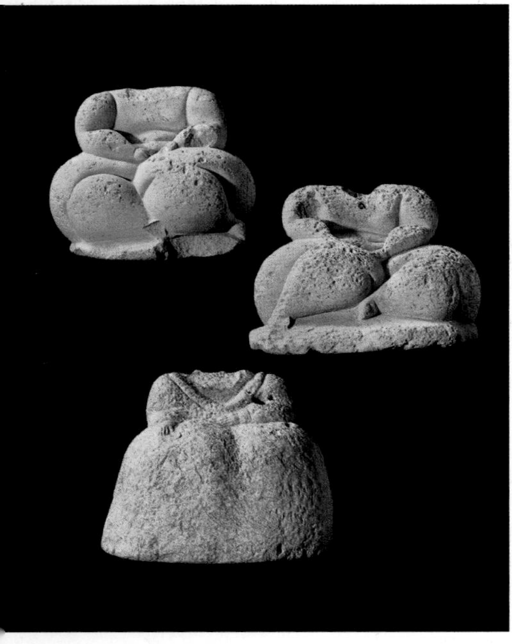

Three of the seated figures from Ħaġar Qim show the 'fat lady' of the Maltese temples in her ample proportions.

Even more securely hidde would have been a slab in th wall of one of the subsidiary ov chambers since it faces not int the chamber but into what woul have been the wall filling, and s would have been invisible at th time. Later destruction has nc only revealed it but removed it upper two-thirds, leaving only tw pairs of feet and one of calves, c the usual bulging form. An alte native interpretation is that it ha

his seated figure from Tarxien has naller ones in relief on the sides, perhaps ildren beneath the protection of their other's skirt?

formerly stood in a more prominent position and is here re-used as mere building material, perhaps after accidental breakage.

If one disregards modern standards of female beauty, and judges them only on their artistic merits, these carvings are superb. In their balance of swelling shapes, with their comfortable solidity, they are works of art of a high order, even if they would score poorly in a twenty-first-century beauty contest.

It must be emphasized that these renderings are in no sense due to incompetence by the sculptors, who were clearly working to well-defined conventions. This is manifest from another piece found close to the others at Ħaġar Qim, unique in following an entirely

CULPTURE TECHNIQUES

Two main techniques were employed. Modelling from clay was usually used only for smaller figurines, such as the Venus on p.101.
For carving, bone and a variety of stones were used, possibly also wood, though none has survived. The latter possibility is suggested by the fact that several of the Ħaġar Qim figures have sockets for separate heads, now missing.
The favoured material was the local Globigerina Limestone, which is admirably suited for larger reliefs or free-standing figures.

different convention. It is a standing female figure modelled in clay, in its present form, with head and feet broken away, 12.9 cm high. The stance is very similar to those just described, but it is in a startlingly realistic style. Admittedly, the proportion of the breasts is somewhat exaggerated, and of the arms reduced, but the modelling of the musculature, particularly of the shoulders and buttocks, is of a very high order by any standard, and very different from those pieces so far described. She has been called, with as much justification as can be expected of the term, the Venu of Ħaġar Qim, rightly putting he in the same league as the femal figurines of the Upper Palaeolith ic. Small enough to be portabl though probably still temple pos sessions rather than personal one are several from the hypogea. Fou show various figures on a clearl portrayed bed. This last is shown i remarkable detail, being rectangu lar, slightly concave, and standin on four short legs.

From Ħal Saflieni, the 'Sleep ing Lady' lies on her right side her right hand under her head, he breasts ample, naked to the wais below which a fringed skirt cover her to her calves. Interpretation o this piece will be attempted late Her bed is 12.2 cm long.

On a companion piece, als in terracotta, a similar figure lie

We can enjoy the superb artistry of the 'Sleeping Lady' of Ħal Saflieni, an artistic masterpiece, even if we are completely baffled in trying to divine her meaning.

nother masterpiece, the Venus
' Ħaġar Qim, has broken with the
range conventions of Maltese
mple statuary.
ıstead, it is a magnificent naturalistic
ndering of the female form.
ike the 'Sleeping Lady', it was modelled
ı clay, then baked to a hard ceramic.
s interpretation is equally unknown,
ut with this piece, we can enjoy it
ithout feeling we need to look for a
eeper meaning.

rone with the arms raised. Head nd skirt are more damaged than on he first, and the posture prevents he breasts from being seen. The hird is only 7.2 cm long, carved n stone and more problematical. Vhile the bed is clear, the figure n it looks more like a fish than nything else.

The Xagħra statuette is another nasterpiece. A more elaborate bed, ts surface decorated with typi- al thorny volutes, is beautifully arved. On it are seated two 'fat adies' closely juxtaposed, their nees drawn up in front of them nder pleated skirts, which leave amiliar bulging calves and tiny eet exposed. Though the breasts re not shown, well-padded chests nd arms are bare. While one head is missing, the other was recov- ered, though broken off. It has the familiar exaggerated thick neck, backward tilted face, and fore-and-aft hairstyle. One of the two holds a cup or bowl on its lap, the other a diminutive figure of the same form and proportions, if of much smaller size. Calves and bedspread are painted in red ochre, and there are traces of black on the skirts and hair. Once more, one has to speculate on the meaning of these figures.

Close to this lay nine other stone figures, so closely packed that they must have been in some form of container. Six, averaging 20 cm, have human heads set on schematic bodies, little more than trapezoidal plaques. None has the one a necklace, waist band, and pleated skirt; one a band and skirt only; three a bare indication of a waistline. The heads are equally varied.

One has severe features and wears some sort of diadem, its peak broken away. Number 2, the one with the necklace, is equally finely worked, very similar but lacking the diadem. Number 3 has the face less finished and wears a hood or cowl. Number 4 is like Number 3 but without the hood, Number 5 simpler still and Number 6, no more than a roughout with the tool-marks still clearly apparent, would have been different yet again, virtually lacking a neck.

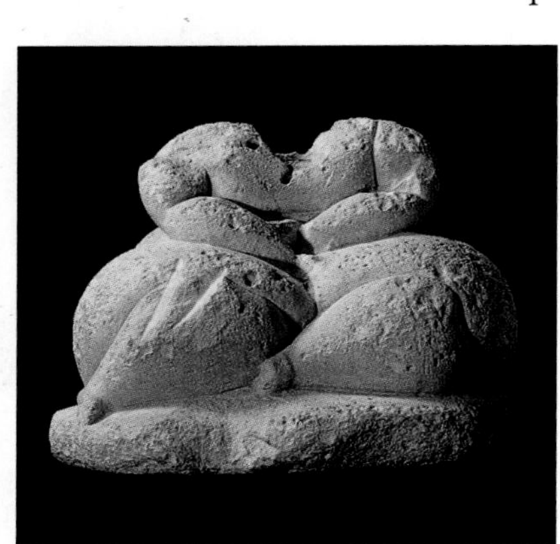

Another of the seated figures from Ħaġar Qim shows the socket to take its separate head, now missing.

The next two have heads very like the 'two-on-a-bed' and many others from Malta, though on very different 'bodies'. The first is on a vertical pillar, far too long to be called a neck, which expands into a broad base. The other is even stranger, emerging from a knob with two short stubs, projecting towards the front and back. Finally the ninth head is not human at all, but apparently meant to represent a pig. Though the mouth is set at the end of a rather pointed muzzle, incised curves on either side strongly suggest tusks.

While the skirts on Number and Number 2 and the heads o Number 7 and Number 8, an the Globigerina from which a are carved, point firmly to loca production, reinforced by th unfinished state particularly c Number 5, these are very strang indeed in a Maltese context.

They must surely have bee used in temple rituals, for late consideration The same probably applies t a series of terracotta seated figurines averagin 7 cm high foun nearby. They wer all more uniforn in appearance though foun scattered rathe than in close association. With thei bulging knee straight forward small backward tilted heads, thei facial feature slightly marked, and with on arm at the side and the othe across the flat chest – thoug two of the 15 have breasts – an all have grossly-exaggerate thighs, they fall very comfortably within the range of Maltes 'fat ladies'.

Less attractive are a few ver roughly-modelled figures, some s gross as to be possibly pathologica A couple were found in Ħal Saflier and several more at Mnajdra. Th

f a different style yet again, by its ery grossness, this small, 7 cm high, gure raises disturbing questions of nterpretation.
he splinters of shell jabbed into the clay efore it was fired hint at a darker side to e temple culture.
is difficult to believe that it was roduced by the same society as the other gures illustrated here.
he context of its discovery in the Tarxien emples is secure.

xact number there cannot be given s it is debatable if some of them re human at all. One from Tarxen has bone splinters stuck into its lay, giving a sinister suggestion f witchcraft. One or two are more learly of animals, though again so ough that one cannot say which pecies of animal was intended.

Many sites have produced fragnents of figurines on the same sort f scale, heads most commonly ut also occasional legs, feet, and ands. While most are broken off, ome appear to be complete, as f intended as votive offerings of fflicted parts.

Finally, there are many even maller pieces, of an even wider ange of subjects, which may also ave been votive offerings but could have been carried around on the person as charms or amulets. The perforated miniature axes, although hardly art, show that the practice was widespread, as do various other pendants and beads, particularly from Ħal Saflieni.

Pendants include animals, probably cattle, birds, and fish, and even a model temple. One V-perforated button from Xagħra was so realistically carved into the shape of a snail that it was only recognized after it had been thrown out on the spoilheap, having been mistaken for the real thing. Most of these are of stone or fossil shell, though a few are of bone.

Some of the heads are tiny and exquisite. One in particular is sensitively carved from a knob

Just as intriguing are these figurines, with human heads on plaque-like bodies. Some were plainly unfinished when buried as a group beneath the Xagħra Circle. Average height 20 cm.

of dripstone, still on its shapeless chunk of rock. Noteworthy also are three from Xagħra carved onto the knobs of small animal toe-bones. The faces on these tiny human heads are barely 4 mm high, with their features picked out in colour, red for the mouth, black for the eyes.

Craftsmanship of a high order is apparent in many of these, from the 2.75 m giant at Tarxien down to those 4 mm faces from Xagħra, though debatable when it comes to the grotesque figures or simple clay twists from Mnajdra. Even more subjective is judgement of their artistry. Some pieces undoubtedly have it – the Venus of Ħaġar Qim, two-on-a-bed from Xagħra, the Sleeping Lady from Ħal Saflieni – others equally certainly do not, but where is one to draw the line? Is a line eithe possible or even desirable? Thes pieces clearly fulfilled a need, o more likely a number of differer needs, whether functional or nc – and some that we would regar as purely decorative might we have been considered by their mak ers as serving a functional purpos Whatever was in their minds, w can still appreciate their achieve ments, four-and-a-half-thousan years or more later. Their product certainly compare well with that c their contemporaries, far exceed ing most.

Having described the architec-
ıre, internal fittings and contents f the temples, what can we say bout the rituals and ceremonies erformed in them, and about the ligious beliefs that inspired them? he only possible answer is – not uch. Imagine those same ques- ons being asked of a tribesman of mazonia or highland New Guinea ıtroduced for the first time into a eserted Roman Catholic church. /hat could he deduce about the ıass, or the tenets of Christianity? (ow much more difficult would e find it if the church had fallen own, its contents smashed, and ıany of them decayed away com- letely? But that is precisely the tuation we are faced with in try- ıg to understand the function, as pposed to the physical structure, f Malta's prehistoric temples.

Fortunately there is a consid- rable body of evidence, so cer- ıin deductions are still possible. hough our conclusions must be ntative, and guesses cautious, e have better grounds for such reconstruction than in the great ıajority of prehistoric societies, just s our Amazonian Indian would e likely to approach closer to the uth in a Catholic church than in much more simply furnished Nonconformist chapel. At least we should make the attempt.

The temples appear to have three zones. Firstly comes the forecourt, often clearly delimited, spacious, open to the sky. This would seem to be designed for public gatherings, presumably with a religious focus given its close association with the temple and its entrance. However, that still leaves a very wide range of possible activities – processions, singing, dancing, sermonizing of some sort, are only a few of them. In many societies, more secular activities take place, encouraged rather than inhibited by the religious setting, markets for example, and other economic or legal transactions such as marriages, administering of justice or

he bench at the foot of the façade and e forecourt in front of the temples at Inajdra hint at communal ceremonies the open air associated with the mple.

taking of oaths, public announcements – the list is endless.

At some sites there is a bench running at the foot of the concave façade, though whether this had a ceremonial use as is likely, or was merely added to give added stability to the façade orthostats is not clear. It appears also on the Tarxien model of a temple façade.

Within the temple, one would expect the religious element to preponderate much more strongly, and the surviving evidence supports this. The first and most obvious activity is perhaps animal sacrifice. The altar in the first apse right of Tarxien South, immediately adjacent to the giant statue (we shall return to it again shortly), gave graphic insights to Tem Zammit when he first exposed it in 1915. The niche behind the trilithon altar was stuffed with the bones of domestic animals. Even more dramatically, the cubby hole in its front, closed with a carved stone plug continuing the surrounding decoration, was found to hold a long flint knife blade and the horn core of a goat. Putting these together, we can hardly be mistaken in thinking that the square stone block was neither more nor less than a sacrificial altar. Nor is it stretching the evidence too far to suggest the same function for the numerous similar blocks in this and other temples.

This stone floored hearth in Ġgantija presumably once played a part in the temple rituals, as did the altar at the back of the apse, now reduced to a single stump.

V-perforation was laboriously cut in
drock outside the entrance to Ħaġar
im.
is tempting to see the purpose of this
be the tethering of an animal until
e moment came for it to be led into the
mple for sacrifice.
'e cannot prove this of course, though it
not easy to come up with an alternative,
ill less a more likely, explanation.

There is supporting evidence. ll undisturbed temple deposits at Skorba for example – produced uantities of animal bones. Sev- 'al of these altars have projecting ones at their base with a perfor- :ion through them, suitable for thering an animal until the appro- riate moment in the ceremony r its sacrifice. Skorba again had good example of this. At both aġar Qim and Mnajdra, there are milar tethering holes in the fore- ›urt or façade, presumably for the ıme purpose. Tarxien in particu- r had relief friezes of animals on ›me of its blocks, as we have seen. hree large flint knife blades were und together in the Xagħra Circle ypogeum. The goat skulls in the re-temple shrines at Skorba suggest that the practice had started early. It should be stressed, however, that, contrary to what many visitors, particularly the younger ones, would like to believe, there is no evidence whatsoever for human sacrifice.

A second practice equally widely attested at many later periods and almost worldwide, was the prominent use of fire. Several temples have centrally placed heat-reddened hearths. What we cannot say is whether these were for burning parts of the sacrificed animals as offerings, or, just as likely, aromatic herbs. Though true incense would not be introduced from southern Arabia until much later, many plants of the Mediterranean area give off a sweet smell on burning. The light from these fires was probably much appreciated also, to counter the darkness of these closed in chambers. The far more extensive reddening at Tarxien is surely the result of the temple's destruction rather than indicative of its use.

It is very noticeable that the interior decoration of the temples is largely, if not entirely, confined to the first pair of apses and the court between them. In most of the temples, that central court is impressively paved, unlike the apses and inner courts. Ġgantija South is the only exception to this, but there are oth hints that its outer apses we later additions to what starte as a three-apse temple.

We can only guess at the function of the laboriously carved huge stone bowl in th first apse of the same temple.

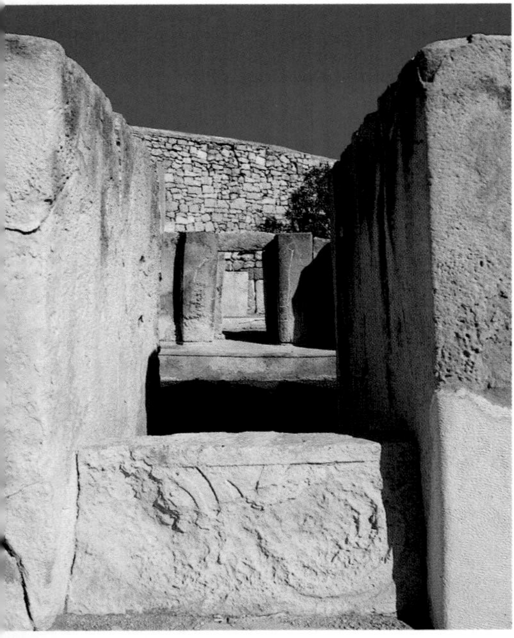

The sill stone with its double spirals (this is a replica, the original in the National Museum is much less weathered) restricted access to the inner recesses of the Central Temple at Tarxien.

All this suggests there were tw zones of access within the temple with a contrast between the out apses and court, to which the ge eral populace – all of it? only son of it? – was admitted, to admi and worship, and a more priva inner zone from which they we barred. A parallel to this woul be offered by a Greek Orthodc church, where only the priest allowed behind the iconostasis, holier but far simpler area than tl main body of the church.

The division between the two zones may be emphasized b

ɪe complexity of fittings in the first
•se right of Ġgantija South leaves us
ɔndering about the temple rituals.

a physical, if only partial, barrier, like the sill stone with its oculus reliefs in Tarxien Central. Nearly always, at least where the door jambs survive, this passage from first to second court could be closed off, as shown by a rebate on its inner side, by V-perforations apparently designed for the attachment of a screen or door, and even recesses on either side to take a massive bar to secure that door. All these, note, were designed to be closed from the inner side.

Admittedly there are a few exceptions to most of this. At the south temples of both Ġgantija and Tarxien, the central altars are decorated, though still directly visible from the outer courts. At the former, both inner and outer passages could be barred. At Tarxien

OOR 'FURNITURE'

Many of the temple doorways have V-perforations and pits in their jambs, as here in the entrance to Ġgantija South. The former were presumably to attach a screen, the latter to take securing bars.

The Oracle Room in the Ħal Saflieni Hypogeum is famous for its ceiling, painted in ochre with spiral designs, and for its acoustic properties. It reverberates eerily to anything spoken into the niche on the right.

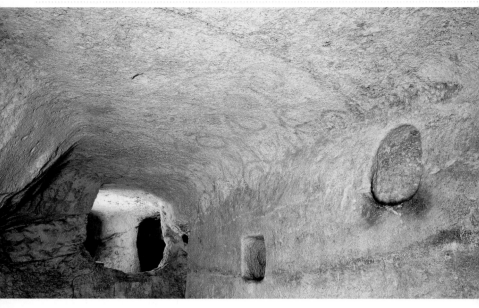

Central, two of the most highly decorated slabs in any of the temples, the spiral-ornamented screens, stood across the side apses, out of view of the outer court. But talking of visibility, we must remember that the interiors of the temples would be profoundly dark, as was pointed out when discussing their roofs. Or would they? That decoration was clearly meant to be seen, so we must suppose artificial lighting was employed, though strangely no obvious lamps have been found. The wall and ceiling painting down in Ħal Saflieni makes the point even more strongly.

Saflieni also reminds us that aural, as well as visual, effects must have been important too. Though it is hard to believe that the reverberations of its Oracle Chamber were designed by those who carved the monument, it highly probable that they wer recognized, and exploited to th full. There must also have bee singing and chanting, perhaps als instrumental music, although n recognizable instruments have su vived. Without them, we can onl guess. Even with them, of cours we would have little idea what th music would have sounded like. we consider again our Amazonia Indian, he would soon realize th capabilities of the church bell, bu would have little inkling of thos of the organ.

Returning to the implications
' that division between outer and
ner, public and private, we have
ıe further significant clue.

In Mnajdra, two carefully carved
›ertures connect the first apse
ght of the South Temple with
ner chambers, one in the thick-
ess of the temple wall, one little
ore than a niche entered from the
ıck of the temple. There is a simi-
r but simpler opening through the
ıst wall of Tarxien East. These are
sually referred to as oracle holes.
hough the term suggests much
ore precision than is justified, it is
reasonable one if not pressed too
r. Clearly these holes provided
ommunication between what we
ave interpreted as the public part
f the temples and an even more
rivate part than the inner court
nd apses. Those inner chambers,
estricted in both size and access,
ıggest, as do the screens and bar
oles, a select few on the one side,
eparated from the general public
n the other. We can hardly avoid
ıe term 'priests' or 'priestesses' for
ıe former, though again we ought
apply the terms loosely if they
re not to be misleading.

But 'oracles'? We cannot know
our 'priests' interpreted the
ill of the gods through them, received offerings or confessions, dispensed advice, blessings or absolutions. None of these uncertainties adversely affects the implication of these holes, that there was clear distinction between priests and worshippers. There is also a strong hint that the relationship between the two parties changed through time. We have already noted that in an earlier period, that of the three-apse temples as first built, the separation of public and private zones of activity did not exist. It was only by the insertion of either a cross wall with a closable doorway, as at Skorba South, Mġarr, and Kordin III, or by the addition of an outer pair of apses, as at Ġgantija South, that this distinction became clear. In the other

his is the finest of the oracle holes in Mnajdra South, and perhaps the best evidence for a priesthood. It communicates with a secret chamber behind. Note also the oversailing courses in the wall above.

five-apse temples it was probably integral, as it certainly was in the case of all the later four-apse temples. The social implications will be looked at later.

In all religions, the rituals and ceremonies are grounded in a body of beliefs. That must apply here also. The main evidence for a reconstruction of these is provided by the carvings, from tiny amulets to the giant statue in Tarxien South. That that represents the goddess herself is a virtual certainty, given its size, prominent position in the most public part of the temple's interior, and similarity to the many

An attractive small clay figurine from Tarxien, only 3 cm high, looks much les like a goddess. Again we must regret th loss of its head.

While patently representing phalli, it is difficult to see why they should have been carved in triplicate (12.3 cm high, from Tarxien).

other representations of the 'f lady'. The arguments for consi ering her female have already be rehearsed: the obesity is only t obvious. But who was she? T most reasonable interpretati is that she is a mother godde Whether the same 'earth moth as worshipped almost worldwi as many authorities imply witho question, or a local manifestation a general idea, is debatable, thou no firm conclusion either way possible now.

Female obesity is widely he to imply fertility, rightly wrongly, though the absence vulva or breasts on most of t statues is strange if fertility w the underlying principle of th

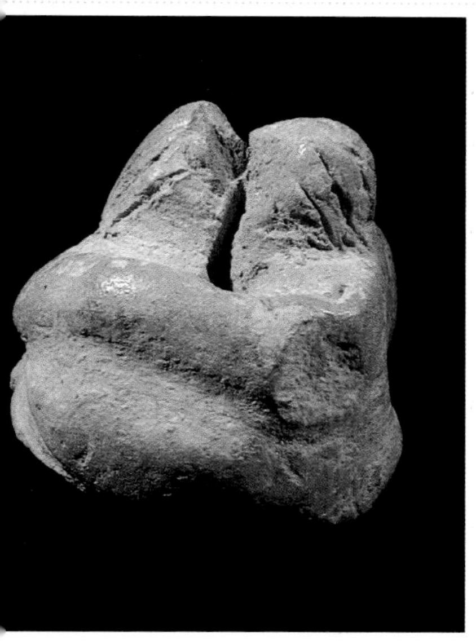

ough somewhat roughly modelled, other Tarxien figure shows an bracing couple. The fertility mbolism is again obvious.

religion. Much more explicit are the small carved phalli from Tarxien, and about these there can be no doubt. Similarly, the juxtaposition on a wall relief at the same site of a very male bull and, given her fourteen piglets at suck, very female sow can hardly be anything but signi-ficant. Two of the seated statues have diminutive figures round her chair, as if to enjoy the goddess's maternal protection.

A small and broken terracotta figurine from Tarxien could be significant here. It shows a human couple in a close embrace, though whether a sexual act or only a kiss is not clear. Presumably the two are of opposite sexes, but this is not obvious in the present state of the fragment.

:MPLES AND THE FIGURINES

ere is an undoubted resemblance in outline between the plans some of the temples and the seated 'fat lady' figurines. Is this ncidence, or was one influenced by the other?

e similarity of shape is the main argument in favour. hat is more, some of the temple models, (p.195), owed that they could be viewed as abstract ns. On the other hand, it is only one form of statuettes, the seated ones, and one of the nples, that with four apses and niche, where similarity occurs at all.

gretfully, any relationship between the o, beyond the fact that both served the ne religion, must be considered unlikely.

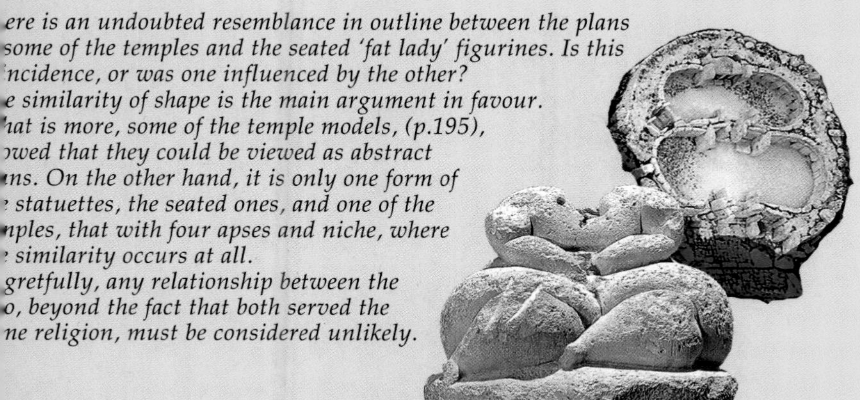

Another aspect of the goddess and her religion was perhaps healing. Models of human 'spare parts' have already been mentioned, and not only the male generative organ. The separate hands, legs, and feet, less certainly the heads, could have been votives, dedicated in the temples as requests for, or thanks for, divine assistance in securing cures. However, the absence of eyes and babies, among the most frequent offerings in later such contexts, could be held to argue against this. Conversely, the grotesque figures from Mnajdra and Tarxien, particularly the one stuck with shell, could also be requests for aid, but against an enemy rather than a disease. One suggestion for tl meaning of the Sleeping Lady Ħal Saflieni is that she illustrat the rite of incubation, where worshipper sleeps in a sanctua in the hope of receiving a cure l divine intervention. But the san rite was also on occasion employ when the aim was informati rather than healing, knowledge the divine will come through tl medium of dreams. Nor are the by any means the only possibi ties for the interpretation of th enigmatic figure.

It has become fashionable interpret many religious practic in the past in the context of shama ism. This also involves mediati between the spirit world and th of every day, often with the obje of curing illness. It has indeed be suggested for prehistoric Malta to

The engraved slab from Tal-Qadi bears radiating lines, asterisks, and a crescent. Can we read an astronomical significance into this, or are they just decoration?

t least the identification of this figure is sy – a snake wriggling up the edge of a ock from the South Ġgantija Temple. s meaning is less secure, though snakes ancient religions were often associated ith underworld deities, and also with rtility, wisdom, and healing. Which of ese, if any, applied here we have no way knowing.

ut the evidence would seem to e strongly against this explana-on here. The shaman acts as an dividual, going into a trance-like ate, often by means of drugs or iolent rhythmic activity. On the ontrary, the temples are patently e result of communal, not indi-dual, religious activity, the sphere f priests rather than shamans.

Could there be any astronomical gnificance, as has been suggested r many ancient monuments? The lans on pages 200-1 show that the mple axes markedly favour the uadrant between southeast and outhwest. Though it is difficult to e what movements of heavenly odies this could be reflecting, it annot be entirely ruled out. It will e discussed more fully in connec-on with that diagram.

Our goddess seems to have had oser association with the under-orld than with the heavens, and so more sinister side. Libation holes rough paving like those in the çade shrines at Tarxien South and the entrance passage of Skorba West imply that the recipient of the liquid offerings was pictured as dwelling beneath the ground. Snakes, as portrayed on the edge of a standing slab from Ġgantija, were frequently associated with chthonic, underworld, deities. The suggestion that the temples were at least in part modelled on tombs could also be telling us something. Both hypogea, Ħal Saflieni and the Xagħra Circle, clearly had religious rites performed within them, being chapels as well as cemeteries. There need be no sur-prise here. After all, one of the main functions of religion is to reconcile mankind with its own mortality. And there need be no contradiction between this and the fertility ele-ment if death was believed to be followed by rebirth.

The concept of mortality leads naturally to a consideration of death and burial in Temple Period Malta. While there may have been other burial rites which have left no recoverable traces, the main one certainly appears to have been interment in rock-cut chambers, a continuation of the practice established at least by the Żebbug phase. It should again be stressed that there is no sign of burials within the temples themselves until after their abandonment as places of worship.

The main difference from earlier practice was one of scale. The

This pilaster in the wall of a tomb at Xemxija, or one like it, was probably the inspiration for the elaborate carving of t Hypogeum.

The side niches in the Hypogeum, carved to represent temple trilithons, held most of the human bone from the site.

few tombs known from the Żebbu phase seem to have been fami vaults, or at most small villag cemeteries, and this still appli to the rather more numerous Ġga tija phase tombs – six at Xemxij single ones at Binġemma and T Ħamet Street, Xagħra. There coul of course, be many others yet to l discovered. By Saflieni and Tarxi times, the great necropolises of Ħ Saflieni itself and the Xagħra Circ were in full use. That part of tl latter so far excavated has yielde the remains of at least eight hu dred people, and Zammit's estima for the former was six thousand! too began in a small way. Among material from that part of the si around the entrance were Żebbı

'he skull, upper arm, spine, and ribs
f this skeleton lay on the floor of the
Xagħra Circle Hypogeum, here revealed
y excavation.

and Ġgantija sherds, while the inner chambers cleared by Zammit had only Saflieni and Tarxien. But those earlier sherds may have been only sporadic, like the corresponding ones in the Xagħra hypogeum.

If they do really indicate use from Żebbug times on, this would mean, as Colin Renfrew pointed out, use of the hypogeum over at least six hundred years. It follows that the total of seven thousand interments no longer poses the enormous problem it was once thought to. At ten burials a year, it need imply a community of no more than three hundred people. We no longer have to assume that this cemetery served the whole island group, for which we have postulated a population of some

URIAL POSITIONS

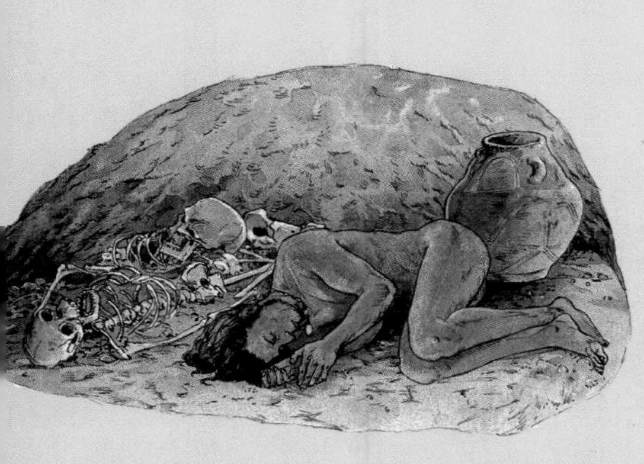

Bodies may be buried extended, flexed, crouched, disarticulated, cremated, or not at all. This covers the most frequent practices, though by no means all. The crouched position was probably the commonest, in Malta as elsewhere. It has two main advantages: it reduces the size of grave pit or tomb chamber required, and by imitating the foetal position, symbolizes either a return to the individuals's origins, or perhaps rebirth into another life.

ten thousand, still less the import of corpses from abroad for burial in this sacred island, as was seriously suggested by some. On the contrary, it seems highly likely that other communities within the islands – Renfrew suggested five more on the basis of the distribution of the temples – would also have excavated themselves their own hypogea.

This argument has been greatly strengthened, of course, by the discovery of Gozo's hypogeum, beneath the Xagħra Circle.

The actual burial rites, however, changed little. Bodies were laid out in a flexed or crouched position, with no obvious preferred orientation. Grave goods were often added, an offering bowl, miniature axe, beads, a terracotta figurine, frequently a sprinkle of red ochre too, though now not so lavishly as had been the case earlier. After the flesh had decayed away and the skeleton begun to fall apart, it could be pushed aside to make space for later burials, just as before. At Xagħra, a particular area was designated for this purpose, a veritable charnel pit beside the entrance, packed with decayed and fragmented bone. The same may well have been the case in Ħal Saflieni, though in the absence of records of the excavation, evidence for such was not preserved.

This change of scale has social implications too. The dead were no longer being cared for within the family group but were absorbed back into the larger community in the vast underground cemeter which that community, by mobili ing the efforts of its members, ha hacked out of the rock to receiv them. At the same time, howeve the elaborate heart of Ħal Saflien its central chamber, the Holy c Holies and the Oracle Room, an the built structures and associate ritual paraphernalia in the centre c the Xagħra hypogeum, show th these were more than just cemete ies. They were temples in their ow right too.

At Bur Mgħeż, Mqabba, natural cave was used for buri in much the same way, thoug without any architectural embe lishment. At least 75 skeletons wer represented here in 1911 and 192 together with sherds of the Ġgar tija and Tarxien phases.

A magnificently carved chamber lies at the heart of the Hypogeum of Ħal Saflien This surely was a temple, comparing closely with those above ground with its porthole-within-trilithon doorway, clearl shown corbelled roof, and V-perforation i the floor.
Perhaps we can regard it as a cemetery chapel since the labyrinthine side chambers and niches held many thousand of human bones.

TARXIEN

TARXIEN

This is the most complex of all temple sites in Malta, though it has sadly lost the atmosphere of a Ġgantija or Mnajdra, being surrounded by modern housing. Four temple units and a square court are immediately conjoined, and there was later reuse of the site.

It was discovered in 1914 by local farmers hitting its great building blocks in their ploughing, and removing many of them for use elsewhere. The saddest damage was to the great goddess statue illustrated and discussed elsewhere. Sir Temi Zammit excavated the site in 1915 – 1917, placing our understanding of Maltese prehistory at last on a firm foundation. Over those years, beginning with the South Temple, he first exposed the cemetery inserted into the ruins in the Early Bronze Ag then successively the Central, Ea and Far East temples.

The South Temple's main façad with a small shrine with libatio holes at either end, opened onto forecourt with a large water cister at its centre. Its walls were reduce to near ground level, the doorwa welcoming visitors being a reconstruction of 1960. Many other block were capped at the same time to prevent erosion.

Immediately inside the doorwa is the most highly-decorated are of any of the temples. Of particul note are the spiral decorated alta block with niche above on the righ close to it the giant goddess statu and in the opposing apse, mor blocks decorated with relief spira

Of the façade of the South Temple, only the bench at its foot survives, even the entrance doorway being a modern reconstruction. However, the model in the next picture gives a good idea of its original appearance. The wide forecourt has a large water cistern at its centre.

Two fragments of this beautifully carved contemporary model of a temple survive, at top left and bottom right. From these can be reconstructed not only the rest of the model but also the original temples. Compare this with the picture to the left.

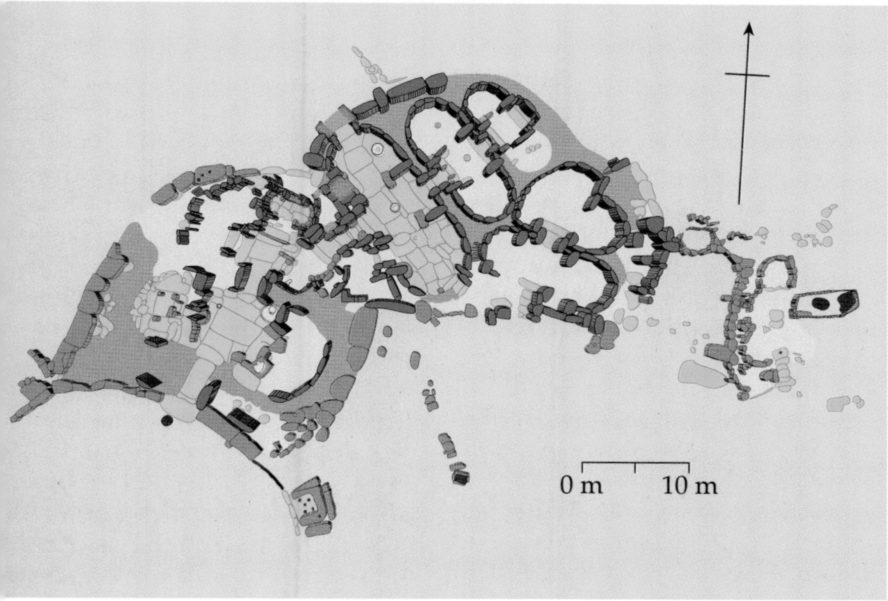

0 m 10 m

espite its comparative complexity, the an of Tarxien can be resolved into its parate elements, four immediately adjacent temple units. The small 5-apse on the right was the first to be built, the 6-apse in the centre the last.

single slab of stone was carved to form hrine at the east end of the South mple's façade. There was probably a cond at the west end.
e five holes through its floor probably rried libations to the underworld.

Dominating the first court of the South Temple was the giant statue of the goddess, now sadly reduced to waist level. Here is the replica on site.
For the original see p.95.

and others with rows of animals. All these are modern copies, the originals now in the National Museum of Archaeology in Valletta.

The second pair of apses is less ornamented, though the central altar bore first all-over pitting, this then cut away to be replaced by a complex pattern of relief spirals. This copy is now badly weathered, reinforcing the decision to remove the original for safe keeping in the museum. The second apse right was adapted to give access to the Central Temple. Note the bar holes and V-perforations in the door jambs.

The first pair of apses of this second temple are massively floored, though this had to be boarded to protect it. A block to the right has been lifted to show that they are not mere paving slabs but substantial blocks. The walls are all of close-fitting orthostats, preserved better than those of the South Temple b the steadily rising ground. They ar however, all heavily reddened by th fire which destroyed the buildin A bowl in the centre was appa ently also used for a small fire an a much larger carved stone bowl the left for some unknown purpos Of particular note is the chamber the thickness of the wall to the righ famous for its reliefs of two bul and a sow.

The inner part of this temple cut off by a high sill stone, anoth replica, decorated with a pair spirals. Within it, the two beaut ful spiral-decorated screens, no in Valletta, masked the second pa of apses. Unusually, another pa sage led to a third and final pair apses with central niche. The inn apse left has the evidence of arch roofing already discussed, and neat little stone cupboard; that c

The blocks around the first apse on the left are decorated with spirals, animals, and graffiti of boats. The wall behind had been demolished to ground level, and was replaced in misleadingly small rubble. Imagine one more like that behind the bowl opposite.

Two decorated blocks in this apse have friezes of animals in relief, 22 horned sheep on one, four sheep, a pig, and a ?ram on the surviving half of the other. The last three are illustrated here.

e right has traces of the Roman llar which largely destroyed it.

The East Temple, the third, much much plainer, but with traordinarily well-cut slab walls, ab walls provided with notches for anoeuvring. Two oracle holes open the right. Its second left apse was so removed by that Roman cellar. otice also another good example bar holes and V-perforations in e front door, and more remark- ly the flight of steps apparently ading to either an upper chamber, the roof.

Beyond a square court is a much naller temple, originally with five oses. The hole in the rock below nnot be dated. This temple was

is altar block is famous for the flint ife in its 'cupboard' and the animal nes behind the porthole. It provides the st evidence for animal sacrifice.

e central altar in the South Temple, a plica, has trilithon altars standing on it. e original is illustrated on p.92. Inner ses open to left and right.

The giant bowl stands in the first apse left of the Central Temple. The closely fitting wall slabs and massive paving of the floor are also well shown in this view.

the first to be built, its form and contained sherds confirming erection in the Ġgantija phase. The South and East Temples were added in the Tarxien phase, the Central Temple being inserted some time later.

The cellar already mentioned and a cistern just outside the bulls-and-sow chamber were cut into the ruins later. The oven in front of the East Temple was a medieval addition. The site then remained undisturbed until the farmers began their depredations, with Zammit's much more careful investigation following shortly after.

While all the major finds from the temples are of course in the National Museum of Archaeology in Valletta, together with the originals of the giant statue and decorated blocks, a replica of the sacrificial altar and a number of lesser pieces are kept in the custodian's hut at the entrance to the site. They include one dec rated slab having both pitting a a curious sleeved effect, and tv pillared altars resembling those Ħaġar Qim. Stone bowls, one them also pitted, are included wi the group, one of them curious having no bottom – a cylinder rath than a bowl, so perhaps deliberate to let liquid libations through, rath than to hold them.

The large globular object on t right as one leaves was assumed be a stone ball like those piled in t South Temple forecourt, but a cust dian, Charles Borg, recently point out that the base is a little flattene with a slight bulge low on the w and hollows above. Could it be much-battered human head? If s it would be much of a size with t one which must once have stood the shoulders of the giant statue, intriguing possibility.

In an obscure inner chamber, this orthostat with its relief carving of a bull and sow with piglets is a striking feature. There is a second bull on an adjacent orthostat.

A stone roller is exposed beneath the paving of the Central Temple. Doubt has been cast on its being used to move the threshold slab above it into position.

the heart of the Central Temple, can seen the closely fitting orthostats with eir tops sloping inwards, the neat little cupboard and the replica screens decorated with spirals on a pitted background.

low level view over the East and entral Temples is confusing, but from e higher level of the photo overleaf, it all comes much clearer, and the groups of sitors serve to show the scale.

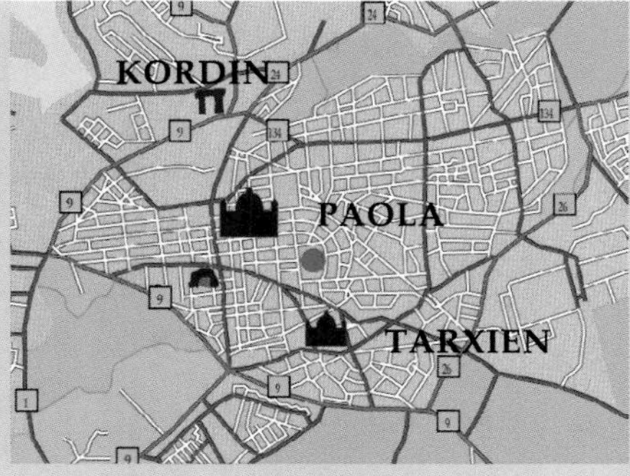

The road to Tarxien Temples is very well marked on the road signs as one approaches the villages of Paola and Tarxien. The easiest way by car is to drive by the Addolorata Cemetery on Vjal Santa Luċia, then on the roundabout, turn first left into Tarxien on Triq Ħal Luqa, and then right on Triq Ħal Tarxien, turn left on Triq is-Sorijiet and then right on Triq Santa Tereza and you will see the Visitors' Centre.

ĦAL SAFLIENI
PAOLA

Under the crowded streets of housing south of of Paola Square built around 1900 lies a unique monument. Apparently some natural cavities were adopted as a suitable repository for the bones of the dead of a flourishing community residing above the head of Grand Harbour. Before their entrance, a setting of large blocks of stone was erected, though its original form was ruined by modern developments. As the cavities filled up, new chambers were cut progressively deeper into the Globigerina rock of the area. Later additions to the site were elaborately carved into what can only be called a cemetery chapel. The importance to us is twofold.

Firstly, the funerary deposits, excavated by Father Magri from 1901, Temi Zammit from 190 yielded a wealth of archaeolog cal material, deposited with tl deceased. This material include much pottery, mainly of the pha we call after this site, though spa ning Żebbuġ (a little only, aroun the entrance), Ġgantija and, in gre quantities, Tarxien as well. Wi the exception of the cistern, to l mentioned shortly, there was no of later periods. There was also great number of personal orn ments such as beads and amulet the latter in the form of miniatu polished stone axes, little carve animals and birds, and larger fig rines. Of these the 'Sleeping Lady is discussed on p.100.

Secondly, while many side char bers have simple oval plans, parts

The entrance area of the Hypogeum, in grey on the plan opposite, had rock-carved chambers to the left and a built trilithon to the right in this view.

The giant water cistern, top right on the plan opposite, provided the site with its water. It too was carved from the rock, leaving pilasters to support the walls. It remained in use long after the rest of the site was sealed off.

0 m 5 m 10 m

TOP LEVEL

MIDDLE LEVEL

LOWER LEVEL

PASSAGEWAY BETWEEN LEVELS

e three levels of the Hypogeum were ·wn successively out of the rock to a ·ximum depth of 10.6 m.

The blocks in orange stood above ground level. Those parts of the Top Level open to the sky are shown in grey, the cistern at top right.

·m the central chamber of the site, ·nings lead into the side niches where main burial deposits, with their ·man bone, pots, and ornaments, were ·nd.

The deposit of red earth, after the bone and cultural material had been sorted from it, was returned to this side chamber to give an idea of how the contents of the site appeared when first found.

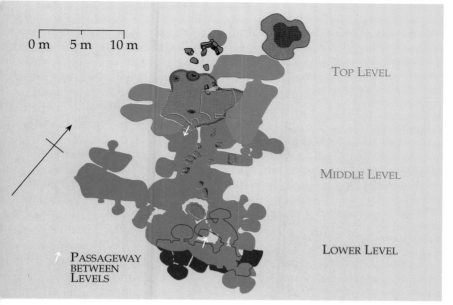

the site were clearly carved to imitate the temples built above ground. Unlike those, these were not subject to weathering by the elements, nor, with the entrance sealed off, by human interference, both of which have done damage to the temples proper. This Hypogeum thus shows us details of, for example, the corbelled roofing, and in two of the chambers the interior decoration of spirals and honeycomb cells rendered in red ochre, which no longer survive above ground. In one small patch there is even a chequered panel of black and white squares.

Sadly a third value was not recognized sufficiently at the time of excavation, and so was not exploited. This was the wealth of information which could have been recovered from careful study of the vast quantity of human bones found. Zammit made a rough calculation by extrapolation from the bon recovered from one small area th the total had amounted to arou seven thousand. Such a study h to await the re-excavation of t Xagħra Circle 75 years later.

We can only guess at the acti ties in this mysterious place. T burials are obvious, though t actual funeral rites less so. We mig assume that the bodies were plac probably in a crouched position, the side chambers, together wi those personal possessions. Ev in this vast labyrinth there is hard space for seven thousand compl corpses, or even skeletons, so alm certainly bones, as they fell apa were pushed to the back to ma room for their successors, th descendants, century after cent ry. Considering the duration of use those vast numbers need n surprise us. The central chamb

This chamber at the centre of the site has elaborately carved trilithons, entrances to further chambers. Its walls are ochred and on one is a panel of chequer pattern in black and white squares.

A second wall, to the left of the last, has two storeys of side niches. These also contained numerous human bones and grave goods.

oubtless witnessed religious cermonies, honouring both the dead nd the gods (I use that latter term the general sense to avoid repeatg the discussion of the nature the god, goddess, or gods conrned), though we can no longer cover them. The reverberations the Oracle Room may well have ayed a part here. The vast cistern one side, certainly contemporary ough kept open for use until much ter than the rest of the site, as its ntents showed, provided water r use in those ceremonies. The nction of the lower level of the te, descending to a point 10.6 m

e 'Holy of Holies' shares many features th the temples, comparing closely with ose above ground although it is not built t carved from solid rock.

e Oracle Room has an ochre-painted ling too, but also side niches for rials. It is the further and higher one ich generates the echo for which the om is famous.

The inner Painted Room bears a sort of honeycomb pattern on its ceiling, turning into a row of spirals where it curves down to the walls.
Whether this had some symbolic significance or is merely decorative we can only guess.

below the rock surface, is more problematic, for the storage of the community's grain (one remembers the Kordin III quern) is at least a possibility, where few others make much sense.

The end of the site appears to have been quite sudden, as enlargement of the chamber behind the Holy of Holies was interrupted, and perhaps that lower level would have been brought into more obvious use if the temple culture had survived a little longer.

The baffling problems of interpretation merely add to the mystery, and to the powerful feeling of religious awe this remarkable monument inspires.

So much for the site itself. Visitors have the chance to enjoy an informative introduction in the foyer. After passing through the ticket office, they are offered number of well-displayed pa els giving some description of t site, its discovery and exploratio They then pass into an auditoriu for a short video show, with con mentary in a choice of language which gives further explanation Although a valuable foretast none of this is a substitute for t visit to the site itself.

This took many years to b adapted with carefully controll air conditioning, together wi the removal of some, though n all, of the overlying houses, t emptying of water cisterns an re-routing of services, to ensu the long-term preservation this unique site. Additionally, a steps, pathways and hand rai have had to be replaced, as t safety of visitors has to be consi ered as well as that of the site.

Here is a particularly fine example of a carved porthole-within-trilithon, to compare with those in the built temples like that on p.72. The horizontal slabs on the right roof over the staircase to the Lower Level.

Inner chambers open off outer ones in labyrinthine fashion in the Lower Level. The original tool marks can just be mad out on the right hand wall.

n the left is an opening into the Central ıamber, on the right the so-called 'Holy Holies' or innermost sanctuary. ıe steps in the centre form the roof to the access passage to the Lower Level. Note the pitted decorations on the vertical pillars.

ur side niches open from the lowest vel of the site. The one on the left reaches e maximum depth of 10.6 m. The slab in e centre once acted as its door.

The easiest approach is along the Vjal Santa Luċia (next to the Addolorata Cemetery), then on the roundabout turn first left into Tarxien on Triq Ħal Luqa, then left on Triq Palma and then left on Triq Ħal Saflieni. The entrance is in Triq Iċ-Ċimiterju. Only a small number of visitors are allowed to visit the Hypogeum every day. It is recommended to book early in advance from the Visitor Centre at the Hypogeum in Paola or from the National Museum of Archaeology in Valletta.

This oblique view of the Middle Level of the Hypogeum has its roof cut away to show the labyrinthine complexity of the site.

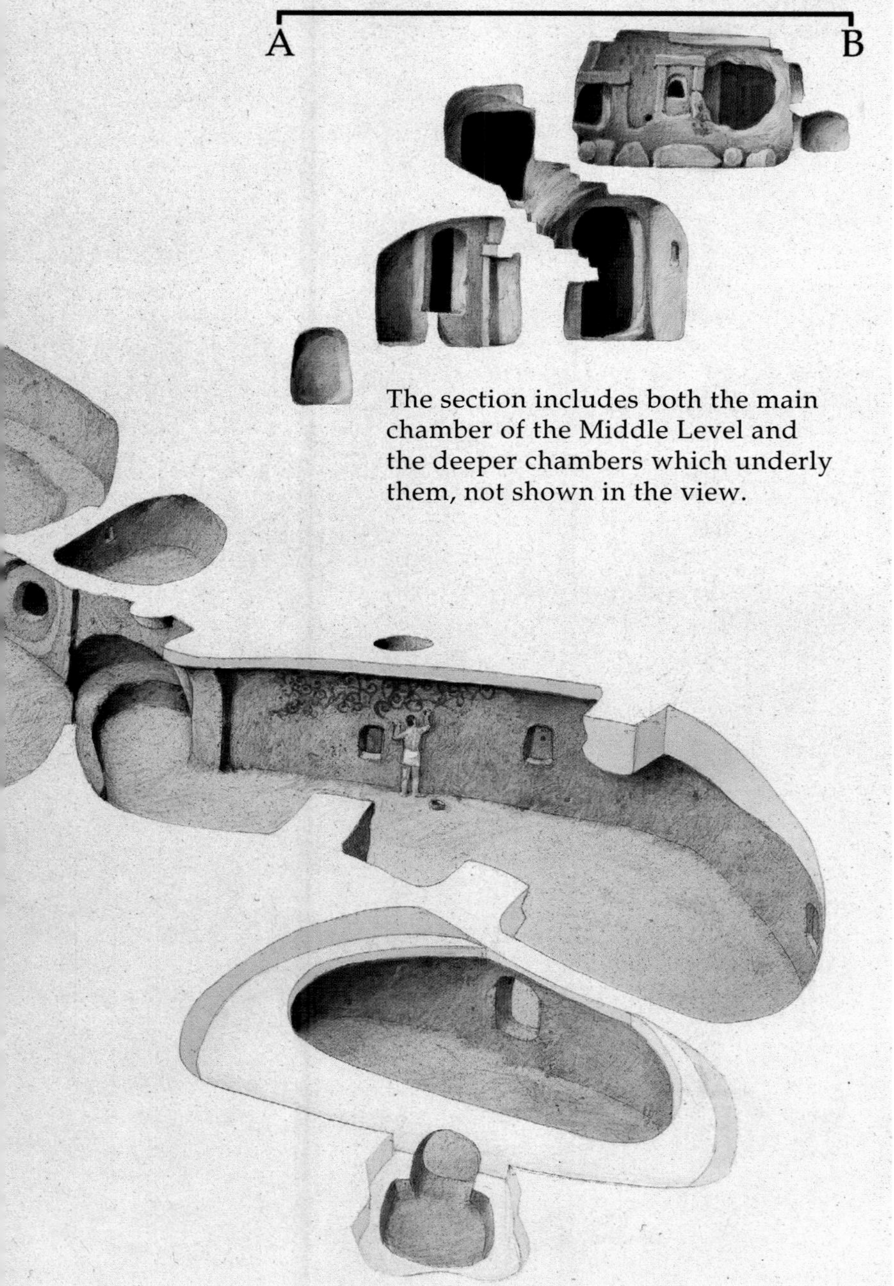

A B

The section includes both the main chamber of the Middle Level and the deeper chambers which underly them, not shown in the view.

KORDIN III
KORDIN

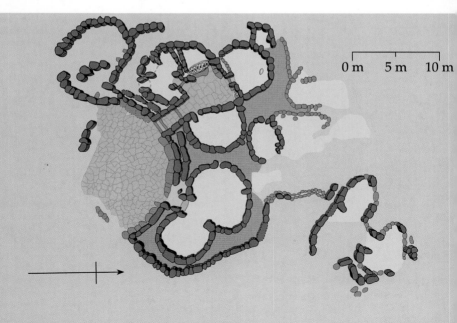

The site is closed off with a boundary wall. Goi… towards Paola, turn onto Triq Sir Paul Boffa and th… up Triq Kordin. Once you see the mosque on t… right, turn left and you will find the site's bounda… wall on the left of the church. The site is under t… care of Fondazzjoni Wirt Artna (fwa@waldonet.net.m… It is open daily during the week.

On the Kordin or Corradino Heights immediately above Grand Harbour, closer to it even than Ħal Saflieni and Tarxien, once stood three temple sites. The first two, dealt with later, are sadly no longer extant. The third, now in a walled enclosure between the Government Technical School and the church on its right, is happily still preserved, although it received a direct hit from a bomb in WWII. The site was excavated by Dr Thomas Ashby of the British School at Rome in 1909.

While the main temple itself is a standard trefoil, of appropriate Ġgantija phase date, it has several features of interest. It is, for example, the only temple whose forecourt, in front of the concave façade, is stone paved. The entrance passage leads as usual into a cen… tral court, also paved. The thre… apses opening off it are all at lea… partially walled off, though it wa… not realized that this was a lat… alteration to the plan, probably i… the Tarxien phase, until the sam… phenomenon was recognized, an…

roved by excavation, at Skorba. he most important feature of this te is undoubtedly the massive multple quern lying across the entrance the left apse. Whether it was rought to the site from the nearst outcrop of Coralline Limestone, ear Żabbar, a kilometre or more the northeast, during the initial uilding of the site, or only added ith the Tarxien phase alterations not clear. It certainly cannot have een inserted later. At one time it as thought that the grooves in it iight have been the result of grinding up potsherds for *deffun* roofing recent times, but the deliberate itroduction of this block of nonocal stone in the Temple Period, nd the raised moulding round the p, show that both the block and its se for grinding, surely for grain ither than building material, were ecurely contemporary. Some religious and social implications are discussed in the main text. To the right of the main temple is a small group of chambers opening from the same forecourt and each other. It is tempting to see this as an irregular lobed temple like Ta' Ħaġrat East, a forerunner of the neater and later trefoil temple alongside. Priority cannot be proved since dating sherds from both temples are attributed to the Ġgantija phase.

Earlier still, and this was demonstrated by excavation in 1960, a village covered an extensive area behind the temples. Many fragments of walling are still visible, though it is not easy to make out a coherent plan. Pottery from here went back to at least the Mġarr phase. This case, of course, parallels that of Skorba and Ta' Ħaġrat, where most of the other temples were erected on new, 'greenfield', sites.

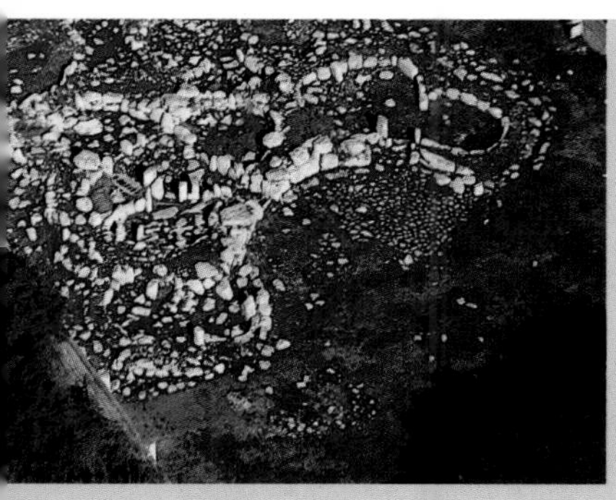

f the three Temple Period buildings hich formerly stood on the Kordin eights overlooking Grand Harbour, only ordin III survives. The two adjacent mples here, which opened onto a stoneived courtyard, are both of early forms, bed and trefoil.

The most remarkable feature was this multiple trough or quern, lying across the entrance from the paved central court into a side chamber.
Huts of an underlying village, earlier than the Temple Period, were found on this temple site.

TAS-SILĠ
ŻEJTUN

While the excavations of the Italian Archaeological Mission at Tas-Silġ in 1963-72 were designed to investigate the remains of the Punic and later temples, the excavators came quite unexpectedly on a prehistoric site beneath them.

Tas-Silġ is a rounded hilltop overlooking the head of Marsaxlokk Bay, so-called from the convent of the Madonna Tas-Silġ (Our Lady of the Snows) on its flank.

At the heart of the Punic temple was revealed a D-shaped setting of large irregular blocks, the foundations of the outer enclosing wall of a temple-like structure. Within this, barely surviving the later drastic alterations, are scanty traces of apses. To the east, the wall is interrupted by a threshold sla[b] pierced by three libation holes. Th[e] western side has a further settin[g], concave this time, which could b[e] the foundations of a façade, thoug[h] later again much confused by th[e] classical alterations and add[i]tions.

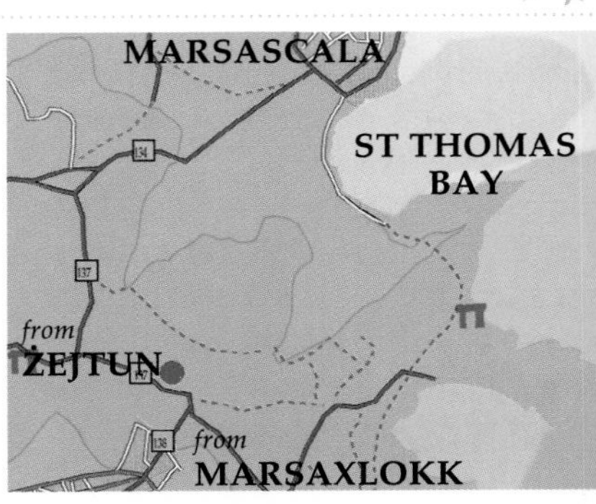

The site is closed off with a boundary wall. Entrance by appointment can be made by calling the head office of Heritage Malta, Valletta, or e-m[ail] **info@heritagemalta.org**. Go towards Marsaxlokk on Triq Marsaxlokk, then go left on Triq Axtart, up Triq Bir Rikka and continue on Triq Tas-Silġ.The site is on the first road on the left.

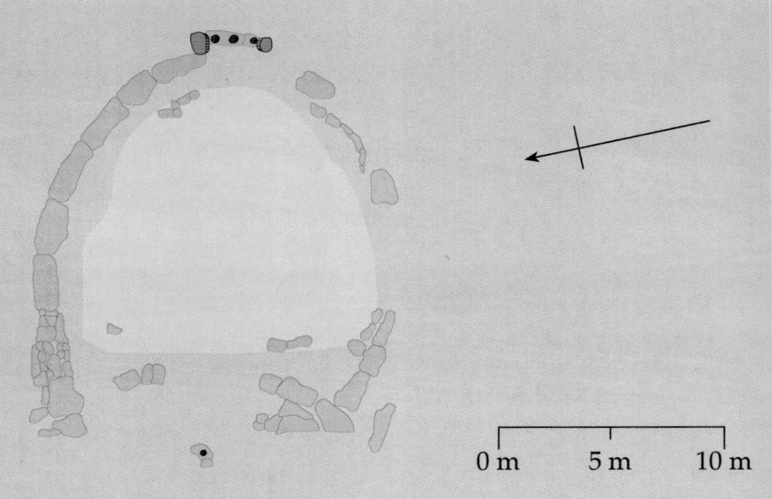

Indeed, a baptismal font was xcavated into the remains when was turned into a monastery in ıe fourth century AD.

That those blocks had formed art of a prehistoric temple was ıown by the associated sherds nd, even more clearly, by a anding 'fat lady' statue.

This appears to have been eliberately defaced and buried a hollow where one of the build-ıg blocks of the façade had been emoved. This in turn implies that hile the Punic temple incorpo-ıted upstanding remains of the ırlier temple, there was no conti-uity of sanctity, despite plentiful org in-Nadur phase pottery on ıe southern slope of the hill near-y. Either way, those remains were ıen levelled, even if their plan as respected and was used as a asis for the new one.

Also a problem is the form of the Neolithic temple. As already mentioned, to the east is what looks very like a threshold slab, and thus an entrance facing the east or southeast, like so many of the others. However, the setting of large blocks outside the remains of the apses to the west appears to be the foundations of a curved façade facing in that direction. Either the threshold was in an inner corridor, or this temple, like Ħaġar Qim, had two entrances, or we are somehow misinterpreting these scanty remains altogether.

ost of the visible remains are of the ınic temple and succeeding Early ıristian monastery, but incorporated to these, mid-right-centre on the r photograph, was the much earlier ructure.

A horseshoe-shaped setting of large blocks has obvious affinities with the temples, confirmed by the discovery of not only broken pottery but also, though badly damaged, a 'fat lady' statue. The original form of the building, however, is very puzzling.

BORĠ IN-NADUR

BIRŻEBBUĠA

Borġ in-Nadur is the tip of a flat-topped spur which overlooks St George's Bay, an inlet on the west side of Marsaxlokk, just above the village of Birżebbuġa and 500 m south of Għar Dalam. While the site of a major Bronze Age village, to be described later, occupation began long before. In the Tarxien period, a temple was erected near the tip of the promontory.

At its heart is a typical four-apse temple, opening from an oval forecourt, 22 m by 15 m, with bed-rock as its floor. Unusually, this was closed on the outer side by a megalithic wall which, indeed, is now the most obvious feature of the site, most of the rest having crumbled into untidy ruin. Behind the usual concave façade, the plan of a four-apse temple ca[n] just about be made out. Still dis[tinguishable] are two orthosta[ts] once flanking the inner passag[e] and bearing pitted decoratio[n] now toppled.

The site was excavated by Dr Margaret Murray between 192[?] and 1927. With only shallo[w]

The site is situated in open fields. Drive towar[ds] Birżebbuġa along Triq iż-Żejtun until you arri[ve] to St George's Bay. Turn on the right (next to t[he] Bus Stop) up Triq A.M. Galea and then right in[to] Sqaq in-Nadur.

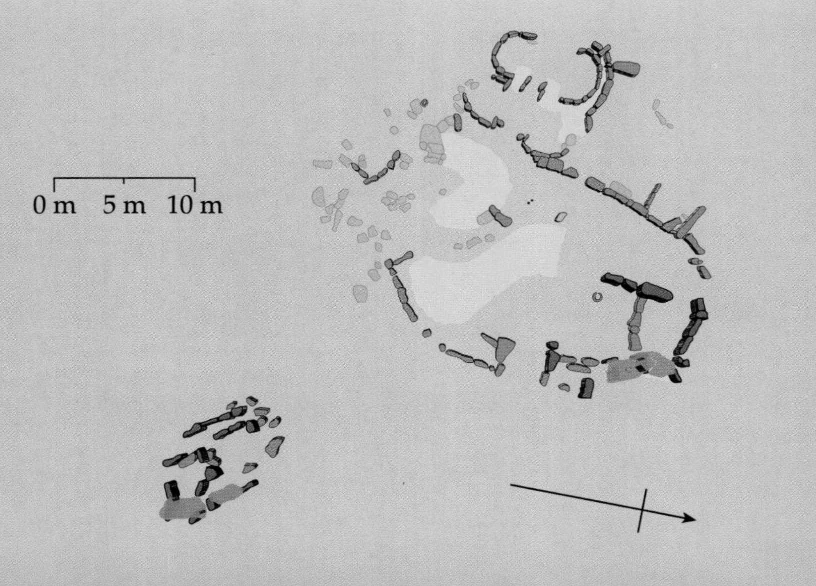

verlying deposits (the heaps ehind and to the left of the temle still show how much spoil as pulled back from the whole ea), and even those mostly the esult of the Bronze Age occupaon, little evidence was recovered n Temple Period activity. Most teresting would have been any ues on the re-use of the temple ructures during the Bronze Age. owever, in the virtual absence f Tarxien Cemetery material on is part of the site, it is probable at it was a long-abandoned ruin efore the Borġ in-Nadur phase ettlers re-occupied it. It would ave been particularly helpful if e Mycenaean sherd from here ad had a reliable context.

In fields some 9 m to the southast is another small group of egaliths, so ruinous that their riginal plan is unclear. They undoubtedly belong to the Tarxien rather than the Borġ in-Nadur phase, but little more can be said of them.

The extensive Bronze Age remains on the site are dealt with in a later chapter (p.288).

It can be assumed that there was a village of the Temple Period somewhere in the neighbourhood, exploiting the resources of Marsaxlokk Bay and its hinterland. The nearby temples of Tas- Silġ and Xrobb il-Għaġin probably served the same community.

lthough difficult to make out on the ound, the published plan includes a dly slighted four-apse temple, somewhat scured by the spoilheaps of the 1920s cavation.
further group of megaliths stands out the field in front.

One apse of the temple appears in the foreground here, but the main upstanding structure was a megalithic wall which uniquely closed in a roughly oval forecourt.

ĦAĠAR QIM
QRENDI

This temple, standing proudly on its hilltop 2 km southwest of Qrendi, has its walls somewhat fretted by erosion on the southern, seaward, side. Here the wind and rain in really rough weather bear some corrosive salt spray, making them even more damaging. This is because the only rock available here was the less resistant Globigerina.

Basically it consists of a single temple unit, though whether a four- or five-apse one is unclear since, very puzzlingly, the terminal apse or niche is replaced by a second doorway to the outside. The forecourt and façade are typical, particularly noteworthy being the larger orthostats at the corners, notched to take the second of the horizontal courses above, exactly as on the Tarxien model. Apart from the replaceme of a few original but fallen block including the lintel over the mai doorway, no restoration has bee done here. There are plans to ad a protective roof to prevent furth decay.

Within, the first pair of apse is more firmly screened off tha normally, access being limited t porthole slabs. The only decora tion here was a single displace sill stone with a pair of oppose spirals like Tarxien's, and the mo attractive of all the free-standin altar, this now in Valletta with replica on site.

Through the next doorway, th right-hand apse has a curious settin of low orthostats forming a sort c pen as if for animals, though thi

The main façade of the temple here is impressive, with its judicious restoration, but the seaward wall, on the left of the picture, has been seriously eroded by the weather. For an overall view, see pp.146-7.

The largest single block is that in the northeast wall, with the attractive external shrine beside it.
The jumble of stones on the left formed part of slighter subsidiary buildings.

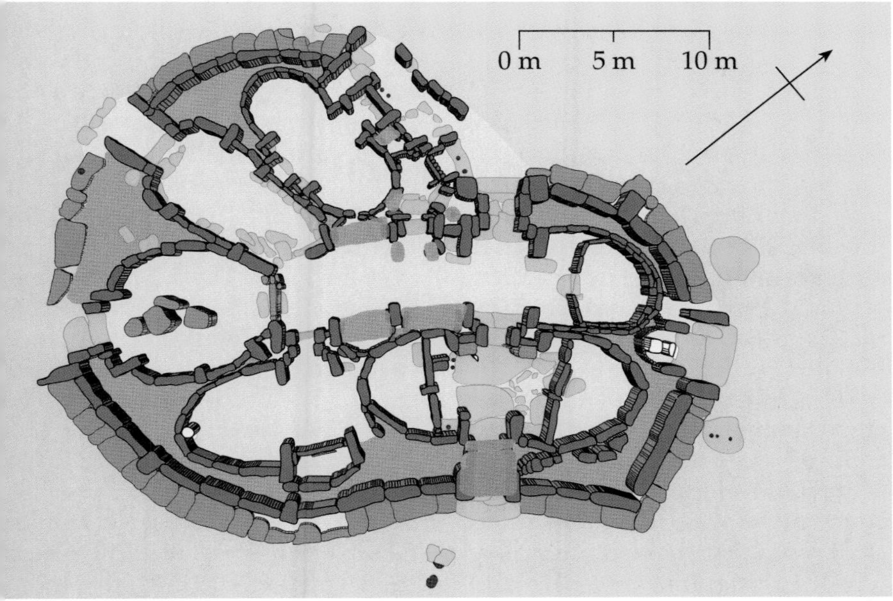

0 m 5 m 10 m

he plan shows clearly how the ɛntral passage of the temple ends not ɩ a niche but in another doorway. lso evident is the way additional chambers, some apsidal, some oval, were tacked onto the four-apse nucleus.

ı the external wall of the southwest ıamber, the severed feet of two standing gures can be made out, just to the left of ɛntre in the picture.

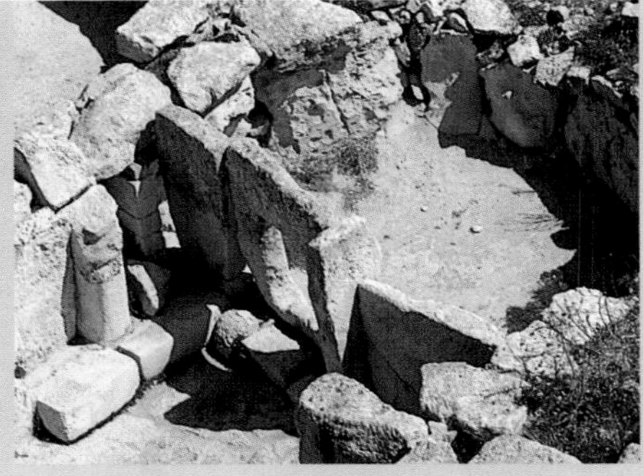

Side apses were screened off from the paved central court with orthostatic walls and porthole slabs. Decorative elements were confined to the court, the inner parts of the apses being left bare.

can only be a a tentative interpretation. A hole, possibly an oracle like Mnajdra's, pierces the wall. The central 'niche', as already mentioned, leads straight to the outside again. The left-hand apse has a high trilithon altar on its left and three more tray-on-pillar altars, two on the right with yet another in a little chamber behind. Less an apse than a passage, this gives access to one of the additional chambers.

This opens up steps to the left, steps under which was found the cache of seated 'fat ladies'. It consists of part of a temple unit, a central court, niche and right apse, tacked closely against the main temple. A low-standing pillar or betyl stands at the end of the apse. A more complete unit – entrance, court, niche, and one pair of apses, lies to the north, and two simple oval chambers to the west.

In the external enclosing wal the first orthostat behind the rig hand corner of the façade is o of the largest in any temple, 6.4 long and estimated to weigh clo to 20 tonnes. Beyond it, an attra tive external shrine is describe in the main text, with the orac hole beside it. The 5.2 m high me hir beyond, with a step at its ba to prevent any lateral movemen seems to have no logical functio though its builders must have ha some reason to justify the ext effort needed to raise it. Roun on the west side, just before th second oval chamber, is the sla facing out into the wall fill, bearin the two pairs of 'fat lady' feet. was either meant to be deliberatel hidden, or moved here from els where, perhaps after breakage.

Thirty metres to the north, an quite separate, are the remains

The pedestalled altars in the photograph above stood in an inner apse, while the particularly finely decorated one on the left (now kept at the National Museum of Archaeology) was found in the first central court.

five-apse temple. Its left-hand nd central apses are still clearly pparent, whereas those on the ght had been removed before e excavation. It was cleared long ter the main temple was emptied ck in 1839 – 'excavated' would putting it too kindly. A small tail worth mentioning is how rt of an orthostat was preserved om weathering by a threshold ab being set against it, that hori- ntal slab being removed later. hile the five-apse form suggests Ġgantija phase date, sherds from floors would place it later, in e Tarxien phase. This anomaly unexplained.

Between the two temples and little to the west is an irregular oup of blocks, clearly megalith- but the shape of the structure ey originally formed part of is w beyond recovery. Finally, a complex of slighter walls to the east is popularly, and imaginatively, known as 'the priests' quarters'. There is no confirmatory evidence.

It is not beyond the bounds of possibility that somewhere beneath, or at least near, this complex is another hypogeum, perhaps as elaborately carved in the local Globigerina Limestone as that of Ħal Saflieni. That remains at this stage merely wishful thinking.

Overleaf: This complex site can be understood better from the oblique air photograph than from either the remains on the ground or the plan on p.143 back. While basically a four-apse plan, additional chambers have been attached to its south side, and a separate temple some 30 m to the north.

f to the north lies a five-apse temple, ubstantial building though eclipsed its better preserved neighbour. It undecorated, but its plan is readily parent.

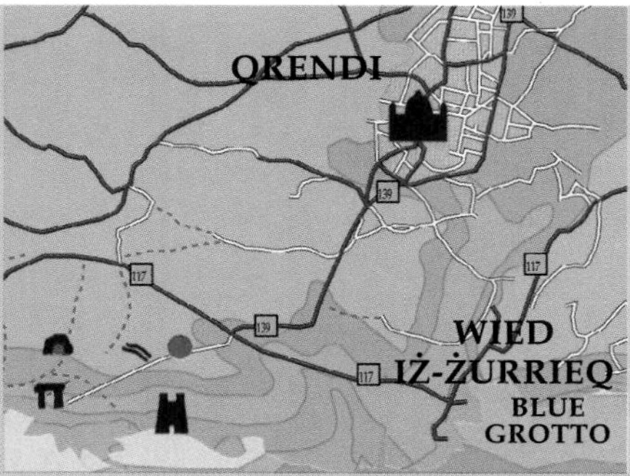

Go towards the village of Żurrieq and pass by the village on 'Triq Wied iż-Żurrieq' to approach the Blue Grotto and Wied iż-Żurrieq following the road signs. Instead of going down to Wied iż-Żurrieq turn to the road on your right continuing on 'Triq Ħaġar Qim'.When you come to the bus stop on the left of the road turn left, up the road, to arrive at the parking of the site.

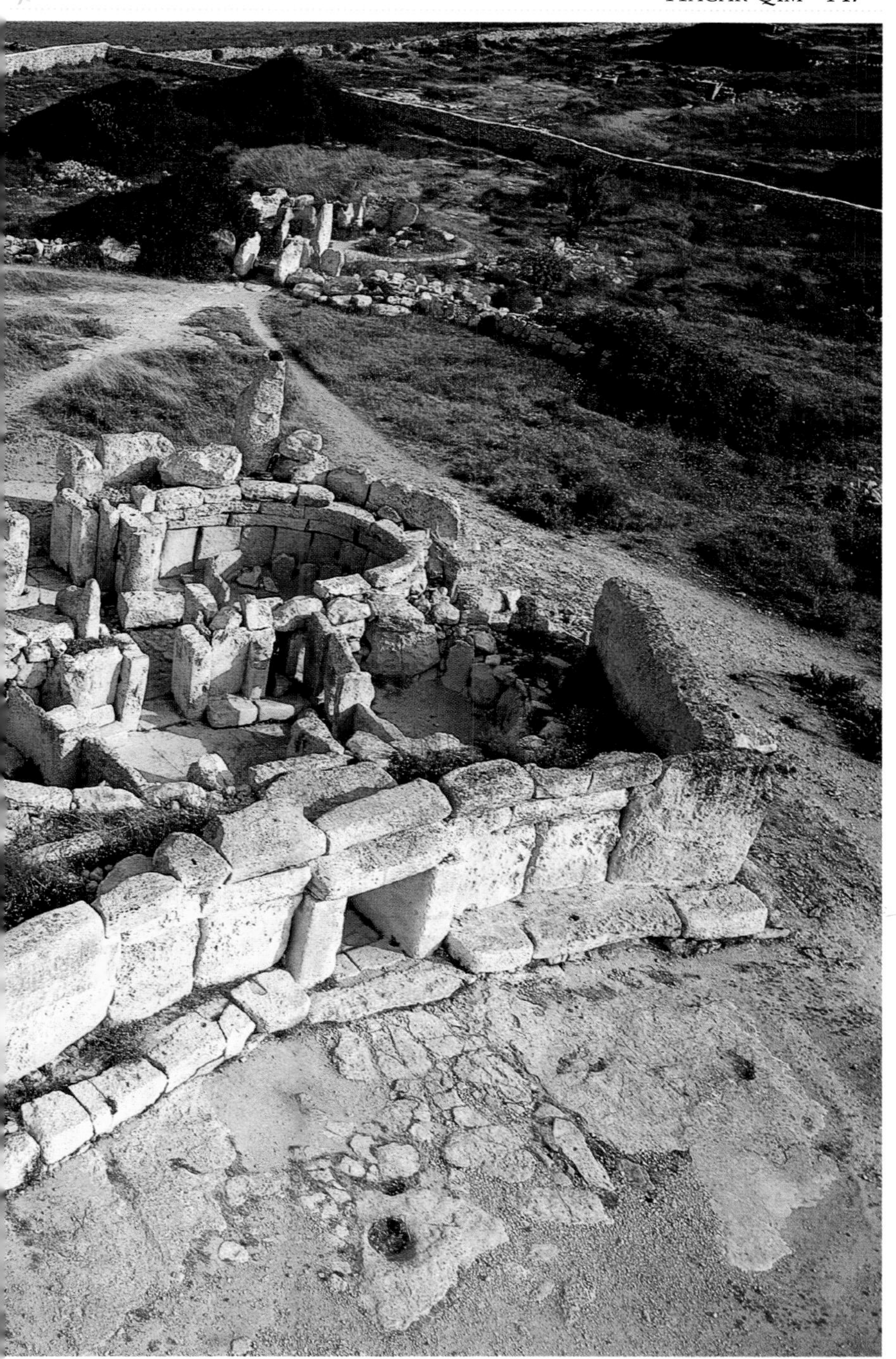

MNAJDRA
QRENDI

Probably the most atmospheric of all the temples, Mnajdra is tucked into a hollow of the southern cliffs, with no modern development in sight, only the flowery slopes, the sea and the rocky islet of Filfla in the distance.

This makes the attack on the site by vandals in 2001 particularly regrettable.

It was another of the early clearances, a year after Ħaġar Qim, some of the finds being preserved but with no record of their exact findspots. It has three temple units opening from an oval forecourt, 30 m across. We should dearly love to be able to people it with its original worshippers, dancers, processions, etc. A sound track would be equally valuable.

The first and oldest temple is simple trefoil of the Ġgantija phas All its small rubble walls are mo ern reconstructions, the *torba* flo showing their former position. Th few modest uprights are origina with their pitted decoration. Th recent suggestion that the irregul lines of dots is some sort of cale dar seems on the face of it a litt far-fetched.

The most famous of the thr temples is surely the third, with i largely intact façade and bench, th former extended by a free-standin wall of long-and-short work.

Through its entrance lies the fir court. Most dramatic is the portho niche to the left, framed in its tr lithon and two strangely tapere orthostats on either side. All a

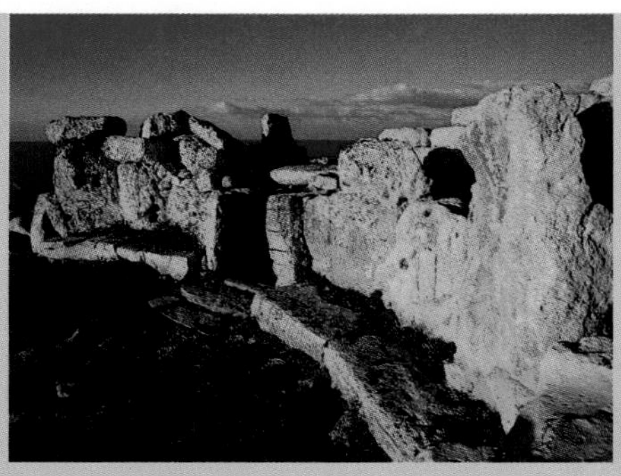

The façade of the South Temple catches the early morning sun, bringing out the rich golden colour of the stone.
Its concavity and the bench at its foot are very evident in this view.

The North Temple had a curious double entrance, the central one an enormous porthole slab, the largest in any temple. However, only its right hand jamb survives. The second entrance has lost it lintel too.

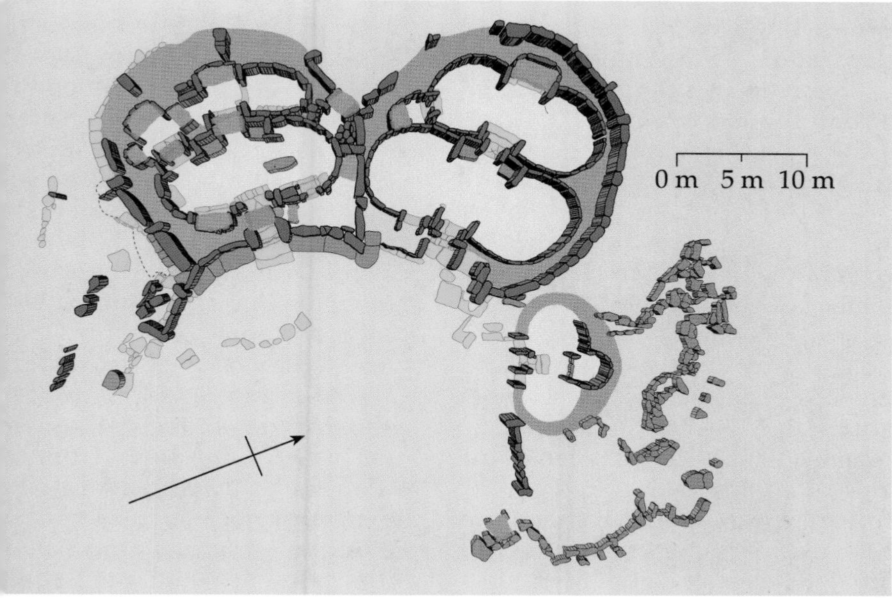

0 m 5 m 10 m

he plan makes even clearer the oval
recourt with the three temples opening
f it, two of the 4-apse form, and a
naller and earlier 3-apse clover-leaf.

Like Ħaġar Qim, there is a group of irregular buildings of unknown function alongside.

elpful though the plan is, the air
iotograph gives an even better idea of the
onument's general appearance.

The first apse on the right is the one which has the two oracle holes, clearly visible in the orthostats, centre and left of the picture. The exit to the forecourt is to the right.

ornamented with typical dotted decoration. Through the porthole can be seen an altar supported on a central pillar (p.90).

Though this is very photogenic, the right hand apse is even more interesting. It is noticeable that its wall slopes inwards to narrow the opening which had to be spanned by the now-missing roof. From right to left in the apse wall are a port-hole doorway at the top of a flight of steps giving access to a chamber within the thickness of the wall, an oracle hole, actually a notch in the side of an orthostat slab, opening from that intra-mural chamber, and then another finer oracle hole in a rebated recess, this communicating with a smaller chamber accessible only from the back and outside of the temple. Within the first side-chamber is another altar, this one very elegant on a double-hourglass shaped pillar. Here particularly th slight convexity of all slabs gives th impression of comfortable solidit

The third temple was inserte between the other two, set at higher level on a sort of terrac mostly modern reconstruction. It unusual in having had an enormou porthole slab, now sadly broke as its main entrance, though wit a second doorway beside it. It apses have walls of orthostat slabs of modest height, toppe by horizontal courses, all of Gl bigerina brought down from th hilltop above. Of particular note the engraving of a temple façade o the first taller orthostat to the le of the passage to the inner apse These are of similar constructio with a tall trilithon altar at th centre and another side chamb with porthole and pillar-supporte altar on the left. It is this pillar i

This intriguing representation of a temple façade is engraved into a major upright on the left of the Central Temple. It shows orthostats flanking a doorway and four horizontal courses of masonry above. Compare it with the model on p.193

The inner apses of this temple are of standard construction, with a portholed side chamber at their southern end. The principal, lintelled, altar is on the right, the passage to the first apses on the left.

articular, tapering towards the ase, which at one time suggested connection with Minoan Crete, where the same phenomenon had een observed. Like the 'Mycenae-n' spirals at Tarxien, this can now e categorically ruled out by the ates, Mnajdra's pillars being by ar the older.

Another astronomical alignment as been suggested here. At dawn n the winter solstice, the sun's rays end a narrow shaft of light diago-ally through the entrance passage touch the right-hand edge of the itted upright on that side of the ourt. At the equinoxes, the whole entre of the temple is bathed in ght. The fact that at midsummer a nuch broader splodge of light hits ne left hand upright at no particu-arly significant point rather spoils ne argument, leaving coincidence distinct possibility.

As at Ħaġar Qim, there is a group of small subsidiary chambers to the east of the temple block, of unknown function.

Standing in Mnajdra's fore-court and looking up at Ħaġar Qim, one can hardly doubt that the two belonged to the same community, to form one of Renfrew's 'clusters'. As mentioned under the latter site, there should be that community's rock-cut cemetery somewhere in the neighbourhood. Its water supply doubtless came from the Misqa Tanks on the hilltop above. But where was its village? We wish we knew.

eering from beneath the central altar, ie sees the connecting passage, the oken porthole slab of the front door, and e blue Mediteranean beyond.
was this temple that suffered the most the vandal attack on Good Friday of 001, though the damage has since been eticulously repaired.

Go towards the village of Żurrieq and pass by the village on 'Triq Wied iż-Żurrieq' to approach the Blue Grotto and Wied iż-Żurrieq following the road signs. Instead of going down to Wied iż-Żurrieq turn to the road on your right continuing on 'Triq Ħaġar Qim'.When you come to the bus stop on the left of the road turn left, up the road, to arrive at the parking of the site. Pass around Ħaġar Qim and follow the passage (no cars) down to Mnajdra.

MISQA TANKS

QRENDI

Some 250 m north of the Mnajdra temples and on the top of the hill, an area of bare rock has had a group of deep cavities carved into it. Without major clearance, it is not easy to say exactly how many there are as some have more than one opening. While some are dry, with a partial filling of loose stone rubble, most fill with water every winter, making study difficult. These still serve as cisterns for irrigating the surrounding fields. It is virtually certain that they were indeed originally cut for water storage.

They are much larger than Bronze Age and recent bell-shaped cisterns (see p.291) and their curvilinear shape would rule out a Roman date. The nearest in form is undoubtedly the one attached to

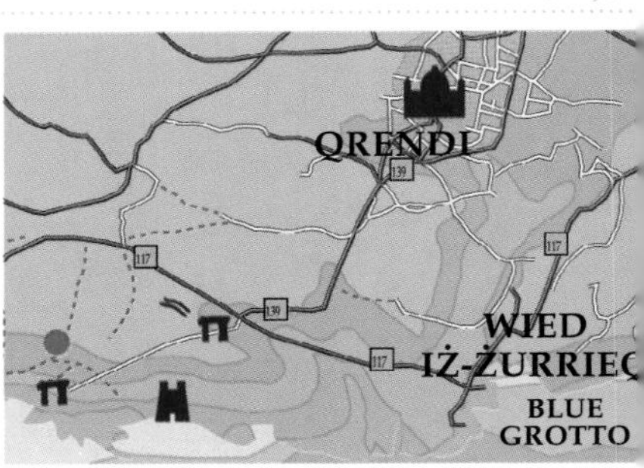

The Misqa Tanks can be found on the top of th slope next to Mnajdra. To reach the site follow th path/road leading off the road between Ħaġar Qi and Mnajdra. A large fig tree is visible from th path, the tanks are next to it.

the Ħal Saflieni Hypogeum, whic is securely of the Temple Perioc That, and their proximity to Mna dra, make it near certain that thei purpose was to provide that templ with a secure water supply. Unfor tunately this cannot be prove since they have been repeatedl cleared out since, removing an datable deposits.

Dr Louis Vella has recently ɔticed that the rock surface ·ound bears several engraved ɜures. These appear better in the ıotographs than in any written ɜscription. They are both prob- matical in interpretation, and of .eir nature also undatable. Apart om their being found so close · the tanks, there is nothing to ıggest they belong with either .e tanks or the temple, yet admit- dly, no more to associate them ith any other particular phase Malta's long past.

ɔttom opposite page:
eneral vite of the site from the air.

ght:
:is, the clearest of the figures, consists of :ross with pairs of lines depending from e tips. There is a vague resemblance to :bbuġ anthropomorphs.

hile the Ħaġar Qim and Mnajdra ·mples are well known, the Misqa Tanks ove the latter pose their own problems. :e tanks are cut in bare rock, but why e there so many? Grooves to control e inflow of water are clear on the otograph, as are the stone 'lids' on two them.

Their bell-shaped form becomes apparent when the camera is pointed vertically upwards to the sky above the opening. Though here in Globigerina Limestone, their cutting was still a major undertaking.

TA' ĦAĠRAT
MĠARR

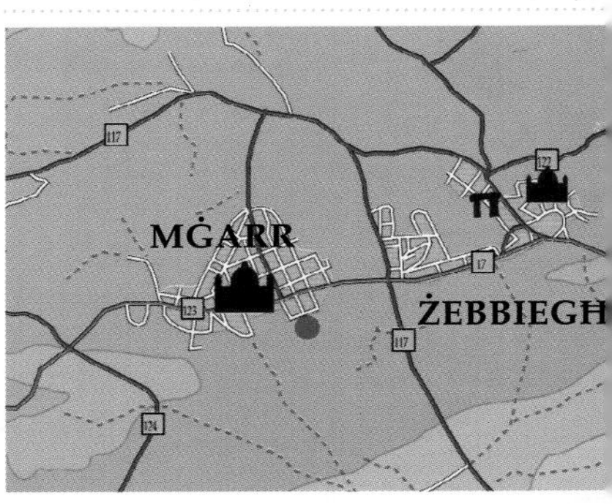

Go towards Mġarr along Triq iż-Żebbiegħ and th into Triq Fisher towards the village centre. O you pass the government school on the right the road turn into the first road on the left, T Ta' Ħaġrat. The site is closed off with a bound wall.Entrance by appointment can be made by call the head office of Heritage Malta, Valletta, or e-m **info@heritagemalta.org.**

The temple here was dug by Zammit in 1925. It lies in the eastern outskirts of Mġarr village, about a kilometre from what was doubtless its partner Skorba. It is smaller than many of the others but better preserved. The major temple to the left has an upstanding façade with bench at its foot, and a monumental doorway, with some restoration.

The central court is massively paved, and the three apses around it were partially walled off in a later constructional phase, probably Tarxien, as only Ġgantija phase sherds were recovered from the packing within the outer walls. No decorated blocks were found here. The most notable find was the little model of a temple, discussed elsewhere (p.192).

Tucked behind this temple on the right is a smaller and mo irregular one, a typical lobe example. Although its plan shou make it earlier than its larg trefoil neighbour, excavatic unfortunately failed to bear th

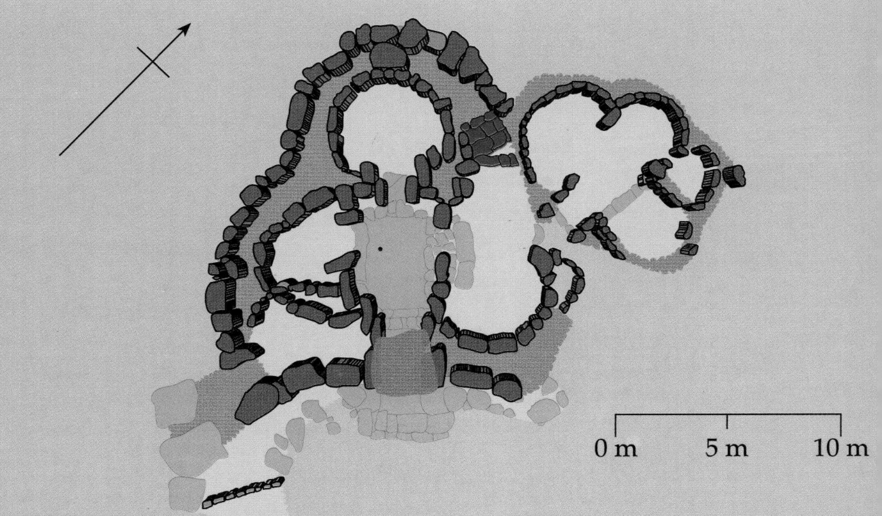

ıt, suggesting instead a Saflieni ıase date. The problem is more .lly discussed in the main text. is possible, of course, that the .nction of these chambers was ore analogous to those of the riests' quarters' at Ħaġar Qim, hatever they were, than to those the trefoil temple.

The flight of steps between .e two temples could be part Zammit's consolidation of e site, though the similar ones Tarxien are certainly contem-ɔrary. Perhaps they provided :cess to a chamber in the wall .ickness at this upper level, ther merely to facilitate roof aintenance, or could there ıve been an oracle hole at ceil-g level in the inner apse of the rger temple?

Plentiful pottery of earlier date ıows that here too the temples replaced a village. Indeed, the pottery which gave its name to the Mġarr phase came from the village rather than the temple, which misled Zammit into one of the remarkably few mistakes he made in his interpretation of Maltese prehistory.

The view of the South Temple façade, with Mġarr village's twentieth century church dome rising behind, is one of the most both evocative and picturesque. A few years ago, an almond tree which grew from the façade, adding an even more attractive touch when in full flower. Sadly, its roots were doing serious damage to the structure and it had to be removed.

Where there is conflict between conservation, research, and picturesqueness, they must be placed in that order of priority.

:e plan and air view show how the two nples at this site, the larger trefoil and ? smaller lobed one, relate to each other. :e central court and entrance passage ? massively paved, the apses torba-*ored.*

While its lintel had to be replaced and the lower steps added, the main temple's façade survived largely intact.
Nothing is to be seen of the underlying village, nor, in this view, of the modern one beyond.

SKORBA
MĠARR

Even its staunchest advocate could not claim the Skorba temple as Malta's most attractive, though it was amongst the most informative, particularly for its earlier levels considered in the last chapter.

Two temples stood side by side on the northern edge of Żebbiegħ, with an interesting suggestion of earlier religious structures, the Red Skorba shrines, on the same site. The main reason it could tell us so much in the 1960s was that it was left untouched through both the first phase of temple digging in the 1820s and 30s, and the second, in the 1900s to 20s. Equally, more would have been learnt if it had waited until now. But of course, knowledge would never advance if all research was halted until we could do it better.

The West Temple had thr
periods of use. In the first, in t
Ġgantija phase, the deposits built u
by the earlier village were scarpe
back for the erection of a typic
three-apse temple. A paved entran
passage, pierced by five libatio
holes, gave access to a *torba*-floore
central court.

Of its forecourt and façade, on
a single standing stone beside t
passage remains, for long consi
ered an isolated menhir. The nor
wall of its apses, however, is
much better shape, to either sic
of two almost as massive uprigh
Somewhere at this time there we
at least two standing blocks wi
pitted decoration.

In the Tarxien phase, the pi
ted blocks were relaid as a ste

Seen from the gate to the enclosure, little sense can be made of the site at first glance, though in the winter months, the contrast between green carpet and white stone is striking.

The shape of the West Temple is more apparent as one approaches.
Though its façade has vanished, the entrance passage, central court, and doorway to the inner apse all become clear.

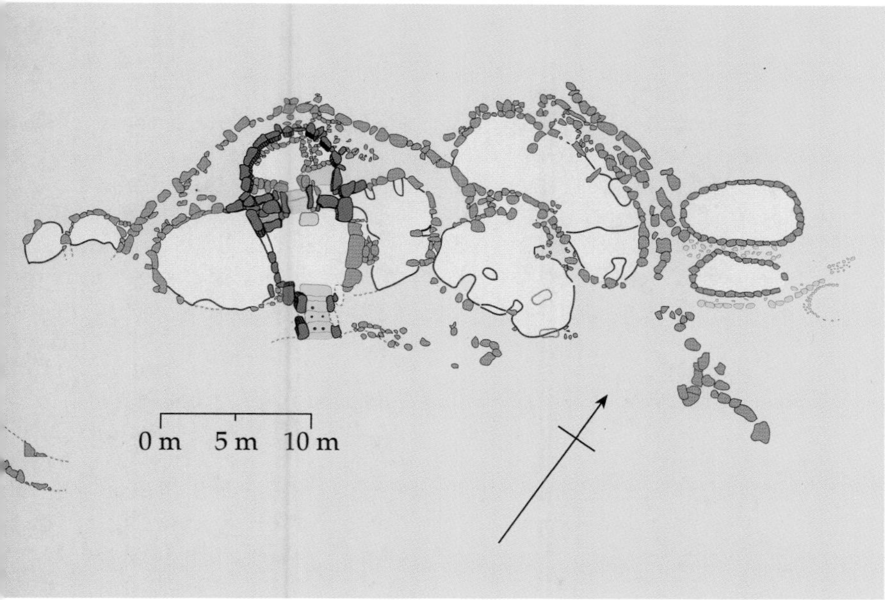

:e 4-apse East Temple was built onto
: side of the Ġgantija phase West one
ring the succeeding Tarxien phase.

The oval chambers to the left were temple out-buildings, those on the right the much older Red Skorba shrine.

vertical view from the top of the
enhir' shows the libation holes through
paving of the entrance. They were
esumably plugged when the site was in
e, or ankles would surely have suffered
ury.

In this view, one must imagine an open court, the blocks in the foreground replaced, one on top of the wall on the left, the other as a lintel on the two squared uprights forming a doorway into the inner apse.

to the right apse (nowhere else is there pitting on horizontal, traffic-bearing, surfaces), with a porthole doorway behind it screening that apse. It was probably at this time that two trilithon altars were added at the back of this apse.

The left-hand apse was also given a step but no screen. Much more importantly, the central apse was walled off, with a central doorway and four altars in the angles inside and outside that wall.

The doorway's lintel is still present, though fallen forward into the court. The implications of the added crosswall are discussed in the main text.

Finally, after the temple had gone out of use, with large chips already knocked out of its doorway, squatters in the Tarxien Cemetery phase added internal walls and a bench to that central apse, and scattered their ow debris on the floors amongst th of the temple users.

At some time during the se ond phase, part of the eastern wa of this temple was demolished that a second could be built clo up against it. This was of typic Tarxien phase four-apse-and-nic form. It was more seriously dan aged, and its presence was on realized at quite a late stage in t excavation of the site.

Despite the thinness of t deposits, a layer of charcoal ga a valuable clue to the method roofing (see p.238). Much of t outer eastern wall survives, toget er with blocks visitors will noti in the wall of the lane which giv present-day access, possibly on part of a façade shrine like Tarxi South's. There are also parts of tw outbuildings to the west.

From the back of the West Temple one can see how its inner apse has been reduced in size by the Bronze Age alterations, described on p.251.
In the distance rise the Binġemma Hills.

The walls of the East Temple survive to much lower height, which is why it was not recognized until a comparatively lat stage in the excavation. The structure c the skyline is a fragment of the modern field wall.

:e West Temple is clear in the aerial otograph, the East one obscured by the ›tpath crossing it obliquely outside the closure fence.

Four blocks of the original forecourt terrace can be seen on the extreme left of the picture.

e outer wall of the East Temple is under : bushes on the left.
e main feature here is the southern amber of the much earlier Red Skorba ·ine.

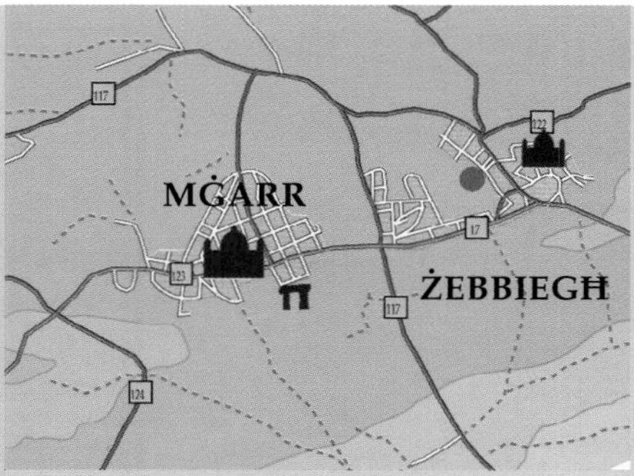

Go towards Mġarr along Triq iż-Żebbiegħ and turn to the right once you come to the first buildings, along Triq Sir Temi Zammit. On the second road to the left you should see a small square (actually Sant'Anna Street). The site is behind the square. The temple site is closed off with a boundary fence. Entrance by appointment can be made by calling the head office of Heritage Malta, Valletta, or e-mail **info@heritagemalta.org.**

TAL-QADI
NAXXAR

A curious site, made more attractive by being planted as a garden. It overlooks the plain of Burmarrad, and indeed, at the time of building, that plain may still have been an arm of the sea.

The most notable part of the site today is the tumbled external wall on the north, beside the lane, which looks more like a dolmen than a temple. However, within this the ground plan of a pair of inner apses is substantially complete, with a niche or small central apse between them. The steps descending behind this are modern. A passage way communicating with a now-vanished outer pair is clearly apparent, as is the paving of an entrance passage. No other trace of outer apses or façade survives.

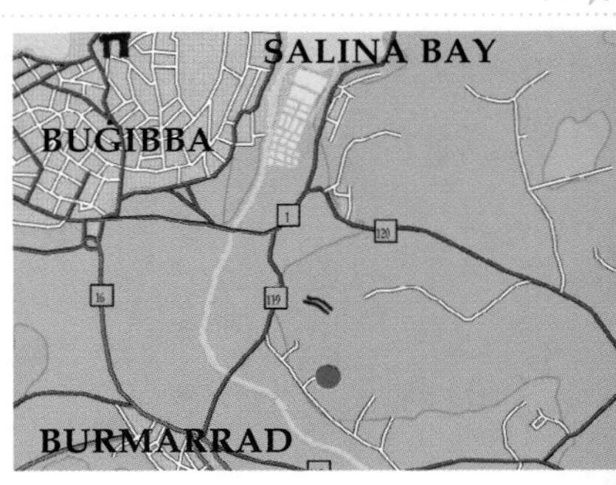

Drive along the Coast Road towards St Paul's B. After the road to Naxxar and before Kennedy Gr take the road on your left. Follow the map abo to find the area of the site. The temple is at end of the road on the left once you arrive at glass-houses.

The oddest feature is the orientation. The temple would seem face quite the wrong way in comparison with the others, uphi and to the east-north-east. Th precise orientation cannot be spec fied since the niche, passage, ar entrance are each on slightly di ferent alignments.

The huge blocks beside the lane, though obvious, are somewhat confusing, being no longer in their original positions. They once formed part of the temple's north wall.

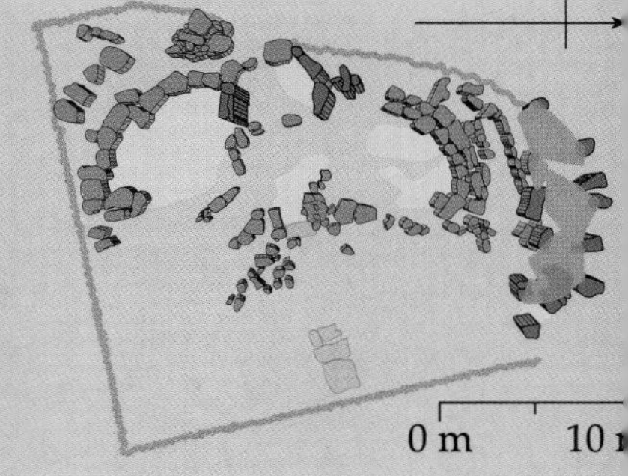

Much of the plan of a four-apse temple c be made out in the adjacent garden, wit view across to Burmarrad and the Bidni Ridge. The sea can no longer be seen fro here, but may have come much closer in antiquity.

UĠIBBA
ˇ PAUL'S BAY

ke Tarxien, the Buġibba temple has .d its setting drastically altered in cent times. Whereas a generation ;o it shared the peninsula between lina and St Paul's Bay with only farm, a small radio station, and a ıights' tower, it is now engulfed in oustling tourist village. It survives ıly as a 'feature' in the courtyard of arge hotel. We should at least be ateful that it was not swept away together.

What can still be made out are ro orthostatic blocks of the façade, entrance passage and recogniz-le parts of an outer pair of apses. aces of the *torba* flooring were und in 1928, implying an inner se or apses, destroyed by a later all. The capstone of the entrance rvives, though displaced.

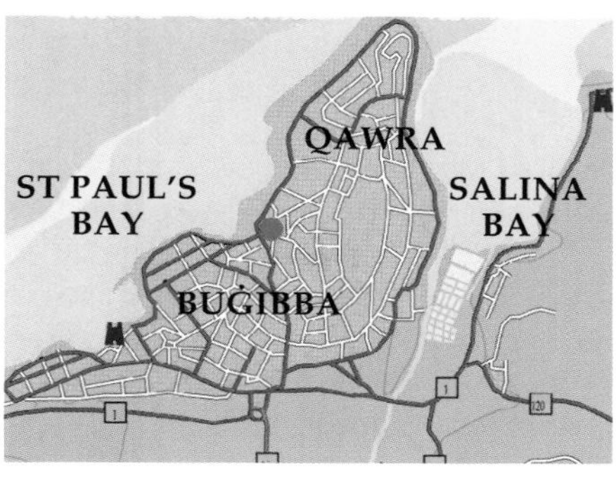

Go into Buġibba and drive along the coastline (Islets Promenade) and, after passing Bay Square, you will see the New Dolmen Hotel in front of you. Ask at the reception of the hotel to go in the hotel's central courtyard where the temple is situated.

Three altar blocks were discovered in the excavation. The two decorated ones, one with a fine pair of spirals and the other with 'fish' designs, are now in the National Museum of Archaeology. Pottery finds, also now at the Museum, placed the site in the Tarxien phase.

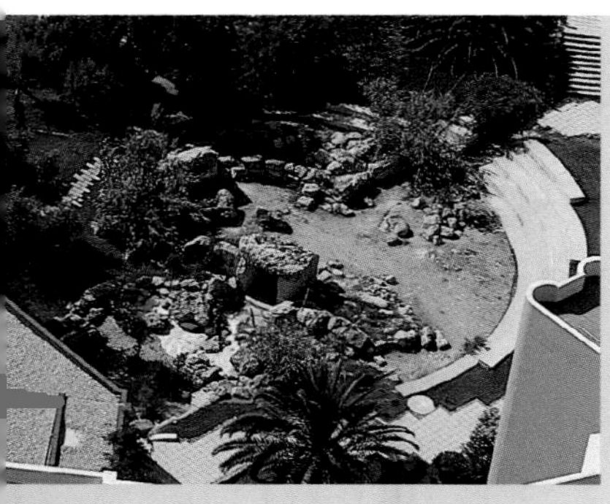

e Dolmen Hotel is misleadingly med since the structure in its central ırtyard is not a dolmen but the rights and lintel, now replaced, of a nple entrance.

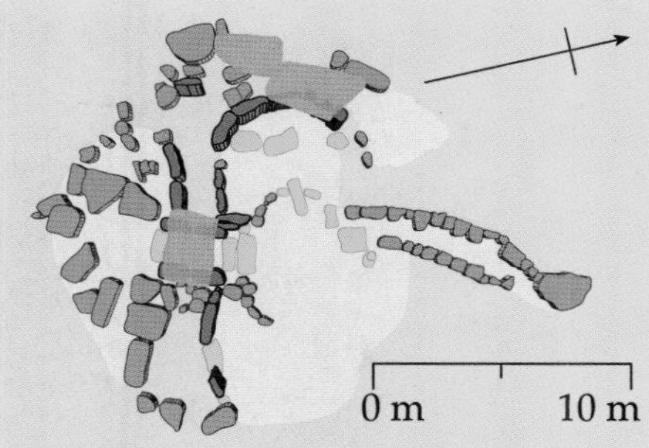

The plan shows how much of the original temple can be traced, as described in the text. The double wall on the right, for example, was an irrelevant later additon.

XEMXIJA
ST PAUL'S BAY

This is another of those sites from which the finds are more instructive than the structure. It lies on the eastward slope of the hill overlooking St Paul's Bay on its north side, now behind the Mistra Village, close to the crest of the hill. John Evans excavated six rock-cut tombs in 1955. All consisted of a vertical shaft cut into the rock, some with one or more steps left to give easier access, with a kidney-shaped or lobed chamber opening off the bottom of it. Each probably once had a stone slab to serve as a door to its chamber. Each shaft has recently been given a neat little cairn nearby as marker, to make it easier to find.

Tombs 1 and 2 both have three rough lobes and are so close together that the wall separating their chambers has broken through. Tombs and 4 are separate, with simple ki ney-shaped chambers.

Tomb 5, that lowest on t slope and thus the first visito will reach, is the largest and mo complex. To obtain the greatest ar of floor space, without imperilli the stability of the roof, the cha ber was enlarged by chipping o five lobes rather than leaving t large an unsupported span. It w Evans who pointed out the simil ity between this plan and that of t lobed temples, going on to sugge a formative connection.

Tomb 6 was thought to be ju like 3 and 4 until a second chamb was recently found on the oppos side of the shaft to the first. Its ro is partly collapsed.

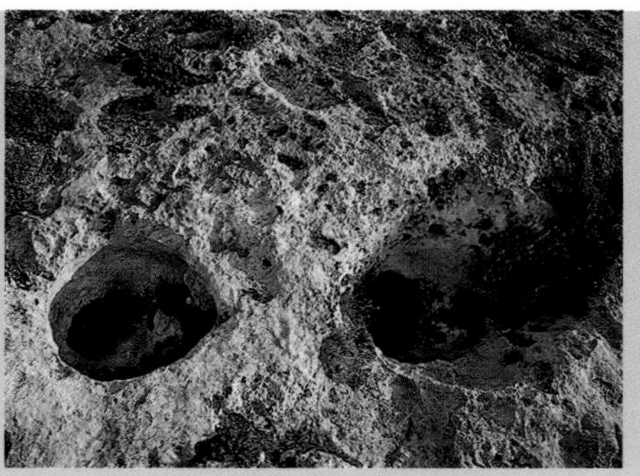

Looking like a V-perforation as in the temples, tombs 1 and 2 were cut separately, though their chambers connect below ground. This must have been accidental as access between them is not easy.

Tomb 3 has the simplest plan, a vertical shaft and single oval chamber. One wonders how the bodies were manipulat through those narrow entrances.

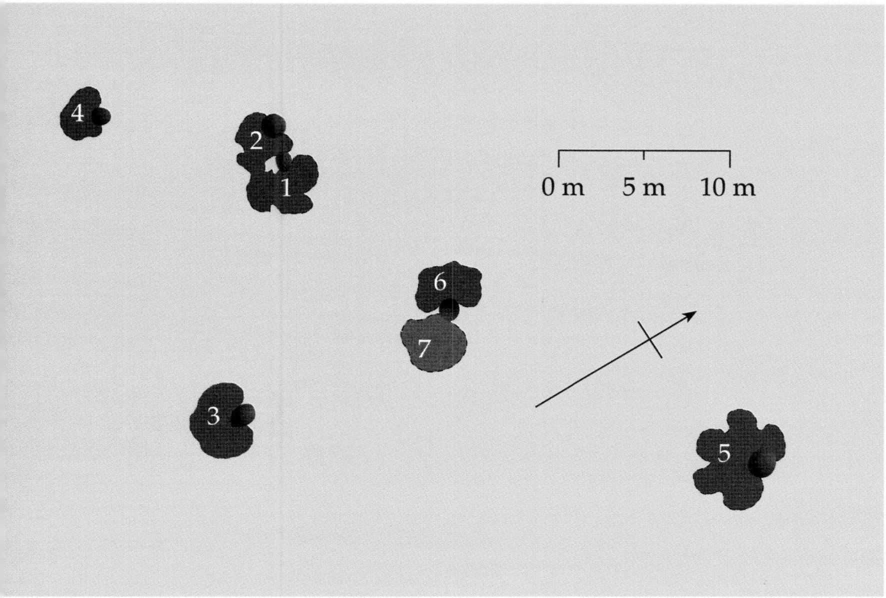

4 2 1 6 7 3 5

0 m 5 m 10 m

e six tombs form a close cluster on ? eastern slope of the hill. It is to be voutly hoped that modern buildings will not be allowed to encroach any further.

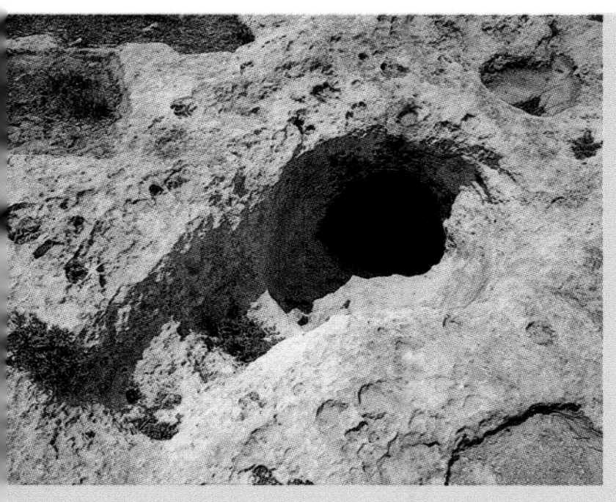

least with tomb 4, a flight of steps s provided to make the task easier. e much-weathered rock, almost devoid vegetation, shows clearly on all these otographs.

Tomb 5 is the largest and deepest, though the chamber entrance is now somewhat obscured by vegetation. The stud at the bottom left was one of four holding a protective iron grill, but it was so frequently vandalized that it had to be removed.

The majority of the finds were of the Ġgantija phase, giving a wide range of restorable vessels, several of them not previously met with. There were a number of Tarxien sherds and some tombs were reopened to receive later interments in the Borġ in-Nadur Bronze Age. Axe amulets were also noteworthy among the finds. The bones were generally in poor shape and so did not receive detailed study. After the Bronze Age, the tombs were lost to sight for over three thousand years.

Other antiquities in the neighbourhood may or may not be associated. A scatter of sherds above and below the cliffs to the north, overlooking the Mistra valley and the main Mellieħa road, are also of the Ġgantija phase and may represent the village to which the tombs belonged. Over the crest of the hill to the west is a cave, reused in recent times so without the ancie deposits it may once have had. Fi hundred metres or so further west few megalithic blocks in the unde growth could be the remains o temple-like structure, too ruino for certainty. Almost certainly mo recent are cart-ruts running rou the slope between the tombs a Triq il-Preistorja – an appropria name since its houses overlie a destroy more ruts.

The shaft and tomb entrance towards the top of the picture were all that was visible of tomb 6 until the roof of the nearer chamber gave way. Re-examination of the other tombs has not revealed any more undiscovered chambers.

The interior of tomb 1 shows how the rock was laboriously pecked out to creat the chambers, no easy job in Coralline Limestone. This photograph was taken just after the excavation of the tomb in 1955.

extra-wide-angle lens is needed to w as much as possible of the lobed form omb 1's chamber.

A step was left in the rock immediately beneath the doorway at the bottom of the shaft.

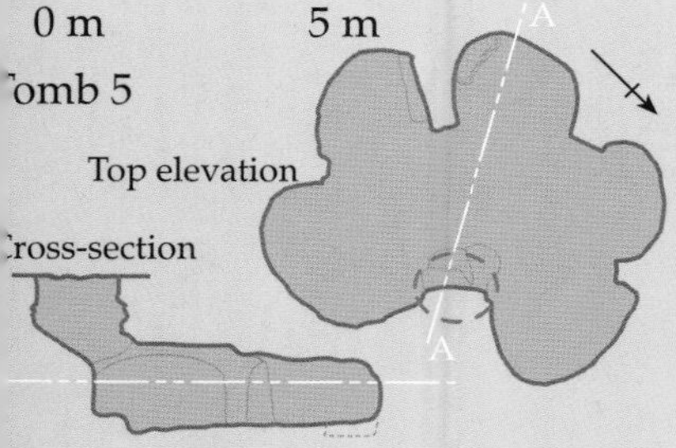

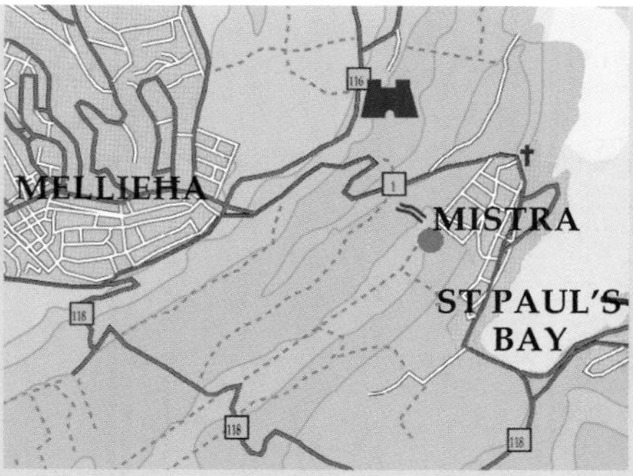

nb 5 is both the largest and the most borately lobed, providing a possible piration for the plan of the earliest ıples (p.87). On the plan, the entrance ft is represented by the dashed circle.

Pass St Paul's Bay and keep on driving towards Mellieħa along Xemxija Hill Road. Once you see the church in front of you, turn left as if to drive into the Mistra Village Hotel. Take the first road on the left (Triq Raddett ir-Rota) and then take the steep road on the right (Triq il-Fuħħar) and turn left on Triq l-Imġiebaħ. At the end turn right on Triq il-Preistorja. The tombs are off this road towards Mellieħa.

KUNĊIZZJONI
(QORTIN L-IMDAWWAR)
BAĦRIJA

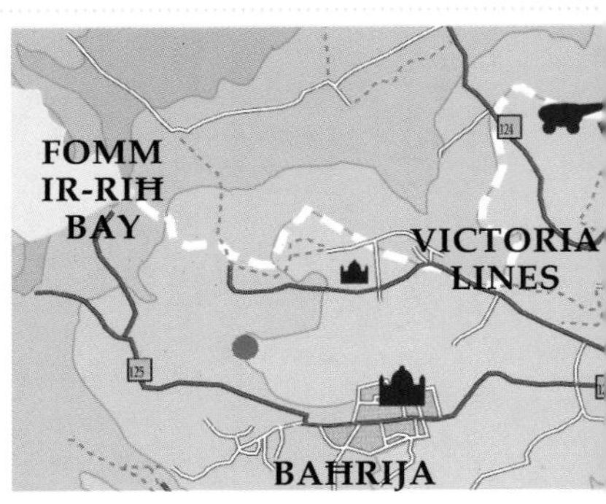

This is one of the most difficult sites to find, an lies on private land used for trapping birds. P through Baħrija and drive down towards Fo ir-Riħ bay. On the way down to the bay before steep downhill you will see a field path closed with a barrier.
What is left of the temple is at the end of this f path in the middle of a birdtrapper's trap bef the edge of the cliff.

Scanty remains of oval chambers were excavated here in 1938. The site would hardly merit a separate entry but for two factors. Firstly, it stands in a dramatic position on a bare limestone plateau north of Baħrija village, as the name Qortin implies. The alternative name comes via the Italian *Concezzione Immacolata*, the Immaculate Conception, the dedication of a chapel standing on the nearest road, 800 m to the east. Like the Bronze Age village of Il-Qliegħa, Baħrija, it has magnificent views across the northwest coast of Malta and across to Gozo.

Secondly, despite the ruinous state of the structure, a considerable quantity of finds was recovered. The pottery was effectively all the Tarxien phase. Since much o had ochred incrustation, a practi common earlier, this might imp the occupation fell, or at least sta ed, early in that phase.

This line of rocks might have been dismissed as of no archaeological significance but for the Temple Period sherds lying around. Excavation in 1938 added little information on the site.

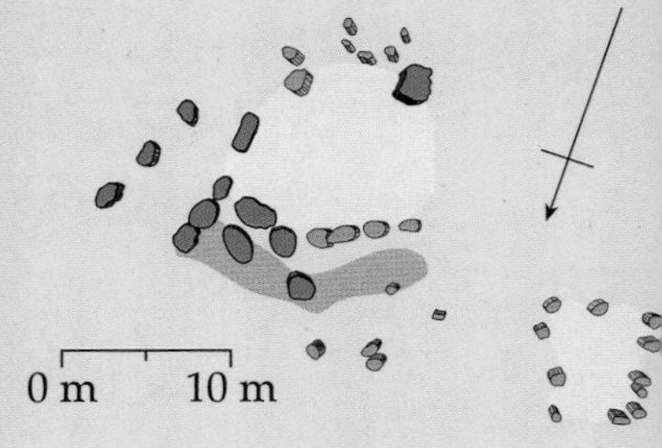

Try as we might, we cannot fit this setting of stones into a recognizable temple plan, though undoubtedly assembled by the people who built the temples.

)THER SITES (MALTA)
ARIOUS LOCATIONS

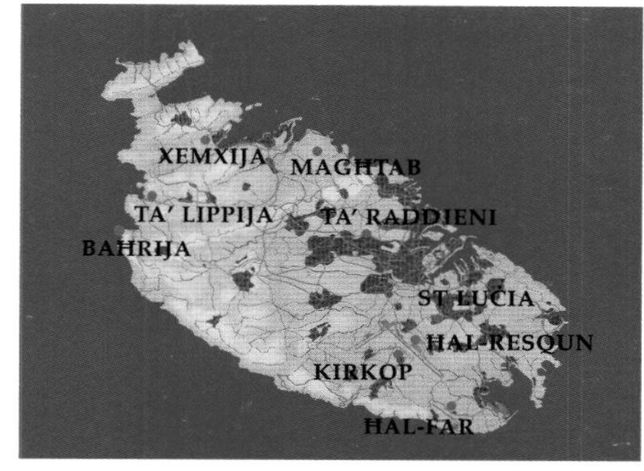

Dotted around Malta are other megaliths, clearly moved by man, some more, some less, convincingly of the Temple Period.

ndoubtedly there must once ıve been many more megalith- Temple Period sites, though hether any of them were ever mples of classic form is now ıknowable.

Evans (1971) listed seven prob- ›le ones: Ħal Far (Birżebbuġa), ·Tumbata (Luqa), Għajn Żejtuna Iellieħa), Ta' Lippija (Mġarr), aliet Marku (Naxxar), and Sqaq Bagħal (Qrendi). All had a few rge stones and prehistoric sherds, ıt none a surviving recognizable an. Several of them, indeed, have nished and are known only from rly records.

Care has to be taken with these. vo more on Evans' list, Qalillija abat) and Ras il-Ġebel (Mġarr), produced Bronze Age rather than Temple Period sherds. Even more notable is Ras ir-Raħeb, a certain archaeological site with two substantial orthostats, but no sherds earlier than Punic. As will be noted on p.190, Debdieba might fall into the same category.

Evans also mentions a ten-metre 'covered way' at Magħtab

e two orthostats on Ras ir-Raħeb are tainly part of a structure, but of the nic period. The Bronze Age village of Qliegħa dominates the skyline behind. sitors should take great care on the fs which surround the site.

A natural cave was discovered during development of the housing estate of Santa Luċija, 1 km south of Paola. Prehistoric sherds and human bones found in it showed that it had attracted attention in the past.

(Naxxar), with rough walls and capstones but no recorded sherds. Its date is quite uncertain. Others reported from time to time have no associated pottery and can almost certainly be dismissed as natural.

However, the best claimant, showing that discoveries may still be made, came to light at Ta' Raddiena during the construction of the Birkirkara By-pass. Six blocks in a curved line are visible, two of them set radially, the other four face out. They are up to 2.3 m long and 1.55 m high, and many Temple Period sherds were recovered around them. These must be the remains of a structure like those previously described, though what its original form was, we do not know. There are more megaliths at L-Iklin, a short distance to the north.

Almost as convincing, thoug without associated sherds, is setting of stones setting of ston at Ħal Resqun, 300 m west of B Miftuħ chapel, Gudja. This t might repay archaeological inve tigation.

How many more are the awaiting discovery, and ho many more once existed but ha been utterly swept away, lea ing no recognizable trace? Aft all, the erosive forces of natu have been at work on them f four-and-a-half thousand yea not to mention the far more rap and drastic attacks of farmers a builders in more recent times.

Megaliths on the ridge southwest of the Xemxija tombs may once have formed part of a temple or temple-like structure. The site is too ruinous to be sure.

The blocks beside the road at Ħal Resqu Gudja, close to the entrance to Malta International Airport, look convincing a Temple Period structure. Excavation would be needed to confirm this by finding appropriate pottery associated.

hese massive blocks at Ta' Raddiena, irkirkara, face out and edge out, must : part of a temple-like structure, and ierds around confirm this. Again, only excavation could recover a meaningful plan. The small rubble above is a modern field wall.

Vhen Ħal Far airfield was constructed, single standing stone or menhir stood nbarrassingly on the line of the proposed ınway. It was moved to become a feature : the garden of the RAF Officers' Mess, ow the ETC complex.

Another menhir stands beside the road just outside Kirkop. The name Is-Salib referred to a stone cross once mounted on its top rather than to the one engraved on its face, both intended to Christianize a pagan monument.

ĠGANTIJA
XAGĦRA, GOZO

This is in many ways the most impressive of all the temples. In fact, it is two temples built side by side, enclosed within a single massive boundary wall and opening onto a common forecourt, itself raised on a high terrace wall.

The southern temple is both the larger and the older, sherds from its wall-filling showing that it goes back to the phase named after this site, about 3500 BC. It has five apses connected by a central corridor, the inner pair the larger, measuring 23 m from end to end.

But it is the surviving height of the walls, just over 7m high in both the façade and the inner left apse, which is the most striking feature. These blocks have never been disturbed, the scaffolding currently disfiguring the façad being intended to ensure that thi remains true.

The first apse right has sev eral altar blocks on which relie spirals can be made out when th light falls at the right angle. The have been much weathered sinc Charles Brochtorff painted ther soon after they were first expose by Col. Vance's excavation i 1827. The inner side apses als had altars, though undecoratec Those on the left needed additiona vertical supports in recent times t prevent their collapse. The snak pillar, now in the Gozo's Museur of Archaeology, once stood on thei left. The altars on the right are nov reduced to near ground level. Th central altar is also massive, it

The sheer size of Ġgantija – the choice of name is hardly surprising – is difficult to take in at a a glance, and the crumbled central section does not help. That it has survived at all is remarkable, considering its antiquity.

Here, at the southern corner of the façade it still stands over 6 m high. The placing of horizontal courses over orthostats, standard procedure in the temple architecture, is very evident in this view.

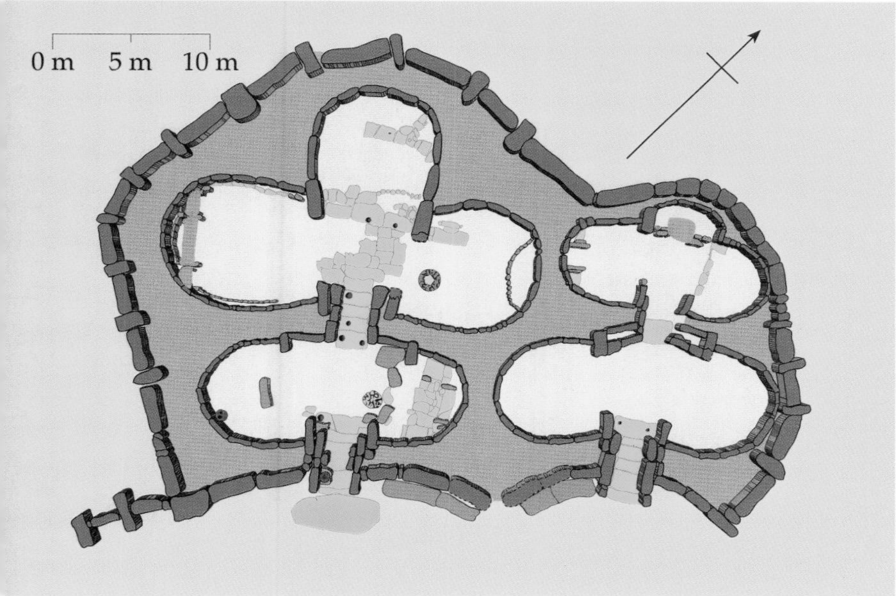

0 m 5 m 10 m

oth temples of which Ġgantija is ɔmposed have a neat, uncluttered plan, of -apses in the southern one, 4-and-a-niche in the later one on its right. They thus offer a useful comparison of the two forms.

'he northeast end of the temple façade ırvives to a lesser height. The smooth ɩlobigerina Limestone of the door jambs f the North Temple contrasts with the ɔugher and greyer Coralline Limestone of ıe façade and external walls.

The rear wall of the temples includes the largest megalithic blocks, as the group of visitors beside them makes apparent. The kink in the wall between the first and second orthostats to their right marks the junction between the two temples.

front bearing dotted decoration, though much more widely spaced than usual, and without the relief frame. This might suggest an earlier date.The passages and second central court are massively stone paved, one block bearing a supposed Phoenician graffito. There are traces of reddening where fires were once lit on their floors. The largest flooring block of all, however, is the great external threshold slab.

The rough appearance of the walls is misleading. They were constructed of local irregular Coralline blocks, where all finer work, the passage walls and altars for example, are of Globigerina. This had to be dragged to the site from outcrops well below the level of the plateau and over a kilometre away. However, traces of plaster infill, including fallen fragments painted in red ochre, show that the walls were once smoothed off by tha means, giving a much finer finis than is presently apparent, one indeed, comparable to the smoot ashlar of the other temples.

Late in the Ġgantija phase o early in that of Tarxien, part of th temple's north wall was remove to allow a second one of four apse to be built close alongside. On of the former outer wall orthos tats can still be seen in the secon apse left. Its anomalous vertica position would of course not hav been visible behind the now miss ing plaster. Another fragment o the earlier wall is visible where th façade has fallen away between th two temple entrances.

This temple is plainer than th first, though the mildly concav Globigerina uprights on the inne side of its first court are striking They mirror the slight concavit

The inner left apse of the South Temple has one of the most complex altars, three trilithons between four uprights. The two somewhat confusing central pillars were added in modern times to support the cracked horizontal slabs.

Looking down the axis of the same temple to the forecourt beyond, one can appreciate the complex doorways of nesting trilithons, one within another. Again one notes the contrast between the dressed stone of those doorways and the rough rubble of the walls.

f the apse walls. It should be ›peated that this rough Coralline ›alling could not have supported ıe weight of a complete corbel ault in stone.

Equally remarkable are the uge orthostatic slabs in the exter-al wall round the back of the ›mples, alternating face out and dge out for greater stability. It › unsurprising that local folklore ttributed the construction of this .te to giants.

Few finds were preserved from ıat early excavation, the most ımous being two heads carved om Globigerina. By contrast, a ump of pottery found in a cave) m to the north in 1947 contained ıormous quantities of Tarxien hase offering bowls. These had een smashed and deposited here › prevent their being desecrated y re-use in secular contexts.

While Ġgantija itself is clearly a major monument, it was not the only one locally. Quite apart from Santa Verna and the Xagħra Circle out to the west, separately described, there are the scanty remains of megaliths between Ġgantija and the carpark by 8 September Avenue, and more above the Għar ta' Għejżu across the road to the west again.

Ġgantija appears particularly dramatically on the air photograph overleaf, looking east on the axis of the South Temple. The rear wall is one of its most striking features.

ıe rough masonry is even clearer in is photo, but one must remember that, use, these walls were all smoothed off th plaster and painted red (see p.74). ıe internal fittings in this right hand se were unfortunately found slighted to ound level.

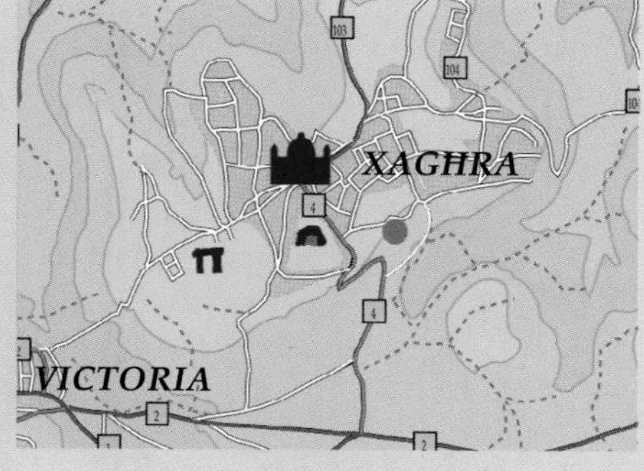

Go up to Xagħra on the main road (Triq ta' Ħamet) and when you enter into the buildings (Vjal it-8 Ta' Settembru) you will see a playing field on the right of the road. Turn right after the playing field into Triq il-Maqdes. There you will see a wire fence. Pass through the gate and walk down the road to the Visitors' Centre.

XAGĦRA CIRCLE

XAGĦRA, GOZO

A unique monument for the Maltese islands was first recorded by Jean Houel in the eighteenth century, dug into by Otto Bayer in 1826, painted by Brochtorff at that time (it is sometimes referred to as the Brochtorff Circle) but then refilled and lost. It was reidentified by Joseph Attard Tabone in 1964 and re-excavated by Drs Stoddart and Malone in 1987-94.

The early artists portrayed a circle of juxtaposed orthostats, effectively a wall, 45 m in diameter, a single gap to the east being flanked by two much taller blocks. They may once have supported a lintel, to provide a trilithon entrance, but if so, it had already vanished. Ġgantija temples are in direct line from here, 350 m away. All but three blocks of this wall have since di appeared, presumably carried o as building material for more rece structures.

At the centre of the circle, Ba er's workmen exposed a deep cavi with a setting of trilithon altars its floor. In one of Brochtorff's wate colours, another workman passes human skull out of a cave to one si to Bayer himself. Of his discoverie this is sadly the only record.

The recent excavation re-opene and emptied the 1826 pit an extended excavation into undi turbed parts of the site, above ar below the rock surface, with, as only to be expected, much mo careful digging techniques and, consequence, much more inform tive results.

Charles Brochtorff's watercolour shows the Circle as it was in his day. The ring of orthostats was then substantially complete on the north and west. Two taller uprights on the east, presumably the original entrance, had already lost their lintel.

Brochtorff's second watercolour shows Otto Bayer's 1826 excavation. Though the orthostats in the background framing Nadur church, and all the structure visi below ground level, had been destroyed, reinvestigation in 1987-94 confirmed bo the presence and importance of the site.

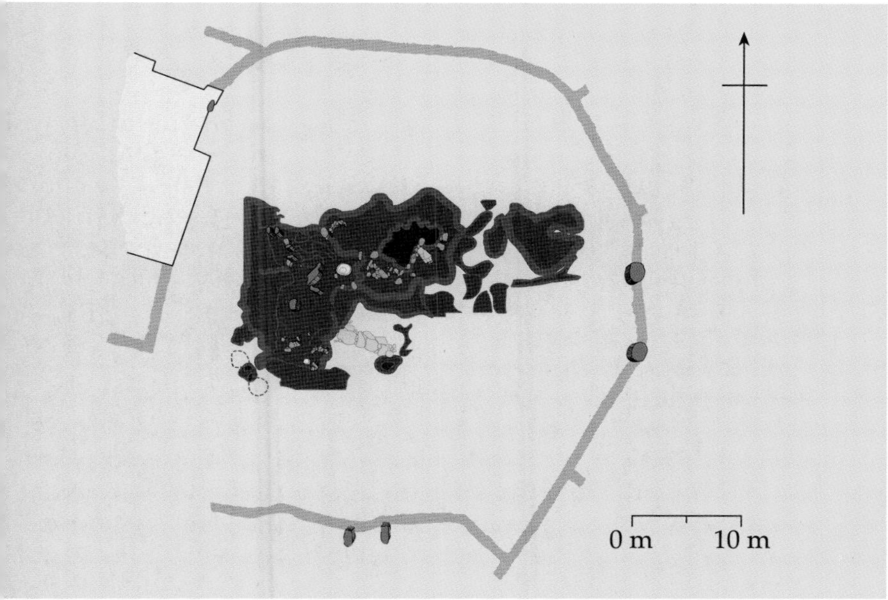

n this plan, the black area represents yer's hole, grey the area cleared in e recent re-excavation. The bistre line ows modern field walls following the line of the former circle, though only three original blocks survive.

e busy scene is of the excavation in 94. A team of diggers is working on e burial deposits on the floor of the ypogeum, the roof having collapsed long ice (p.298). Xagħra village stands on e skyline behind.

At the centre of this photo is this typical Temple Period construction. The Globigerina Limestone blocks were imported to the site for finer structures like this. Its further face bears pitted decoration and there are traces of red ochre on it.

A village of the Żebbuġ phase left much broken pottery across the site but no structures other than a single rock-cut tomb with two chambers (p.60).

Then in the Tarxien phase, probably through the sinking of another tomb shaft, a series of natural caves in the rock was discovered. These were then extensively enlarged, it not being too difficult to cut into the decayed rock once the hard crust had been broken through. Unfortunately for us, this rock is Upper Coralline, quite unsuitable for the delicate carving of Ħal Saflieni. So although what we have is undoubtedly a second hypogeum, it is nowhere near as striking as that site. At least its builders tried, by importing blocks of Globigerina from a kilometre or more away, to make altars such as those Bayer found. A smaller setting had survived, together wit a huge carved jar, if only in frag ments.

As well as the building wor below ground and the stone ci cle itself, and presumably at muc the same time as both, a mega lithic threshold and paved are were constructed on the surfac giving access to the hypogeu below, probably by way of step now missing.

As at Ħal Saflieni, at the en of the Temple Period the unde ground part of the site was seale off again, though a settlement the Tarxien Cemetery phase wa established above.

The main function of this si was clearly for burial, making it veritable necropolis. Study of th bones, still continuing, has give a tally so far of at least eight hu dred individuals.

While most of the skeletons were completely jumbled, a few, like this one in a pit beside the threshold slab, were found undisturbed, just as they were laid to rest. The crouched position is typical.

Over most of the site, the bones had been moved around after the flesh had rotted from the bodies. The result is the sort of confusion seen here.

While still well short of aflieni's six thousand, this has rovided an invaluable sample for etailed study, going a long way owards compensating for the loss f the remains from that site. It hould be added that the total will ery probably rise considerably s study continues, and the site as been far from completely emped. How much further it extends elow ground is not known as afety considerations prevented e clearance of side chambers, ith their roofs of badly shattered ock.

All in all, the reinvestigaon of the Xagħra Circle and s hypogeum has advanced our nderstanding of both the prehisoric population and its burial rites a remarkable degree. How many ore hypogea are awaiting redisovery in Malta and Gozo?

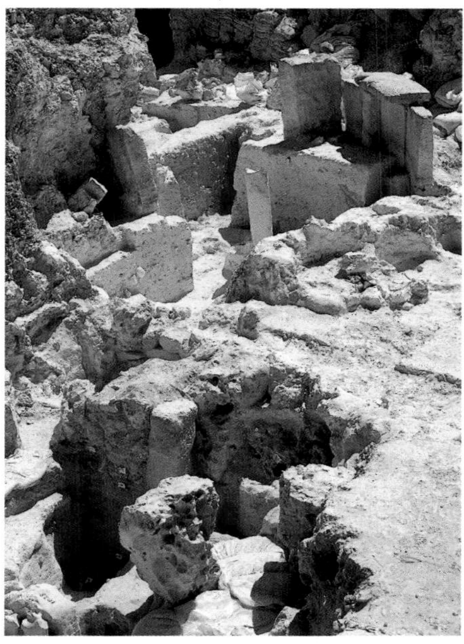

While yielding hardly any settings of stones like Bayer's, the recent work produced far more evidence, thanks to modern techniques of excavation.

n the surface of the rock, a row of egalithic paving slabs formed a onumental threshold giving access to e cave system. Unfortunately the steps own into the Hypogeum did not survive.

The excavation site of the Xagħra Circle is not open to the general public and is closed off with a boundary fence. The excavation 'hole' has been filled up with sandbags for protection. Very little is to be seen at present.

Go up to Xagħra on the main road (Triq ta' Ħamet) and turn left after the second bend into Triq ta' Qaċċa. On this road you have to walk up a narrow alley on the right of the road. The site is at the end of the path off this alley.

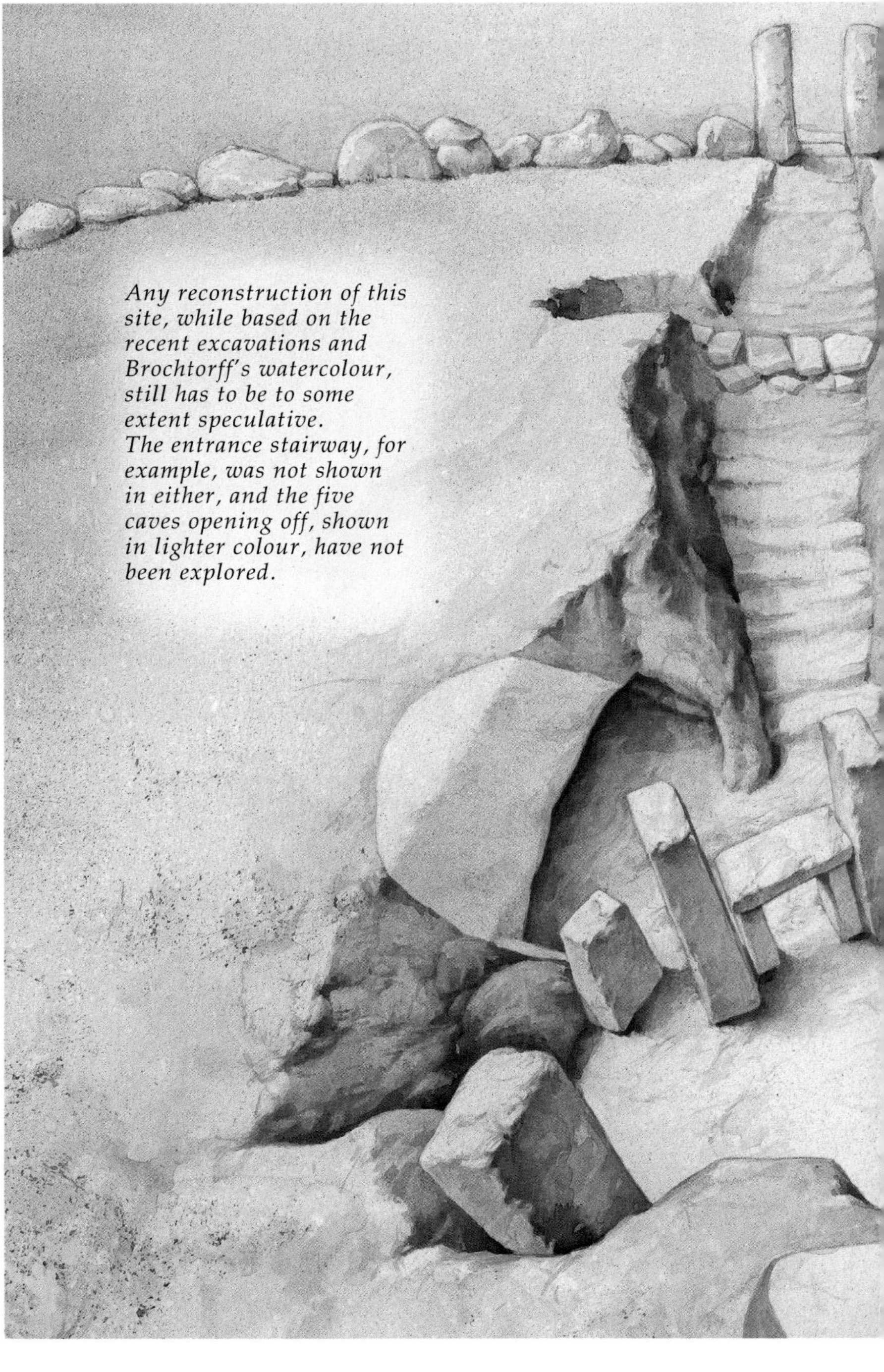

Any reconstruction of this site, while based on the recent excavations and Brochtorff's watercolour, still has to be to some extent speculative. The entrance stairway, for example, was not shown in either, and the five caves opening off, shown in lighter colour, have not been explored.

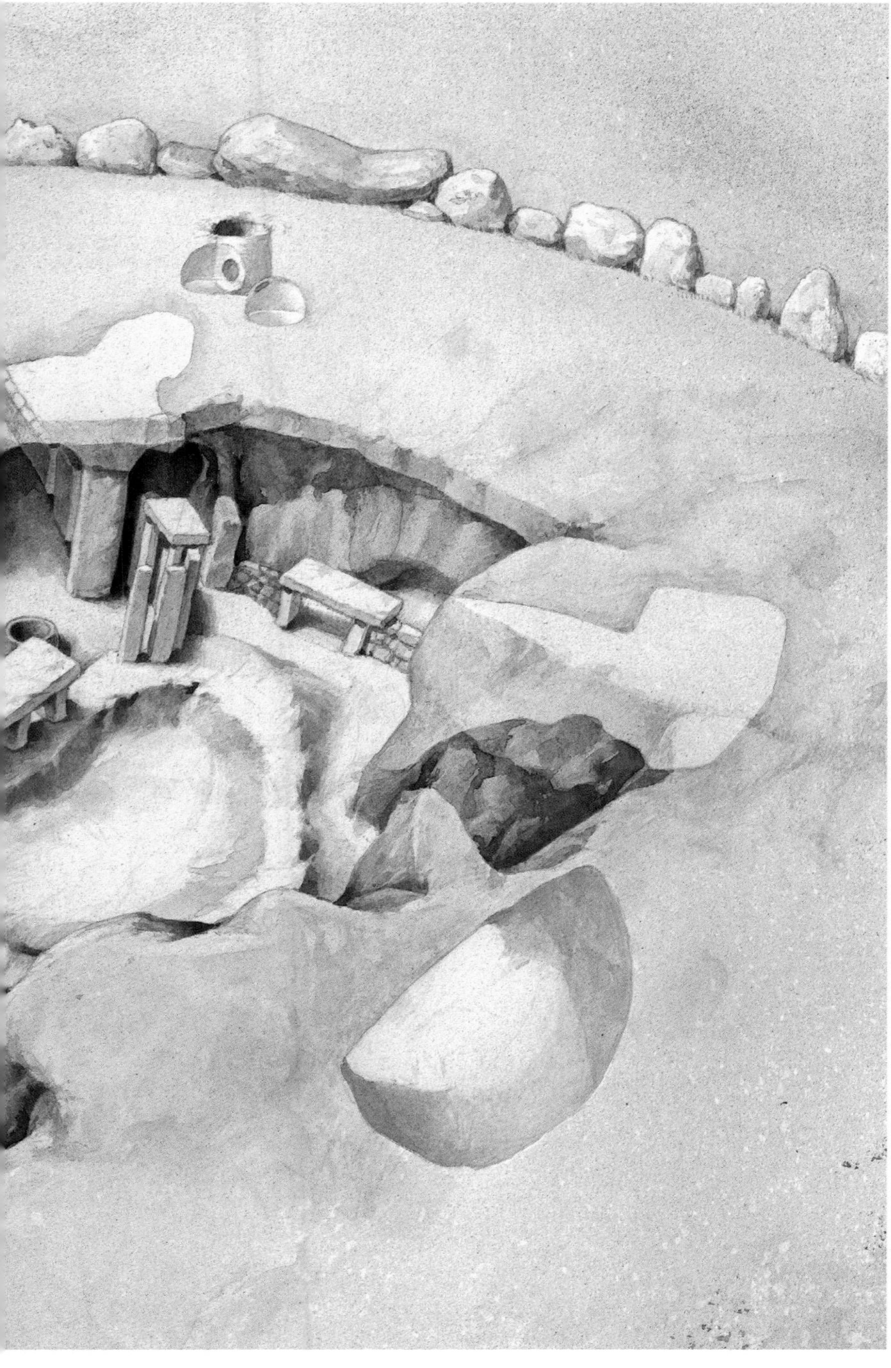

SANTA VERNA
XAGĦRA, GOZO

A sad site these days, with no more than three rather shapeless blocks standing in an open field. It lies 700 m west of the Xagħra Circle, near the southern lip of the plateau, and is approached by way of a lane from the end of the road off San Anton Square. Apart from a scatter of sherds in the fields around, it would be hard to believe that a complete temple once stood here.

When Ashby and Bradley dug it in 1911, they revealed a spread of *torba* alongside the standing stones, the shape of which seemed to indicate the plan of a small trefoil temple, the three blocks having formed part of its façade. In 1960 further trenches found deposits of much earlier date, since the temple had, like Skorba, Kordin III, and Ta' Ħaġrat, been built over the site of much older village, going back to least the Grey Skorba phase.

This site was presumably an outlier of the scatter of sites extending westwards from Ġgantija along the southern lip of the Xagħra plateau.

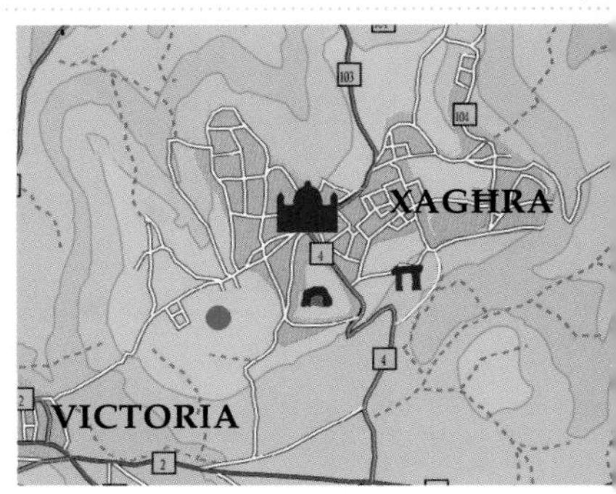

Go up to Xagħra on the main road (Triq ta' Ħam and turn left after the second bend into Triq Qaċċa. At the end, at Pjazza San Anton turn left i Triq San Anton. Walk up a road on the right and the pathway on the inside right (between the bui ings). Walk along the lane until, on the right, y will see the remaining megaliths in open fields.

At the western end of the line of monuments south of Xagħra, Santa Verna has survived in very poor shape. The largest remaining stones probably once stood at one end of the temple's façade, with traces of a stone bench at their foot.

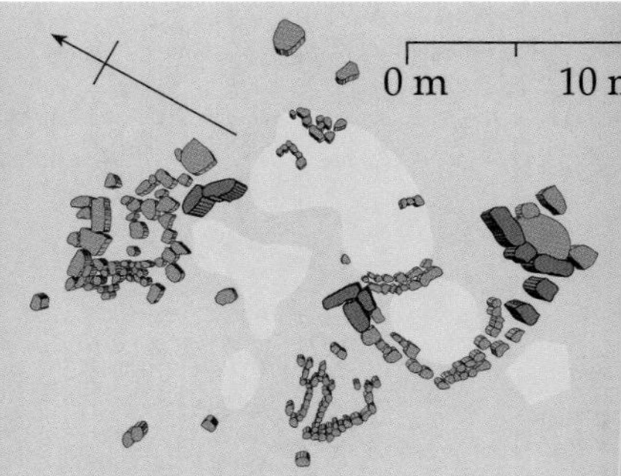

Only the torba *floor, now reburied, hinted at a trefoil plan. Otherwise we would have had no idea of the temple's original shape.*

'A' MARŻIENA

ICTORIA, GOZO

his temple has survived in only arginally better shape, and would e more easily understood if not heavily masked by carob trees. has never been excavated and, view of the thin soil cover, ould probably tell us little if it as, despite the scatter of sherds ound. It lies on the southern lip of e Victoria plateau looking across wards Sannat. A footpath immeately opposite the windmill tower ads to it.

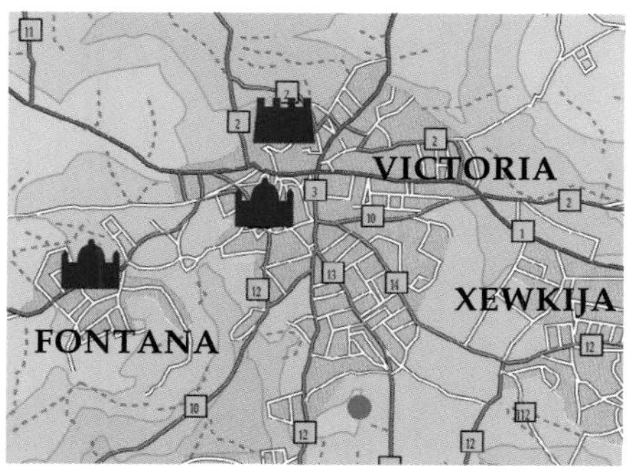

From the centre of Victoria drive towards the village of Sannat along Triq Dr Anton Tabone. As you approach the edge of the buildings at Taċ-Ċawla, turn into Triq il-Mitħna. Walk along a footpath on the left of the road until you see the carob trees at the edge of the plateau. Very little is to be seen at this site.

What can still be made out are ree curved fragments of wall of bstantial blocks. The rear wall of e temple is fairly complete and uite impressive, now serving as modern field wall. Beneath the robs lie the scanty remains of an al chamber, with part of another curved wall to its left. From these it is not too difficult to reconstruct a five-apse plan, assuming the complete apse to be the central one. It has to be admitted that this is somewhat conjectural, even if supported by the sherds of the Ġgantija phase among the surface finds.

n the tip of a separate plateau, ' Marżiena lies south of Victoria, erlooking the fertile central plain. e aerial view shows little but carob es, and some blocks rather larger than uld normally be expected in a field ll.

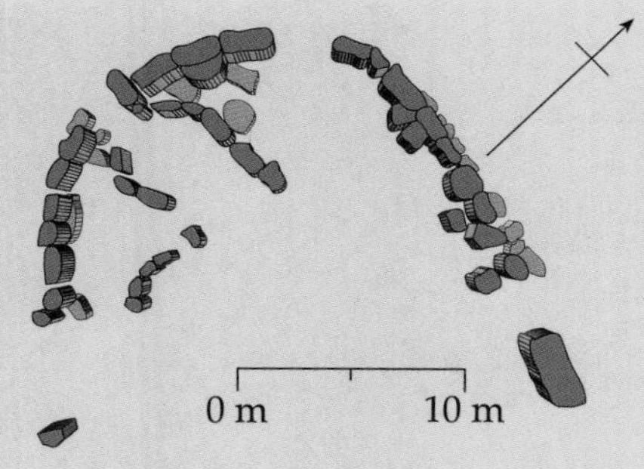

Survey in 1960 was difficult, but yielded a plan which bears a convincing resemblance to better-preserved temples. It is doubtful if excavation of the shallow soil would provide much further information.

BORĠ L-IMRAMMA
SANNAT, GOZO

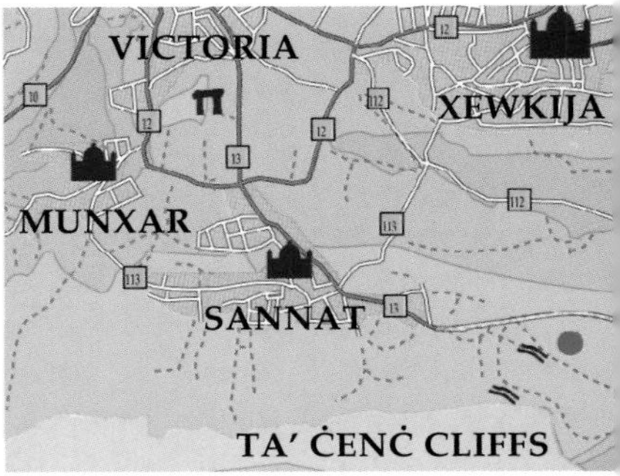

Pass through the village of Sannat and drive towar the cliffs of Ta' Ċenċ. Drive along the dust ro. towards the sea. Park on the side of the road whe the electricity poles turn into the valley, and wa towards the right in the direction of the edge of t cliffs. The low megaliths are in open fields and o has to look carefully to find them.

While undoubtedly a major building of the Temple Period, it is something of a stretch of the imagination to call it a temple itself. It shares few of the characteristics of the usual temple plan. A large roughly circular courtyard, about 20 m across and presumably always open to the sky, has clustered along its north, west, and south sides a number of small, again nearly circular, chambers. An entrance passage to the northwest, of large squared stones, is the strongest clue to its date, supported by sherds around. It has never been excavated.

It lies near the centre of the Ta' Ċenċ plateau, 300 m southeast of the reservoir and due east of the hotel. Cart ruts pass close by its south side, and the Ta' Ċenċ dolmens are n far off to the north, but associatio with either is both unproven an unlikely.

Attempts to prevent hunters fro shooting and trapping around have been only partly successful.

Well away from the other sites, Borġ l-Imramma stands on the open plateau of Ta' Ċenċ. It looks quite unlike any other contemporary building, apparently consisting of a partial ring of chambers round an open court. One doorway strongly resembles those in the temples.

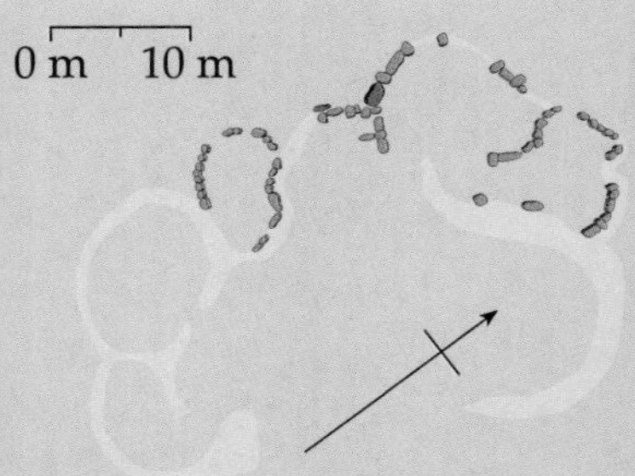

Once more, the surveyed plan gives a better idea of the shape of the site than does the overall view, but still does little to explain it.

)THER SITES IN GOZO
'ARIOUS LOCATIONS

.s with Malta, there are a number ſ sites in Gozo of lesser, in some ıses minimal, importance.

Once out in open fields but now wallowed up by the village of Qala, single standing stone beside the ɔad close to the government sec- ndary school is always referred to s the Qala menhir. A few sherds 'om nearby might mean that it once ɔrmed part of a megalithic struc- ıre, like the 'menhir' of Skorba. If ɔ, housing development all round as destroyed all other traces.

On the northern edge of Għajn- ielem village are three groups f megaliths, some of them still ı position but none yielding a ecognizable plan or sherds. Two ıst north of the Xewkija-Qala ɔad go under the name of Borġ il-Għarib, the third, to the south, L-Mrejsbiet.

A natural cave in the Pergla valley north of Xagħra was more significant, with a good though disturbed deposit of Ġgantija and Tarxien phase sherds. By contrast, nothing of archaeological significance has been reported from

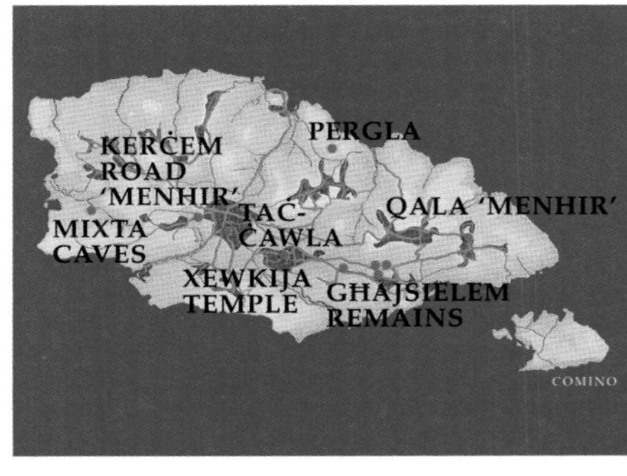

Other and lesser sites of various forms are shown on this map, dotted around Gozo.

'he enigmatic menhir at Qala is a single ɔmewhat irregular standing stone, now ł least quite isolated. It is not known ' that is a true picture, or if missing dditional blocks would have told a ifferent story.

L-Mrejsbiet is now no more than a jumble of rocks in the middle of cultivated fields near Għajnsielem. Its original plan is quite unknown, and it is only assumed to be a former temple site.

Calypso's Cave above Ramla, also within the limits of Xagħra.

Numerous early references testify to a temple site immediately beneath and alongside Xewkija parish church, but only scanty traces survived for Magri to investigate in 1904, and none today.

Of much more importance, the site of Taċ-Ċawla, in the southern suburbs of Victoria, has several times been mentioned in the main text. Little more can be said until it can be properly excavated. The initial exploratory trenches have been refilled so there is now nothing to see on the ground.

Gozo has a second menhir, outside the gate of the government nursery on the Kerċem road. It is of rather different form, being much nearer square in section. This suggests it was more likely of Roman than prehistoric date. There are no associated sherds to clinch th issue.

The Mixta caves round the lip c Għajn Abdul, the small plateau we of Għar Ilma and Santa Luċija vi lage, yielded an interesting group c sherds of Għar Dalam date, but hav since been almost totally remove by quarrying.

Finally, mention should be mad of two sites which get reported t the Superintendence of Cultura Heritage frequently, somewhat t their annoyance. They are promi nent groups of megalithic block near the San Dimitri chapel, at th northwest corner of the islanc and on the summit of Tad-Dbieġ the island's highest point, a littl under 200 m above sea level. Bot are purely natural, being the broke up fragments of an Upper Corallin crust, left stranded on the Globig rina surface.

The western part of the Borġ il-Għarib site is a single row of largish blocks on bare rock, without associated finds. Its blocks resemble those of megalithic sites, but this attribution is uncertain.

A little to the east, more blocks are built into a field wall, this crowned with prickly pears. There may be archaeologica material beneath the higher field behind it, but it has never been sought by excavation.

he Upper Coralline cliffs around Għajn bdul have several caves, of which this is he best preserved. However, the early pottery came from another in the group, now destroyed by quarrying.

standing stone between Victoria and ercem is always called a menhir, though ts neat rectangular cross section might uggest that it was of Roman rather than rehistoric date. No sherds have been ound to settle the matter.

A scatter of blocks on a hill top at San Dimitri, near Għarb, looks quite as convincing as some of the other less well-preserved sites, but is purely natural.

KORDIN I & II
(DESTROYED SITES)
KORDIN

A.A. Caruana in 1896 mentioned five groups of megaliths on the Kordin or Corradino plateau, immediately above the head of Grand Harbour. By 1908, when Ashby explored the area, three of these had already vanished. He left plans of the two he investigated, but these too had disappeared by the 1950s when Evans attempted to locate them. Only Ashby's Kordin South, or Kordin III, separately described on p.136, survives.

Kordin I was a small jumble of rooms according to Caruana's plan, more like the outbuildings at Ħaġar Qim or Mnajdra than a true temple. Kordin II was more substantial, though again employing much smaller blocks than most temples.

Two more sites once stood on the Kordin platea[u]. One disappeared under development, the other i[n] the bombardment of the 1940s.

Three pairs of apses were plotte[d] with a respectable connecting pas[-]sage between the outer two. 'Inne[r]' remains debatable, however, as th[e] next area, if really a forecourt, i[s] both slight and irregular, runnin[g] almost imperceptibly into a tangl[e] of small rooms. Could this really b[e] a second six-apse temple?

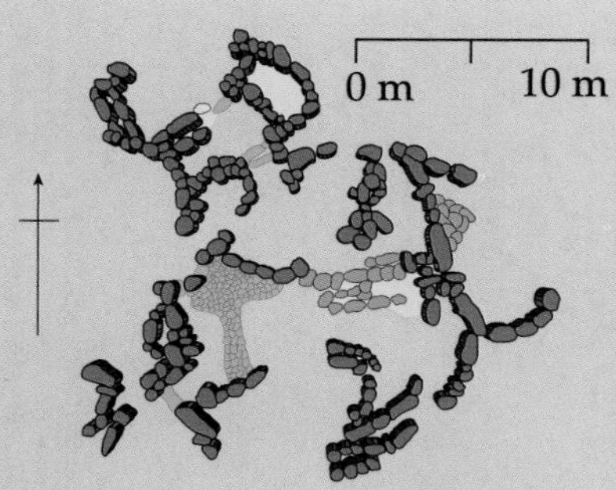

Plans of both were made before their destruction, though that of Kordin I makes little sense in terms of temple morphology. The closest parallels are in the outbuildings of Ħaġar Qim and Mnajdra.

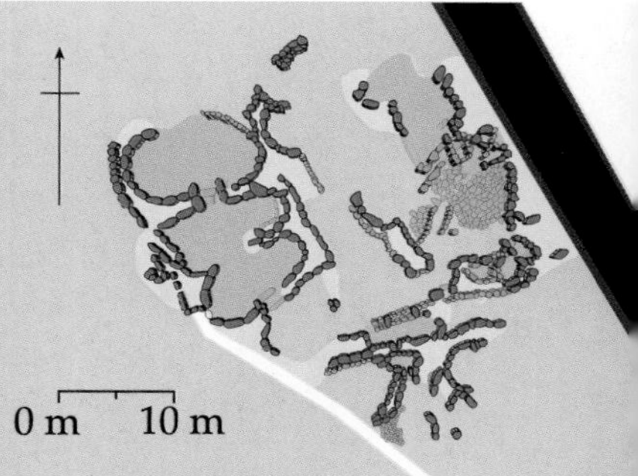

Kordin II at least bears some resemblanc[e] to an apsed temple, though of much slighter construction and with barely a hint of façade and forecourt. Both are certainly of the Temple Period from their associated finds.

:ROBB IL-GĦAĠIN

)ESTROYED SITE)

IARSASCALA

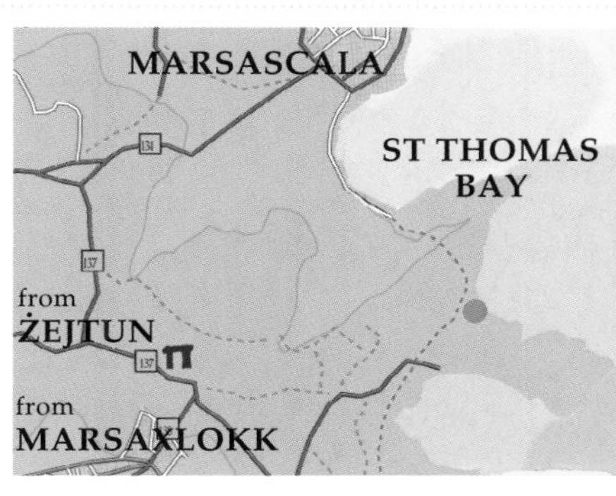

There are practically no remains to be seen at this site. Actually visiting the site is very dangerous since what remains is perilously at the edge of an eroding cliff which is undercut and any weight could cause its collapse.

ramatically but perilously sited on) m-high eroding cliffs, the few last :mains of the temple are in immi-ent danger of falling into the sea. he yeasty water below, the result of at erosion, gives it its name, liter-ly 'spaghetti water'.

The inner part of the temple had typical plan. A paved court and ıner passage gave access to two airs of apses and a large central iche. Outside, the plan was less sual. There was apparently no ıçade. Left of the entrance was an xternal shrine, while erosion has :moved all evidence on the right. he semi-circular forecourt was oored in *torba* and bounded with low wall, as surviving at least. Off the left a strange circular structure was also *torba* floored – perhaps an outbuilding as at Skorba. Finally, two straight boundary walls, well out to the southeast and southwest, seem to have formed a large enclosure, even more extensive than Borġ in-Nadur's. At its centre, a paved entrance passage was set strangely askew.

t the extreme east of Malta, Xrobb il-ħaġin is thought to be a member of the ıs-

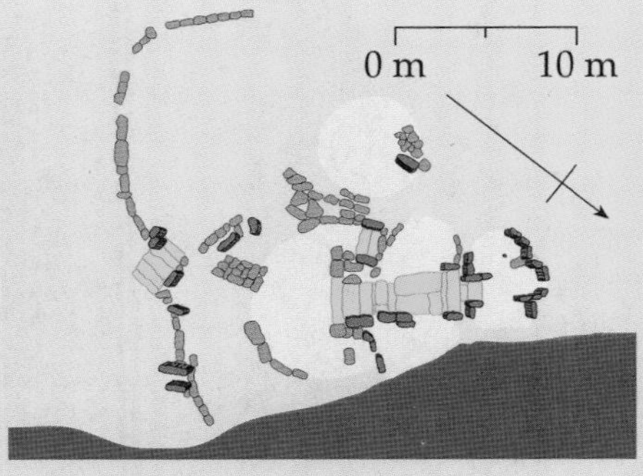

Although the site, or such of it as is left, matches the four-apse plan reasonably closely, the forecourt area is at best anomalous, possibly remodelled later.

DEBDIEBA
(DESTROYED SITE)
LUQA

Little can be said of Debdieba since it was completely removed by an extension to Luqa airport some 50 years ago. Ashby's excavation and plan in 1914 leave numerous problems, the main one being that, whereas sherds of both the last two temple phases were found in some quantity, so were Borġ in-Nadur, Punic and Roman wares, with no clear association between the pottery and particular elements of the structure.

This needs stressing, as the remains, while some of the blocks were up to two metres long, formed markedly rectangular features quite unlike those of any surviving temple building. In the absence of any *torba* flooring, it is quite conceivable that the enti building was of later date, erecte fortuitously over earlier settleme deposits.

However, perhaps I am beir unnecessarily sceptical over thi since that model from Tarxien wi rectilinear chambers is certainly the Temple Period.

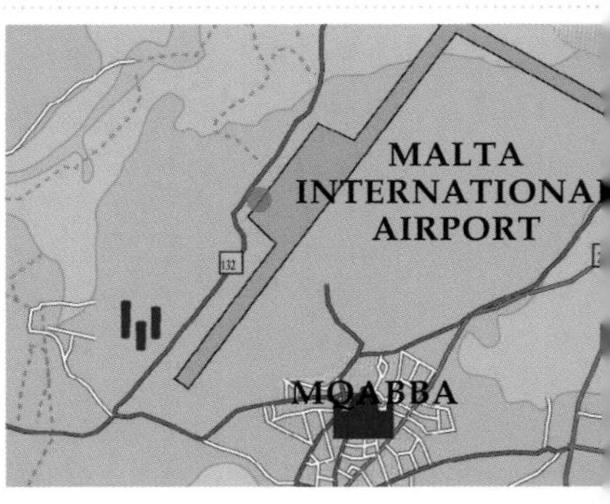

The location map explains why there is nothing be seen of this site on the ground now.

The aerial photograph reinforces the same point. Debdieba was not the only site lost. An attractive Early Christian catacomb was obliterated by the nearer end of the same runway.

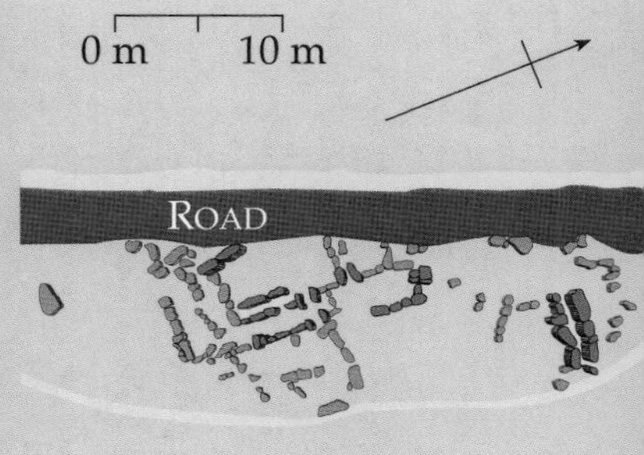

The rectilinearity of the remains and smaller size of its megalithic, raise doubt that this truly belongs to the Temple Period. Although there were prehistoric sherds, numerous later ones were found too. Which of these were genuinely associated with the building?

ĦAL ĠINWI
(DESTROYED SITE)
ŻEJTUN

st across the road from San Nikw chapel, between Żejtun and ıs-Silġ, the site is represented by few blocks still visible in a field all. More may survive beneath e soil since Laferla's excavation 1917 was refilled immediately terwards.

Quite apart from the numerous gantija and Tarxien phase sherds, tails of the structure place it uneıivocally in the Temple Period, ılike Debdieba, though there is tle to suggest a temple proper. ve roughly-square chambers were ıddled together, 13 m over all. At ast two of the doorways had major ving slabs and pairs of orthostat blocks on either side. One of the ıambers, perhaps a central court, was recorded as having a *torba* floor, and two others were also paved.

Just off to the south, a recumbent block 3.5 m long and 0.75 m wide was found, possibly part of an original boundary wall. This is not conclusive in itself since Punic and later sites on Malta can incorporate large natural blocks.

The site of Ħal Ġinwi has been refilled and thus very little is to be seen today. The few megaliths are on private land and the local farmers do not allow visitors to the site.

is site lies in open fields a kilometre st of Żejtun. It is hardly worth the visit. ese few blocks nestle inconspicuously in ield wall, all that survives of once more tensive remains.

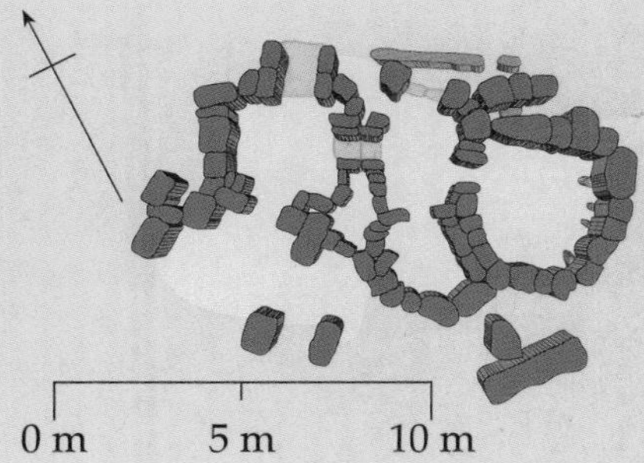

The plan drawn by Laferla in 1917 has details confirming a date in the Temple Period, and there were appropriate associated sherds, but there is nothing standard about the plan.

TEMPLE MODELS

The term, though generally used, is rather misleading. It covers the remarkable group of architectural representations made at the time, and as such almost unknown elsewhere in the prehistoric world. They come in three forms, making them even more extraordinary.

Firstly there is a three-dimensional model, and here the word is fully merited. It was found in the temple of Mġarr and shows a small single-celled structure, oval in plan, with a trilithon doorway – two single block jambs and a lintel. The walls consist of megalithic blocks alternating flat in the wall face and radial, slightly projecting. These are topped by one course of horizontal blocks. The roof is puzzling. Seven transverse bars are shown, but whether they are slabs of stone, for which the span looks excessiv or balks of timber is not apparen The model measures 4.5 by 3.7 cm Since the doorway must be 1.7 t 2 m wide on the evidence of th temples themselves, it gives a approximate scale. From this w can calculate the size of the build ing represented as 10 to 13 m long about the size of the smallest, eas ern, temple at Mnajdra.

Secondly there are four eleva tions of temples. Much the fines is a beautifully carved one from Tarxien. It is broken into four su viving fragments, of which thre join. The first shows the lower righ corner, with part of a door jamb an three facing orthostats on a slightl concave plan. As with the façad of Ħaġar Qim, the outermost is th tallest, with one of the five horizon tal ashlar courses butted against and the second notched into it

The little carved stone model from Mġarr, only 4.5 cm long, shows a fairly typical temple building, although its façade continues the curve of the external wall rather than being flat or concave.

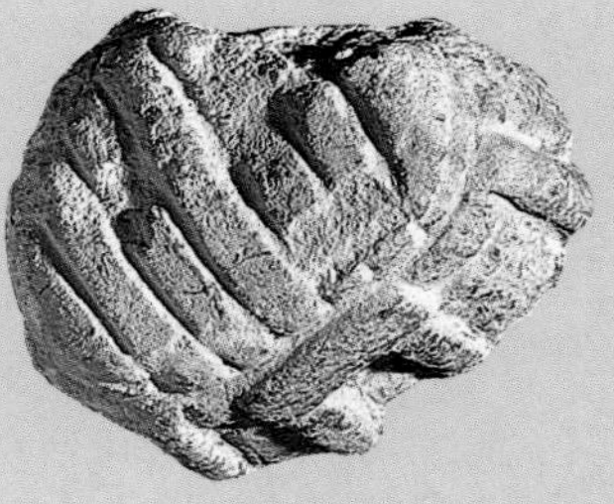

The view from above raises more difficulty. It is not clear what sort of structure this is meant to represent, so it gives little help with the vexed problem o how the temples were roofed.

*he fragments in the pictures
·low are as found. Here they
e assembled with additions* *in plaster of Paris to show how the temple façade may once have looked.*

*ıe upper left corner illustrates the slight
·ersailing of the sides and the projecting
rbel courses, missing from all the extant
·mples.*

The lower right corner, conversely, can be matched precisely in surviving remains, effectively guaranteeing the validity of the other. Note the delicate carving of the stone model.

top inner corner. A bench stands against the wall, its top with rectangular projections at the back of alternating height, exactly like blocks still standing in the first apse left at Tarxien South. All its features can be matched in surviving remains.

The other three fragments are of the upper left corner. Five horizontal courses of blocks oversail slightly to the side and are topped with a projecting corbel course. Above this and set well back, there is one course of facing orthostats, the corner one again notched to take the first of three more horizontal courses. A second projecting corbel course has a last horizontal course set on its inner edge. No temple survives to this height, but we can hardly disbelieve this evidence when the other fragment is so well substantiated, and this has strong support from engineering princ ples, in particular the use of th 'blocking course' on the rear edg of corbels to counterbalance the destabilizing overhang.

If the lowest course of the secon fragment corresponds to the firs above the corner orthostat on th other – it cannot be lower, and higher, the proportions look muc less likely – the whole model woul have stood 33 cm high, and bee about 52 cm across. The back is le quite rough.

A rather cruder representation carved into one of the uprights i Mnajdra's central temple. A trilitho entrance in an orthostatic façad its blocks not separately shown, topped by four horizontal course none projecting as a corbel. It i 24 cm high. Even rougher are tw more scratched on a single ston plaque from Skorba. One show

Only 2.5 cm long, this carved amulet shows another temple-style wall of alternating orthostats, though more schematically. The V-perforations were presumably added for attachment. It was found at Tarxien.

The central graffito on this plaque from Skorba shows another temple façade, to be compared with that from Mnajdra on p.150. A second on the left is even rougher and apparently unfinished.

›ur to five orthostats either side f a shallow pit, presumably the ›ntral door, with two horizontal ›urse above. It measures 24.5 by 3.5 mm. Beside it, a rough square ith central pit and two horizontal parallel lines above would not ave been recognized for a temple ıçade if the rather better one just escribed had not been on the same laque beside it.

Thirdly come two representations of building plans. Two agments of one from Ħaġar Qim ıodelled in clay show the walls of mple apses with doorways. A logial reconstruction would give it five pses and an overall length of about) cm, though neither plan nor size certain. The walls are shown as umps, so the building would not ave looked like this, before, during, r after construction. The external alls, for example, are not shown at all. It is, then, schematic, and more probably prepared before building commenced – with interesting implications.

The last piece to be considered is even more puzzling. Again from Tarxien, and again carved from stone, is a curved, possibly oval, platform of two courses of ashlar masonry with an enclosure wall, now broken off, following its lip. It bears wall stumps and doorways very like those on the Ħaġar Qim piece just described, but unlike in being strictly rectilinear. Parts of seven rooms are shown, only one complete, and one of the doorways appears to be an entrance from the platform. No building looking remotely like this is known from prehistoric Malta. Was it another architect's presentation piece, turned down flat by either the developers or the planning committee?

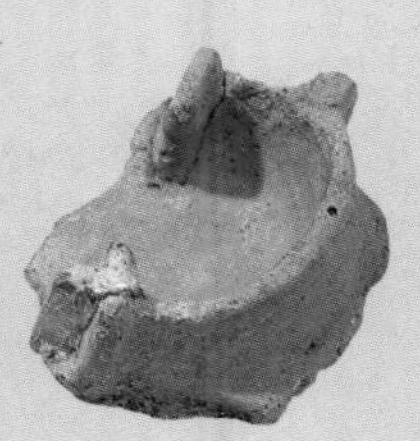

lore puzzling is this ceramic model from aġar Qim, not a picture but a schematic ound plan. Apses and door jambs are early represented. It is a pity more of it as not survived.

While undoubtedly of the Temple Period, and coming from Tarxien, this remarkable piece shows a unique rectilinear building. It again appears as a ground plan, though with a three-dimensional podium.

TEMPLE ROOFING

It is generally agreed that the temples must have been roofed, since the plaster we know was used on their walls (see page 198) would not have stood up to the weather if exposed, and the relief decoration on the altar blocks in the Ġgantija temples has deteriorated markedly since it was painted by Brochtorff in the 1820s, immediately after being exposed by excavation. There is considerable controversy over how this was done. The roof on the Mġarr model (see page 192) appears to show either long narrow slabs of stone or balks of timber, neither of which seems very likely. The two favoured views are that chambers were covered with either a stone-built vault or a flat roof of rafters, brushwood, and clay. The former, as suggested by Ugolini in 1934 and recently revived, is structurally po
sible over smaller chambers, lik
that with the bull and sow relie
between Tarxien South and Centra
half of which was found standin
by Zammit, but not on the large
ones, particularly when the wal
are of irregular rubble, as in Ġga
tija. On that site there is no hint o
oversailing in the 7 m standin
To close such an opening woul
need a far greater weight of ston
than the rough walls could poss
bly support. Further, a roof of suc
height would be expected to sho
on the models of temple eleva
tions (see page 192-5).

A flat roof supported on beam
agrees better with what the eleva
tions show, though not with th
Mġarr model. The excavated ev
dence at Skorba can also be quote
in support. In the inner apses o
the East Temple there, a layer o

Better even than the miniature models, the ceiling of the Holy of Holies in the Hypogeum (see also p.119) offers a full-sized replica of a corbelled temple roof, beautifully carved in the solid rock and saved from weathering by being underground.

A flight of steps between the Central and East Temples at Tarxien gave access to th roof, but whether for ceremonies or merel for maintenance is unknown.
The seventh and eighth steps are cut from a single block.

ıarcoal, with some lumps of clay, ould indeed seem to be the burnt mains of a collapsed roof of this rm.

That, however, is not the comete answer. The Holy of Holies Ħal Saflieni shows oversailing urses of roofing, all carved from e solid rock. In several temples ith more carefully-shaped blocks, e wall face can be seen to incline wards, as in Mnajdra South, first se right. This does look more like e beginnings of a vault, which ould have been more practicable ith well-cut stone, and would have en unnecessary for a timber-rafred roof. Both techniques, then, ere probably used, each in approiate circumstances.

More intriguing are the inner ses of the Central Temple at Taren. Here, the upper face of the wall thostats are cut to slope inwards towards the apse, and this is even more marked on the one surviving block of the next, horizontal, course above. These would seem to rule out the corbel vault, used nearly everywhere else in antiquity, since the oversailing blocks run the risk of toppling inwards. To prevent that, they must be set either strictly horizontally or even sloping a little outwards, to carry the thrust out into the walls. Here the blocks are so well-cut that the inward slope must be intentional, the only possible explanation being that they are elements not in a corbel vault but in a horizontal arch, as opposed to the much more familiar vertical one. They are meant to press inwards, thereby locking into a rigid structure. At not later than 2500 BC, this use of the arch is at least as early as the first record anywhere else, in the tombs of the Royal Cemetery at Ur.

e oversailing courses of stones in the lls of Mnajdra South, first apse right, duced the roof span. Though additional urses are possible, it is thought unlikely at the vault could have been closed in s way.

The same effect is apparent in Ħaġar Qim, second apse right, where the initial course of orthostatic blocks is also illustrated in this view. Top right is the back of the temple's external wall.

TEMPLES AND TOPOGRAPHY

A full GIS (Geographical Information System) study of the settings of the temples might prove informative, or at least throw some new ideas on why they were built where they were. Even without that, however, some generalizations may be made.

All the temples appear to be on or near good agricultural land, though soil erosion has made this less than obvious at Mnajdra. It is indeed difficult to reconstruct the appearance of the landscape at the time in any detail. The temples do not seem to relate to water sources though there are springs near both Ta' Ħaġrat and Skorba..

Few are on the highest point in their immediate neighbourhood. At Ħaġar Qim, Tas-Silġ, and Borġ il-Għarib, the land falls away o all sides, but so gently that it unlikely to have been a signif cant factor in the choice of sit Indeed, nearly all are on eithe level or gently sloping ground

Only three overlook stee scarps. Ġgantija certainly has prominent position, emphasize by the massive terrace wall i front of it. Ta' Lippija would hav been visible from the Ġnejna are but Xrobb il-Għaġin only fro out at sea. Santa Verna and Ta Marżiena are close to, but set bac from, similar scarps. Dominanc over the local landscape seem not to have been an issue.

So far, then, no very clea pattern emerges, though fu ther research would clearly b desirable.

This view from the air shows the setting of Mnajdra excellently, at the foot of its bare rocky slope. The large oval forecourt appears clearly too. Although its retaining wall is entirely modern, it presumably follows the line of the original.

By contrast, Ħaġar Qim stands on the highest point locally, though still hardly in a dominating position. From the camera's viewpoint, however, it is dramatically silhouetted against the sky, with a few windswept trees around.

'EMPLE ORIENTATIONS

/hen discussing the siting of the ·mples, we noted that they showed marked preference of orientation, ıe great majority facing points ustered either side of due south. he diagram on the next page lustrates these individually, the ›mpass rose then grouping them · make the point clearly. Only the ajor temple axes are included, so de entrances are omitted and the ıomalous sites with no clear axis ·e indicated by question marks. wo ruinous sites, Santa Verna ıd Ta' Marżiena, have queried :rows since their axes are less .an certain, and Tal-Qadi's too is ›mewhat hypothetical, being the /erage of the three suggested by s structure.

The lines are too far south to be ıked with the rising or setting of the sun or moon, even at their most southerly. It has been pointed out that the stars of the Southern Cross would have been visible just above the southern horizon at this distant time, but so low, and less brilliant than many others in the heavens, that they are hardly likely to have influenced the temple builders to this extent.

This illustrates well the problems of prehistoric religion. Clearly the builders saw some significance in their alignments, though unrelated to the movements of the heavenly bodies. Whatever the reason for their choice, it is quite impossible for us now to discover what that significance was. Would our Amazonian Indian be able to explain the orientation of Islamic mosques or Christian churches?

view of the entrance doorway of najdra South shows the sun rising over e horizon on the Equinox days. Was this ecisely planned, or merely coincidence, ven a predilection for a south-easterly to uth-westerly orientation?

The enigmatic engraved slab from Tal-Qadi bears radiating lines, asterisks and a cresecent, which could be either astronomically significant, or only ornamental.

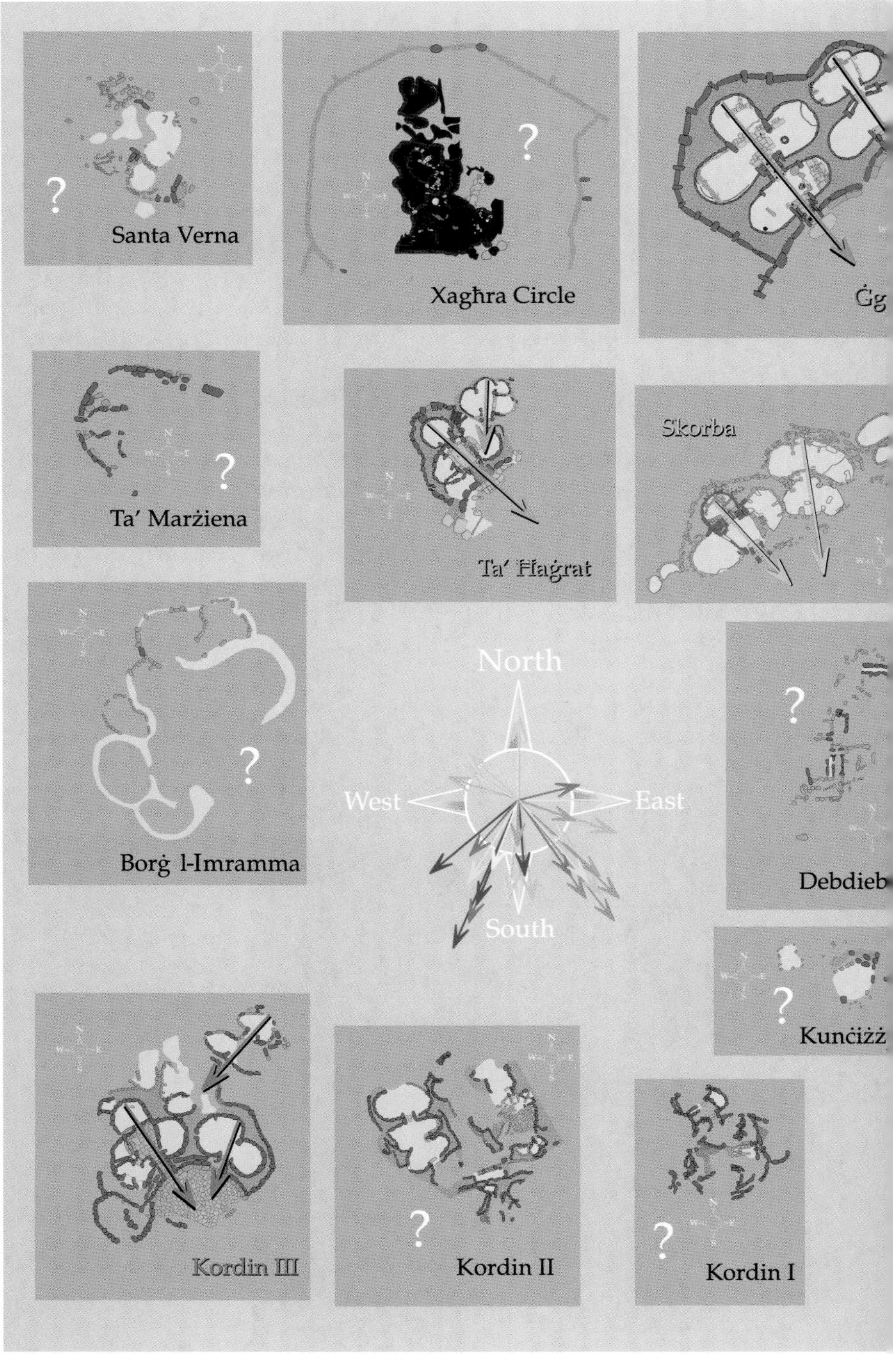

Santa Verna

Xagħra Circle

Ġg

Ta' Marżiena

Ta' Ħaġrat

Skorba

Borġ l-Imramma

North

West

East

South

Debdieb

Kunċiżż

Kordin III

Kordin II

Kordin I

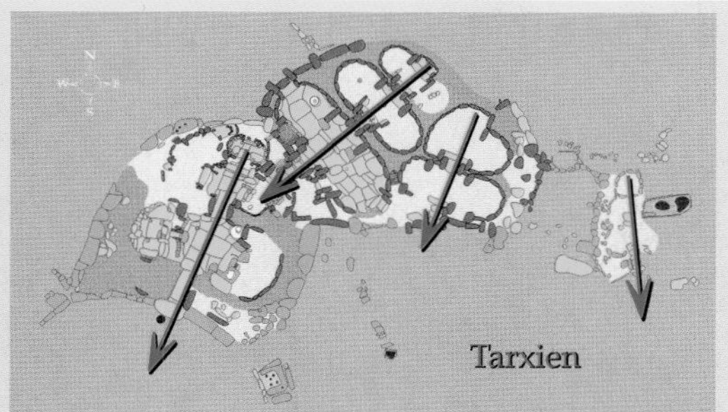

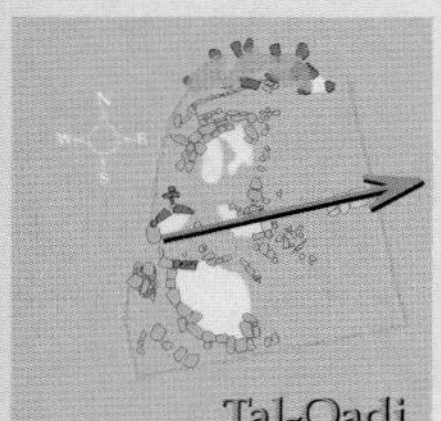

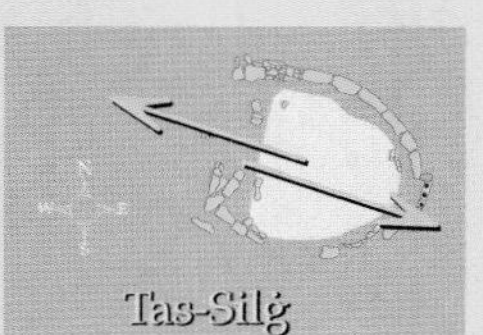

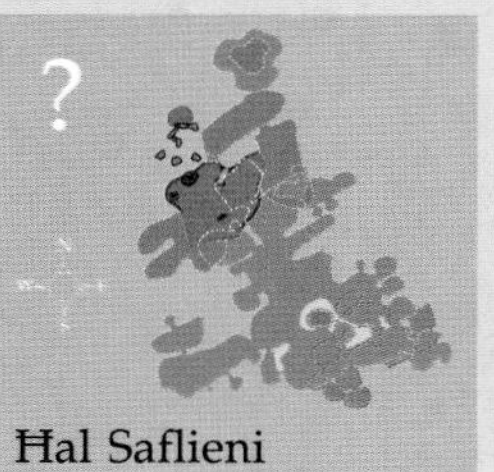

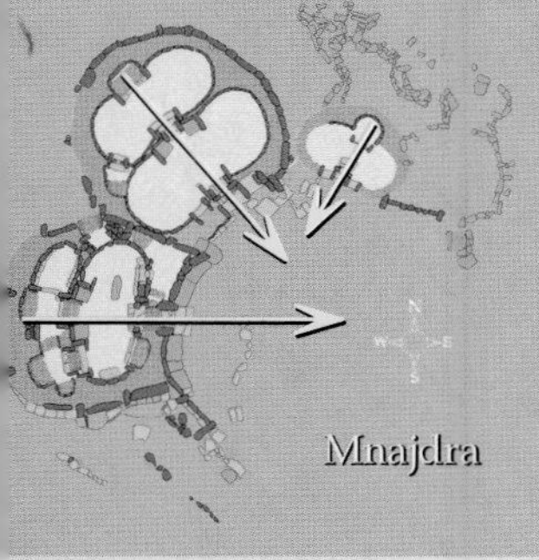

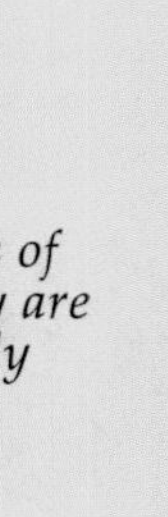

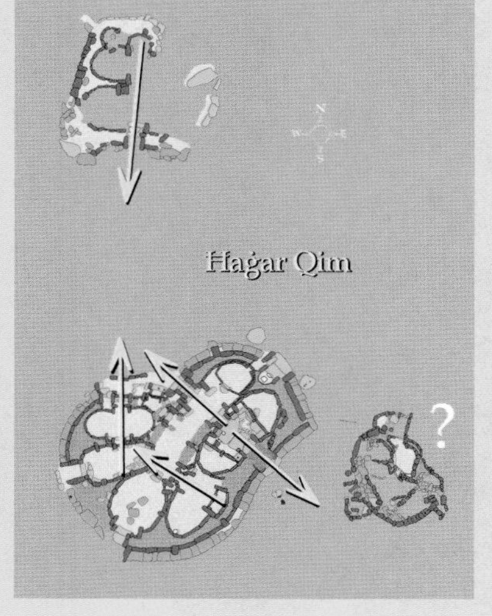

ıe illustrations here show the plans of
ʼ the known temples of Malta. They are
awn to the same scale, and correctly
iented for comparative purposes.

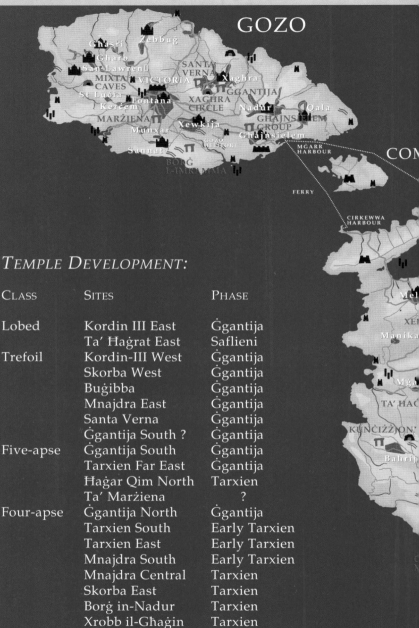

TEMPLE DEVELOPMENT:

CLASS	SITES	PHASE
Lobed	Kordin III East	Ġgantija
	Ta' Ħaġrat East	Saflieni
Trefoil	Kordin-III West	Ġgantija
	Skorba West	Ġgantija
	Buġibba	Ġgantija
	Mnajdra East	Ġgantija
	Santa Verna	Ġgantija
	Ġgantija South ?	Ġgantija
Five-apse	Ġgantija South	Ġgantija
	Tarxien Far East	Ġgantija
	Ħaġar Qim North	Tarxien
	Ta' Marżiena	?
Four-apse	Ġgantija North	Ġgantija
	Tarxien South	Early Tarxien
	Tarxien East	Early Tarxien
	Mnajdra South	Early Tarxien
	Mnajdra Central	Tarxien
	Skorba East	Tarxien
	Borġ in-Nadur	Tarxien
	Xrobb il-Għaġin	Tarxien
Six-Apse	Tarxien Central	Tarxien

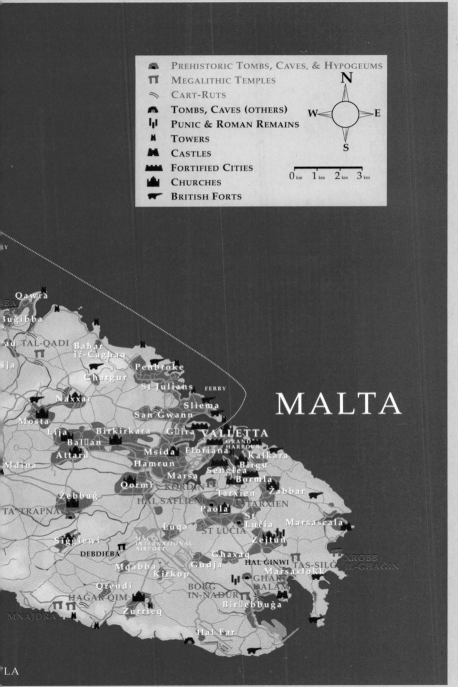

PREHISTORIC TOMBS, CAVES, & HYPOGEUMS
MEGALITHIC TEMPLES
CART-RUTS
TOMBS, CAVES (OTHERS)
PUNIC & ROMAN REMAINS
TOWERS
CASTLES
FORTIFIED CITIES
CHURCHES
BRITISH FORTS

N
W E
S

0 km 1 km 2 km 3 km

MALTA

Qawra
BA
Buġibba
ad TAL-QADI
ija
Bahar iċ-Ċaghaq
Pembroke
Gharghur
St Julians
FERRY
Naxxar
Sliema
Mosta
San Ġwann
Lija
Birkirkara
G□ira
VALLETTA
Bal□an
GRAND HARBOUR
Attard
Msida
Floriana
Kalkara
Mdina
Hamrun
Birgu
Senglea
Marsa
Bormla
Qormi
KORDIN
Tarxien
Żabbar
Żebbuġ
HAL SAFLIENI
TARXIEN
TA' TRAPNA
Paola
St Luċia
Marsascala
Luqa
ST LUĊIA
Siġġiewi
MALTA INTERNATIONAL AIRPORT
Żejtun
DEBDIEBA
Ghaxaq
XROBB IL-GHAĠIN
HAL ĠINWI
TAS-SILĠ
Mqabba
Gudja
Kirkop
Marsaxlokk
Qrendi
BORĠ IN-NADUR
GHAR DALAM
HAĠAR QIM
Bir□ebbuġa
MNAJDRA
Żurrieq
Hal Far
LA

While the temples themselves were an astounding achievement, we need to know much more about the people who developed them, built them, and worshipped in them. This far back in the past, only archaeology can provide this information, yet still leaves many problems unresolved.

CHAPTER 4

THE TEMPLE PERIOD

Despite the massive increase of information on the Temple Period from the temples themselves and their contents, and I include here the closely-related burial sites, we are still woefully ignorant about contemporary dwellings and settlements. Whether or not 10,000 is anywhere near the right figure for the population of the islands, it is patently obvious that many people were needed to build the temples, and fill the cemeteries. They must have lived somewhere, yet to date we have only three certain relevant sites.

Immediately behind the western outbuildings of the Skorba temples, excavation in 1962 found an oval hut with earth floor, stumps of mudbrick walls, on one side constructed on a stone footing. It measured 6 by 3 m. It was securely dated by the Ġgantija phase pottery recovered from it, including

For example, the reader is invited to ask his or her own questions of this delightful but enigmatic carving from the Xagħra Circle. Its significance can only be a matter of speculation. Note particularly the surviving ochre on the legs and volute-decorated bed cover.

A Ġgantija phase hut was revealed behi the later temple outbuildings at Skorba. A quern and rubber lie beside the wall, just as they were left when the hut was abandoned.

two small complete cups and some ten restorable bowls. Eleven saddle querns were found within it, one large one with its upper stone rubber still beside it at the foot of the wall. Beneath the floor, a small pit contained a number of seashells. The hut had gone out of use before, or probably at the time of, the building of the temple, since its entrance passage was sealed off by the temple wall.

A second clay floor, 3.9 by 3.6 m, came to light under the East Temple as a result of plough damage to the latter's floor. It was also dated to the Ġgantija phase by sherds within it, but with Saflieni sherds lying in the thin layer above it. This meant that it had remained in use after the West Temple had been built, though obviously before the East Temple. It was less informative than the Hut of the Querns, with so little of i contents surviving, and none of i walls. Two entrance passages, po sibly leading to other rooms, cou not be followed without removi the overlying temple.

The second site was another ov hut, this time with a *torba* floor ar only traces of mudbrick walls. O side had been cut away by ploug ing, the other by the foundations a modern building, which is ho it was discovered. The only pa preserved was a strip no more th 2 m wide, protected by the fie wall which had been built over it.

ood beside the Mġarr Road on the estern edge of Għajnsielem, Gozo, ıd was dug in 1987 by Caroline alone as an offshoot of the project ı the Xagħra Circle.

This was a more elaborate strucre, 8 m long and perhaps 5 wide. hollow of these dimensions had en cut in the rock surface to a pth of 70 cm and filled with stone ıbble as foundation for a *torba* oor, twice repaired with a new yer of *torba*. A mudbrick pillar ood at the centre. A second pillar ıd stood at its southern end and yond it a similar though slighter ructure, 2 m square. Associated ottery, as with the second hut at orba, was of the Ġgantija and flieni phases.

The third site is at Taċ-Ċawla, uthern limits of Victoria, Gozo. ere a substantial stone wall was und and partially investigated by ark Horton and Nathaniel Cutajar 1995.

Associated deposits contained large quantity of Temple Period ottery, with some sherds of the ırxien phase specifically identifile. The note of hesitation here is ıe to the fact that, compared with her groups, only a small proporon was decorated or of the typical fering bowl form. This makes the oup more interesting, not less, since it suggests that it was an accumulation of domestic rubbish, the first of that phase to be found in Malta. The building itself has not yet been further studied, the site having run into complicated legal problems of ownership. Its investigation promises to fill a glaring gap in our knowledge of Maltese prehistory – the near-total absence of domestic sites.

Certainly there must have been many others. A quantity of Tarxien pottery came to light beside the Għar ta' Għejżu on the west side of 8 September Avenue, Xagħra, in 1990, but no structures were found, and even the pottery looked more like the usual ritual material than domestic. Detailed searches across the Xagħra plateau and to the west,

erds picked up on the surface, like ese from Ta' Ċenċ (see p.184), can be ributed securely to the Temple Period m their fabric, but unlike excavated terial are often too small and abraded be dated more closely.

and more sporadic ones elsewhere, produced nothing convincing, so until they do, or a likely site turns up by chance, Taċ-Ċawla looks the best, or only, opportunity to repair this serious omission in our knowledge.

Those few sites already discovered go some way towards explaining our failures on this front so far. They show, for example, that the standard building material outside the temples appears to have been mudbrick. This is surprising in itself, stone being so plentiful in Malta even if timber was scarc Mudbrick was rarely employe elsewhere in southern or weste Europe, though common in easte Europe, Greece, and the Near Ea where its use over centuries led the building up of the great moun generically known as tells.

Despite the lack of domest sites, we can still reconstruct reasonably full, if indirect, pictu of life and economy at the tim Study of the human bones fro the Xagħra Circle shows that t population enjoyed at least ave age health, and was not under a particular stress. The point nee making as the supposed excessi demands of temple building ha in the past been suggested as a ro cause of the downfall of the te ples. This is discussed further p.238.

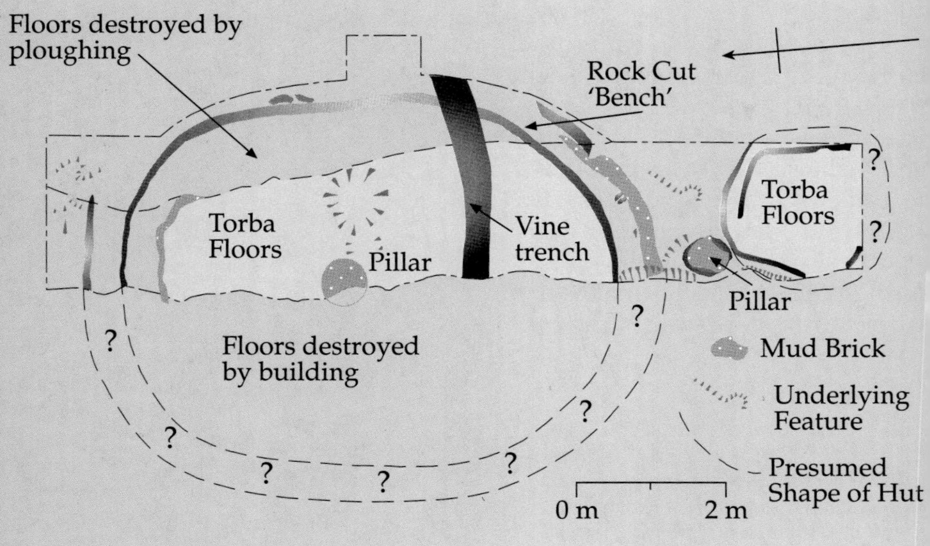

A cross section of this hut by the Mġarr Road, Għajnsielem, was preserved only by having a field wall built across it. It is a precious, though fragmentary, relic of domestic architecture of the period.

om the Pergla Cave, between Xagħra
d the north coast cliffs, a considerable
antity of pottery, animal bones, and
her refuse was recovered in 1913. There
s no built structure and little
suggest the remains were ritually
posited.
alternative explanation is that it
s dumped here from some nearby but
discovered settlement.

There is little to suggest change the way of life at this period, r any further immigration. ere was, however, a substantl increase in the population by tural growth. That is implied by th the far greater quantity of potry surviving from the Ġgantija d Tarxien phases and the major ilding programme manifest in e temples. Yet the few dwellgs discovered, and the refuse sociated with them, show negible differences from what had ne before. Life was based on the me mixed farming, as shown by e numerous querns and animal nes, though more environmental mples from flotation of domes- deposits would be welcome to nfirm this.

One addition was made to the list of domestic animals. The tooth of a donkey was identified by the late Prof. O. F. Gandert from the Ġgantija phase deposit in the Pergla Cave, Xagħra. While ass transport could be highly significant in some areas – the donkey caravans between Assyria and Kültepe in Turkey are an obvious example – within a small island like Malta, the impact of its introduction is not likely to have been very great. Cattle, sheep, goats, and swine surely continued to be much more important, particularly as suppliers of food.

The biggest change was undoubtedly in the organization of religion and society, topics to be discussed shortly. Before that, one aspect of the

Malta used what local materials it could, as with this chopper of chert from the Xagħra Circle. For any superior resources, like flint or obsidian, it had tc rely on imports from abroad.

economy does need to be looked at in rather more detail, that of trade.

The finds from temples and cemeteries show that the import of raw materials continued unabated. Obsidian is found in quantity throughout the period, though generally in very small pieces. Some of this could be recycled from earlier imports, but there seems to be too much to be thus explained away. That no more cores have turned up is less surprising than that those two did in the northeast field at Skorba, a domestic deposit, note. The marked swing at Skorba between the proportions of obsidian from Pantelleria and that from Lipari implies that it came into the island by a different route now. However, at the Xagħra Circle, Pantellerian obsidian continued to predominate. This seems to mean that Gozo and Malta had diffe ent trading partners, an interesti possibility, if, on the face of unlikely. A hint of the same is pr vided by flint. Common at Skor was a light-brown flint which c be matched closely on the Mo Iblei in the hills behind Syracus Xagħra appears to have preferre good quality black flint, distinct different and presumably from different source, though perha in the same general area. At bo sites, the local grey-yellow che very frequent in earlier levels Skorba, has virtually disappear

om use, either as less efficient r flaking and cutting, or simply lacking in prestige value. Ħal aflieni and Xagħra show that oreign stone', a general term to over the petrological niceties of rpentinite, tremolite, sillimanite orolite, and the like, was import- l no less than before, primarily r miniature axes, whether perfo- ted for suspension or not.

These are metamorphic rocks est represented in Calabria. A w were basaltic, from volcanic eposits in the Mount Etna area. ne pendant from Xagħra, a rec- ngular piece with a perforation at ther end, was identified as a true deite, the nearest source of which in the Alpine foothills in Pied- ont. That material from the same urce was also exported as far as itain shows just how widely trade aks could extend as early as 2500 . But then, it has long been known at Baltic amber was reaching com- unities on the Mediterranean, ough none is yet known from alta. Red ochre, another exotic aterial on the islands, probably ming from the Agrigento area, is ll very much in evidence in buri- s. It was placed in the Ta' Ħamet mb in Xagħra in such quantity at the finder in 1927 thought he d discovered a bloody murder.

In the Xagħra Circle hypogeum, many deposits were stained a light pink as a result of its use, either sprinkled on the bodies or in some cases painted onto the stones. There, and on the plaster of the Ġgantija North and Skorba western outbuildings, it was applied as an overall wash, at Ħal Saflieni as painted spirals. In one case certainly, in many others very probably, it served as a background to the relief spirals on decorated slabs. In the Ġgantija phase, considerable amounts were required to encrust the scratched designs on pottery. How much was used in the form of cosmetics to decorate the person, we cannot now tell.

Yellow ochre, equally foreign, is less noticeable in excavation and,

d ochre was prized as a symbol of od and life, as in the Ta' Ħamet Tomb, għra. It is not found naturally in alta, so it must have been imported from ne unknown source in Sicily.

lacking the obvious symbolic significance of the red, was probably much less employed. A fragmented 'fat lady' statuette from the Xagħra Circle showed that it certainly was used on occasion.

Besides raw materials, there is again a handful of exotic sherds of pottery, though surprisingly few. Five groups look out of place among the local products, of which three belong to identifiable overseas cultures. Several, from at least three vessels, are of undecorated jugs with a smeary part-polished surface. They compare closely with material from Piano Quartara, a Copper Age culture on Lipari, and were found in the Xagħra hypogeum.

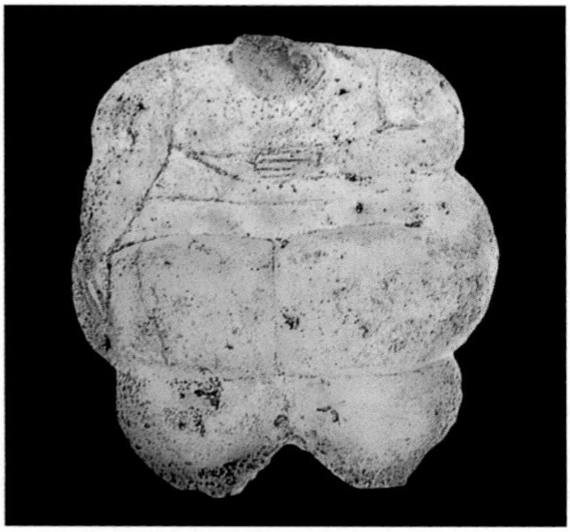

Six cm high, though now lacking its head, this little statuette of alabaster was found in the Ħal Saflieni Hypogeum.

From the same place came a small red-slipped sherd with a slightly muzzy black-painted line. It is well matched in Serraferlicchio, a contemporary group in Sicily. Another sherd of the same type was recognized by Evans from the temple at Borġ in-Nadur, a much disturbed site, though the Xagħra find would suggest it belonged with the Tarxien rather than the Bronze Age occupation there.

Serraferlicchio was followed in Sicily by Sant' Ippolito, another, rather coarser, painted ware, ar a sherd from Xagħra is close i appearance to that. It too, howeve came from a disturbed level.

The Ta' Ħamet tomb at Xagħ has already been mentioned. Tl five small cups or vases within resemble Ġgantija ones in a ve general way, though by no mea precisely. They too could poss bly be of foreign inspiration. O sherd from tl hypogeum nea by and anoth from the Ta Qadi temple loc similar, thoug none exactly li it is known fro abroad.

More intrig ing are five sher and one comple vessel of a ve distinctive forr all from secu Temple Peric deposits. Th needs stressing the form becan very common in the Tarxien Cer etery phase, so it must be suspe where there is any possibility contamination from the latter. Tl complete vessel consists of an op straight-sided bowl on a tall pe estal, its lip thickened on the inn side to give a 2 cm wide beve which is spanned by dot-fille erect triangles (see p.249). Dotte bands decorate the pedestal als and there is a handle joining bo and pedestal. It was found whe

ıe megalithic niche above the dec-
rated altar in Tarxien South was
ismantled to be brought into the
Iational Museum of Archaeology
ı 1958. The sherds are of simi-
ır rims, with nothing to suggest
ıat they also stood on pedestals.
ıdeed, a handle on the outer wall
f one rather implies the contrary.
he rims can be undecorated, or
ear dot-filled or hatched triangles.
wo were found in Ġgantija levels
t Skorba, one inside the Tarxien
ltar in its West Temple, and two
ı the Xagħra hypogeum.

The importance of this group
es in the light it could throw on
ıe still controversial origins of
ıe Tarxien Cemetery culture, in
'hich they become very frequent.
his problem will be pursued in
ıe appropriate place below. While
cattered examples have come to
ght in Sicily, in Castelluccio con-
:xts, and even southern Sardinia,
ıe only place where they look real-
' at home is at the northern end of
ıe Aegean, at sites like Thermi on
esbos and the second city on the
ite of Troy itself. Could they really
e clues to extensive maritime trad-
ıg ventures from that area? Or are
ıe undoubted similarities no more
ıan misleading coincidences? And
' that is not their source, where did they come from? The one fact of which we can be reasonably certain is that, although they may have been imitated in Malta, that is not where they originated.

Perhaps analysis of the clays from which the few early ones were made might solve the mystery. Our account has nowhere else so closely resembled a detective story.

We have already discussed the mechanisms of this 'trade' in an earlier section, whether commerce, gift-exchange, or whatever, and there is little to suggest that they had materially altered by this time. Nor do we have any more evidence than before on the nature or form of the boats which, considering Malta's geographical position, were necessarily employed.

variety of stone types is represented ı the axe amulets from Ħal Saflieni and ther sites, all of which had to be imported ıto Malta.

Certain graffiti on stelae in the first apse left of Tarxien South Temple, visible only when sunlight at a low angle picks them out, are claimed as representations of seagoing boats. This could be so, but they are far too schematic to be informative. A gentle curve with more steeply upturned ends can certainly be described as 'boat-shaped', and the vertical dashes within it may be meant for paddlers, or passengers, but then again they may not. It is quite impossible to reconstruct a practical vessel from this evidence alone. Yet th obsidian, flint, and other ston demonstrate unequivocally tha sea crossings to and from Sicil were well within the capabilitie of people at the time.

Much easier to carry out, thoug much more difficult to demonstrat now, were the economic exchange which must have taken place withi the islands themselves. By and larg each farming community was probably to a great extent self-sufficien However, it is likely that while al communities enjoyed eating fis for example, not all had easy acces to the sea, let alone the boats, th skills, and the time to catch thei own. Conversely, fishermen woul become more efficient at that craft i not obliged to raise crops and stoc to feed themselves and their families as well.

These boats, scratched onto orthostats in Tarxien South, first apse left, do little more than hint at the means of navigation available at the time. They are artificially emphasized in this photograph.

'ig leaves were plucked from their tree ɔur-and-a-half thousand years ago, when potter used them to line a mould for ıaking a giant bowl. This is now in the ntrance hall of the National Museum of rchaeology.
'races of such ephemeral items bring he distant past visibly before our eyes. 'hey also illustrate the intelligence of the ırly Maltese, finding a simple soluton to he problem of the wet clay adhering to the ıould.

While unskilled labour, as we vill suggest, was probably recruit-d from the islands as a whole for he building of the temples, the rchitects who planned and over-aw the work, the masons who uarried and dressed the stone, nd even more the sculptors who roduced their carved or modelled nasterpieces, must surely have een specialists, not just farmers vorking part-time.

The same must have applied o the potters, whether men or vomen, who turned out such great uantities of technically highly ompetent pottery. A fact that rgues this particularly strongly s the presence of several excep-ionally large vessels from Tarxien, ncluding a deep carinated jar with a diameter of 55 cm, two biconical jars with pairs of tunnel handles at 43 and 44 cm, and a monster carinated bowl a good metre across the mouth.

The last shows an interesting detail of how it was made, since the outsloping wall from base to cari-nation bears the imprint of many fig leaves. As it would have been difficult for a wall at this angle to maintain its shape when the clay was still wet, it must have been made in a mould, lined with a layer of leaves to prevent the clay from sticking to the mould. Above the carination, the wall, nearly verti-cal here, would not have needed that support.

The potter who made this vessel could only have been a specialist,

and an ingenious one at that, not just someone knocking up pots for household use in the back yard.

The same goes for the sculptors who carved other gigantic vessels out of stone, another offering bowl at Tarxien, and the great jar from the Xagħra Hypogeum, of similar remarkable dimensions.

Some of the Tarxien phase pottery has such uniform yellow colouring that it must have been fired in carefully-controlled conditions. To produce this fine ware required not only a high level of skill on the part of the potter, but also a closed kiln rather than a mere bonfire heap.

It is most unlikely that anyone but a specialist potter could have afforded the capital investment in plant that this would imply, let alone the skill required.

A second giant bowl in the same hall has a maximum diameter of 85 cm. It bears a light design of running volutes. Both the modelling and baking of so large a vessel would challenge the skill of any potter.

Again, there must have bee some redistribution of resource to allow the skilled craftsmen o women to engage in their specia ized activities. However, all thi must remain speculative, at leas until bureaucratic records begin t be kept, as was already happenin in Mesopotamia and Egypt but nc until very much later in Malta.

In this it resembles the skills c navigation; whatever the form the took, both navigation and redis tribution must have been takin place.

OTTERY STYLES

s with architecture, Maltese pre-istoric pottery reached its highest evelopment in this period, and it probable that the requirements f religion at the time were behind oth. Two distinct strands are vis-ɔle in this.

On the one hand, there is a clear volutionary line in the typology of ebbuġ, Mġarr, Ġgantija, Saflieni, ıd Tarxien wares, in fabric, shape, andle form, and decoration. On ıe other, a number of new tricks ppear, unrelated to what had one before, particularly in the ecoration. Nor can they be traced overseas influence, not being ound abroad either. In fact, they ın be explained only as deliber-:e innovation by the pot-makers ıd, even more remarkably, a will-ıgness by society to accept that ınovation.

This is quite unusual in pre-assical antiquity, where tradition as normally much more highly alued and firmly applied, where-; novelty was suspect and equally gidly rejected.

ĠARR

ırly in the period, it is that first rand which is much more in ·idence. Mġarr pottery is on the whole better made, harder fired, and darker in colour than Żebbuġ. Yellow slip and red paint have both dropped out entirely. Instead, a few sherds bear designs in a curious grey paint, probably the result of the change to more reducing conditions in the firing, leading to greys and blacks rather than reds and yellows. But the continuation of painting, if only in a small way, looks like a half-hearted survival of its earlier use.

By contrast, the gouged line decoration becomes much broader and more assured. The rather ragged chipped triangles bordering the Żebbuġ lines are replaced by a neat and delicate fringe of light scratches. The neatness was even more marked when the new

ıe broad gouged lines are typical of ġarr, often being filled with a white ste. The lower two show the transition ɔm the chipped triangles of Żebbuġ the finer fringes of Mġarr and, later, flieni.

broad cut-out lines still held their white paste infill, which only occasionally survives. A new and characteristic practice was to add a wash of red ochre over the white fill. Designs are not easy to recover as sherds are usually small and no complete, or even fully restorable, vessels have yet been found. They do, however, seem to lead on directly from Żebbuġ ones.

Much the same has to be said of vessel shapes, most developing out of Żebbuġ single-handled cups and two-handled jars. Two new forms are a heavy but low cylindrical vessel, a platter or li
with the base of the wall draw
out into a rib, this bearing a hor
zontally pierced lug or handle. Th
other is an ovoid or shouldere
jar, not unlike Żebbuġ ones bu
differing in having a lip rolled
thickened.

Mġarr pottery has turned u
in mixed deposits on a number
sites, Mġarr itself (where Zamm
thought it came at the very en
of the Temple Period), Kordin II
and others, though nowhere wa
it plentiful. Until a pure level wa
found at Skorba, it could be di
missed as transitional betwee
Żebbuġ and Ġgantija, or even
few distinctive features overla
ping both those phases. Althoug
it does now seem to be a phase
its own right, it appears to hav
been quite short.

This curious vessel probably served as a lid. Its decoration is also transitional between Żebbuġ and Ġgantija, more regular than the former but coarser than the latter.

typical cup of the Ġgantija phase, was found in tomb 1 at Xemxija, ctured on p.162. It has the stinctive rim and shoulder lines and nverging curves on neck and body. ne variation in surface colour, from ack to reddish, shows that it was ked in an open fire, not in a closed ln.

GANTIJA

ne pottery of the Ġgantija phase llows directly on from that of ġarr though, having said that, ere are some major changes and, the other hand, some details, particularly the use of cross-hatching, pear to hark back more to Żebbuġ. ne fabric is virtually indistinguishle from that of Mġarr. It is dark, ten somewhat blotchy in colour, ell-polished, and hard-fired.

Technically, then, it is very mpetent, though the blotchiss suggests poorly controlled ring conditions, and so, bakg with the fuel stacked round e pots rather than the use of a osed kiln. The commonest vessel apes are large cups or bowls of o standard forms.

One, shape 23 in Evans's 1953 classification, has a vertical or slightly in-sloping neck, straight or modestly concave. It stands above a slightly swelling shoulder which curves down into the convex body with a small flattening as base. A single prominent handle stands at the base of the neck, with a small knob diametrically opposite. In the second, Evans shape 22, the neck is rather more concave and distinctly outsloping. There is no shoulder, and the handle, a long vertically-pierced lug, is attached where the neck turns in to the convex body. Almost as common is a third bowl, with neck straight or convex and a smoother profile from rim to base. Its two handles, if such they can be called, are merely slight thickenings of the rim to form a vertical rib with either a perforation through it or, more frequently, simply a dot on the rim to represent such a perforation, no longer functional.

These vessels are all decorated in a manner to be described in the following pages.

A variety of jar forms, with smoothly curved or separate necks may or may not be decorated. None has the swelling neck of the Żebbuġ storeyed urns. The lips are rolled or heavily thickened, these always on undecorated jars or deep bowls. They

The base of this saucer from the Nadur tomb, Binġemma, is quartered to hold erratic converging curves.

A simpler cup has the same rim and shoulder lines, now with a pair of concentric curves on the neck. It offers a better illustration of the Ġgantija symmetrical handle.

often bear transverse dashes, qui
different from the Żebbuġ dimple
though presumably derived fro
the latter.

Three related lid forms would
snugly over short-necked jars. Th
first is a rather thinner walled ve
sion of the Mġarr low cylindric
vessel already described; the se
ond a curved shallow bowl with
prominent rib running round it; th
third an almost globular bowl wi
a similar rib. All the ribs have fo
vertical perforations, and genero
decoration places them all firm
in this phase. Although describe
here as lids, mainly because th
decoration completely covers th
'bases', it is possible, from the pe
forations, that they were in fa

sherd from Ġgantija itself has within its onverging curves close hatching which tains its original red ochre incrustation.

used as hanging bowls. They could, of course, have been used in both ways, though not at the same time. There were other less diagnostic forms, like ovoid jars and small pottery spoons, all undecorated.

Handles follow a similar pattern, some distinctive ones associated with particular vessel forms, others more generalized in shape and use. The prominent strap handles on bowls and cups derive from Żebbuġ ones, but differ in being pinched to something of a point. Instead of a parallel-sided strap, the effect is of two elongated triangles of roughly equal size joining at the tip. The horizontal, vertically-pierced lugs taper markedly at either end, again forming a triangle but this time a very broad short one.

HANDLES

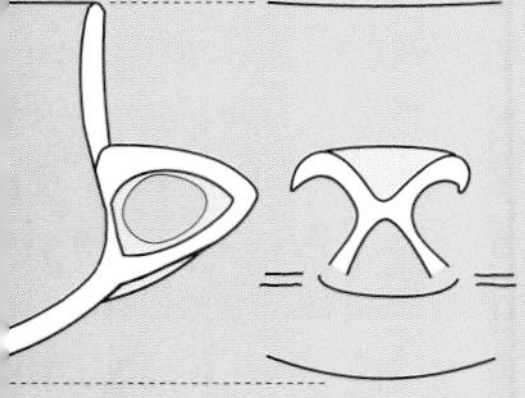

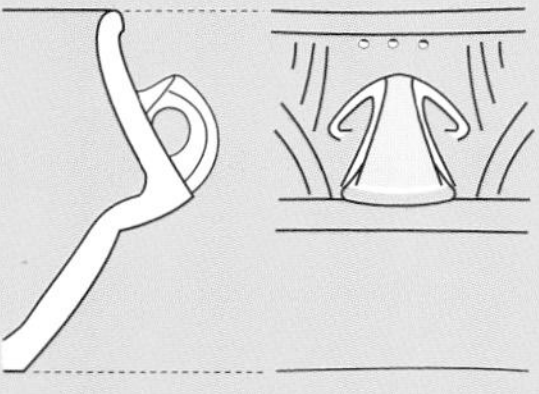

n cups of the Ġgantija hase, handles projected rominently from the ase of the neck, and ere approximately ymmetrical when seen in rofile.

y the Saflieni phase, the pper bar was somewhat duced in size, the wer becoming more convex and approaching triangular shape as the peak became sharper. Tarxien phase cups and offering bowls have developed a more markedly carinated form, and the handles have taken on their characteristic nose-bridge shape. In this, the lower bar is enlarged to a clearly triangular outline, rising to a quite sharp pointed peak, while the upper bar is correspondingly reduced. Indeed, on some vessels, not illustrated here, it is suppressed altogether, the triangular strap curving back into the cup wall.

A decorated globular bowl from tomb 3, Xemxija, shows the second main Ġgantij phase technique, with hatched designs in alternate chequers.

Vertical strap handles on jars do not show the elongation they do on the bowls. On the contrary, the jar wall is often dinted in, reducing the projection of the handle.

Oddest of all, perhaps, are the short ribs running to the rim which look like pierced lugs though the holes never run right through. The bowl decoration runs over these, but otherwise, unlike in Żebbuġ, handles were always left plain.

The grey-on-dark painting noted in the Mġarr phase might have continued into the beginning of this one, as suggested by the occasional sherd with both painting and scratching, but, if so, it seems to have died out early. Certainty is difficult because of the problem of residual sherds turning up in later levels. Instead, all decoration was now carried out in fine scratched lines, revertin then, to the Żebbuġ technique, no always either just before, or mor likely after, firing. The result is thin and slightly ragged line as th polished surface spalls beneath th hard engraving point. This ma sound inefficient but was probabl intentional since the irregularitie would provide a better key for th red ochre wash which was alway applied. Indeed, it was probabl the ochre incrustation rather tha the scratched line itself which wa meant to be seen. The reappea ance of cross-hatching is surely t be explained in the same way, t give a block of colour, though th

chre has often not survived the assage of time, or the cleaning all herds need when recovered from he ground.

As for designs, there are some tandard characteristics, followed y bewildering variation in detail. Decorated vessels all carry a single line encircling the rim on the utside (in Żebbuġ, it will be emembered, if there was such a ne it was on the inner face). Most ave a similar line at the base of the eck, whether there was a break n angle at this point or not. The wall was then usually divided by traight vertical lines into four panls, the body remaining a single ecorative field excluding only the mall flat base.

All decoration was carried out n sweeping scratched curves with oth assurance and exuberance, uite unlike the tentative and untiy Żebbuġ ones. These curves may un parallel to each other, or more requently join at a tangent, like ailway junctions though of single ather than double lines. Blocks of atching between the curves are ommon.

The most distinctive characteristic of all is for lines to stop at a small erminal circle, a 'cherry' or 'comet'. he effect is increased by all curves aving their concavity below, possibly recalling the Żebbuġ arcs or 'rainbows'. An exception to this is found on the globular bowl-lids. These have their necks divided into a chequerboard pattern, alternate rectangles void or filled with cross-hatching, usually with a diagonal reserved band.

SAFLIENI

Although not clearly separated off by Evans, pure levels, if not very rich ones, at Skorba, Santa Verna, and Mġarr have clarified the Saflieni phase, even if it remains little more than a transitional one between Ġgantija and Tarxien.

The finer ware is both thinner and harder than that of Ġgantija, almost metallic. Both the commoner bowl forms continue, with smoother profiles and no longer

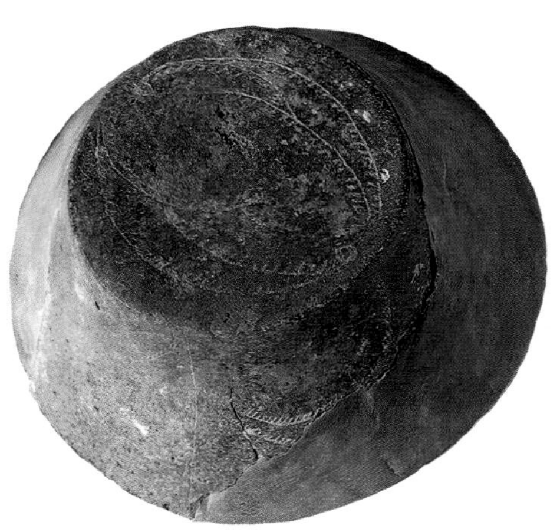

ringed lines, first seen in Mġarr ecoration, reappear on later Ġgantija and aflieni vessels, as on the walls and base f this splay-walled bowl.

any trace of shoulder on the first, the second more widely splayed.

One new form, probably derived from the latter, has a concave out-sloping wall rising directly from a large flat base. A second should perhaps be derived from the hanging bowls. It has an acute carination between the body and the concave insloping neck, which then curves sharply in until virtually horizontal. This hole-mouth was so characteristic of Ħal Saflieni that it can reasonably be called a Saflieni bowl. Two pairs of perforations through the horizontal flange are the only handles, or were they

An elegant sharply carinated bowl with its inturned lip is characteristic of the Saflieni Hypogeum.

Rather clumsier is this deeper example. I has panels with flecked filling, contrastin with Ġgantija phase hatching.

intended to attach a lid? Thes bowls vary enormously in siz from 6 to 40 cm in diameter.

Alongside this fine ware, coarser sandy one, pinkish i colour, unpolished, and quit differently decorated, makes i first appearance. It is used onl for ovoid jars with simple rim and no handles. The wall bear conjoined soft-incised arcs fille with rustication, which covers a the lower body.

The rustication is carried ou by rough vertical scoring, agai patently applied while the cla was still wet and soft. At the ris of introducing jargon, the ter 'arco-striate' describes it wel Otherwise the scratched decoratio

variant of the fork-ended thorny ·lutes, giving a more jagged effect, ·pears on this vessel.

continues the Ġgantija tradition in diluted form. Lines tend to be scratched more lightly, though still ochred. The exuberance has faded, leaving only single arcs, sometimes below straight diagonals.

Rare connecting lines suggest the cross-hatching which is hardly ever now employed. Some curves foreshadow Tarxien volutes. Rim and bulge lines have disappeared completely, as have the ring-headed 'comets'. Two new techniques are introduced, or reintroduced. One is the use of a fringe, now to a fine single line, and the other the filling of areas between back-to-back curves with dots or short flecks. The curves are quite irregular, arcs or complete ovals, and the effect is like pudding stone, reserved 'pebbles' in a dotted or flecked matrix. This is

ɔTTERY VOLUTES

ɜ with the handles, vessel decoration, corresponding velopment of volutes n be traced through the ȝantija, Saflieni, and ɪrxien phases.

the first, a wide ɪriety of converging ɪrves was employed, often with patches of hatching and lines ending in a small circle, the distinctive 'cherry'.

In the second, two curves run parallel, open ended, and usually nestled within an arc with side branches, the so-called 'boat' motif.

In the third, the volute is often closed with a fish-tailed end, sometimes with additional 'thorns' along its sides, as on the altar reliefs.The 'boat' has disappeared, though its side branches can be retained, attached now to the volute itself.

a particularly common design on the open dishes and Saflieni bowls, where the division of the wall into rectangular chequers obviously harks back to the Ġgantija globular bowls.

There is much more variety here, the reserved spaces sometimes growing to leave only irregular-dotted or cross-hatched bands. Far and away the most ambitious is a platter from the Hypogeum bearing a fourfold repeat design of this type on the outer side, and a scatter of nine cross-hatched bulls and a goat (it has not survived complete and on the missing piece there is room for one more bull, or goat).

The protruding strap handle loses its vertical symmetry, the upper triangular bar becoming shorter than the lower. Again, the horizontal handle on the more open bowl is reduced in size and no longer perforated.

A new handle form with descendants in the next phase but no obvious antecedents consists of a triangular strap rising from the rim to a near-point, then bending sharply down as if a second small triangle were attached to its tip, forming a sort of hook.

This simple open bowl has circular studs all over its outer surface, probably once acting as keys to hold a white paste inlay.

TARXIEN

Tarxien pottery, which has su vived in greater quantity than th of all other phases put togethe also shows much greater variet and a certain amount of intern development over time, thoug this has yet to be worked out i detail. In many respects, in fabri form, handles, and decoration, can be seen to follow lines alread started in Saflie or Ġgantija. I others, howe er, again unde each of thos four headings, introduces ne elements withou obvious antece ents.

Fabric firs while the cla is usually bett prepared and th surface more hig ly polished tha ever before, th quality of firin does not alway match these, so that the fine su face can flake off, leaving an almo powdery body beneath. For one off ritual use, of course, this woul hardly matter. The coarser pin sandy ware is much more freque too, though this certainly looks mo domestic than ritual.

Most vessels were baked in bo fire conditions as before, particular some enormous bowls, as their ofte blotchy coloration shows. Othe examples, however, with a unifor

he most numerous single vessel form
'om Maltese prehistory is the Tarxien
hase carinated bowl, often, as here,
ndecorated but elegantly polished. They
'ere recovered in enormous numbers
'om all temple sites and the two hypogea.
Vhile the name 'offering bowl' is
peculative, it is probably a good guess as
) their original function.
he bowl shape and the typical nose-
ridge handle can both be traced back to
ncestral forms in the Ġgantija phase.
'either, however, survives into the
ronze Age.

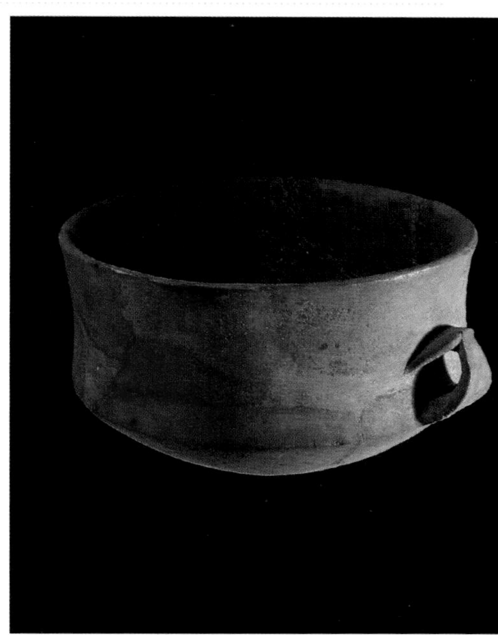

ellow or rose-pink surface, especially those with red inlaid bands, nust have been fired in closed kilns) achieve their uniform colours, epresenting a notable technical dvance.

By far the commonest form is vans's shape 41, a carinated bowl 'ith vertical concave neck, convex ody, and small flat base. While a ew have no handle, most are furished with a nose-bridge handle on ne carination and a D-shaped nib n the opposite side of the vessel. hey are convincingly interpreted s offering bowls, being often too rge to be convenient for drinking 'om. They were recovered in great umbers from all temple sites, and y the hundred from the North Cave ehind the Ġgantija, all smashed, a ump for debris from the temples. Since nearly all our finds have come from temple contexts, they would probably be found to be less massively preponderant on domestic sites when these can be found and studied.

Practically the only variation on this form is in its size, from miniatures barely 3 cm across to monsters up to a metre. The overwhelming majority, however, fall within a few centimetres of 20 cm diameter. One or two stand on low pedestals.

Nearly all have the characteristic nose-bridge handle, if they have a handle at all. Like the Saflieni one, it consists of two conjoined triangular elements, but now the upper one is much reduced, nearly flat and horizontal, the lower correspondingly enlarged and convex. The upper triangle may indeed be suppressed

altogether, the elongated tip of the lower curving back to reattach to the neck. In a more exaggerated form still, it rejoins a triangular projection of the bowl rim, which in turn can be drawn out into a long point, tipped with an animal head, or bent sharply down into a hook reminiscent of that already noted in Saflieni.

There is much more variation in a second carinated bowl form, lower in proportion, its neck straighter and sloping in to a rolled rim. This too can have the handle and nib already described, or alternatively two handles and no nib, one handle and three equispaced nibs, four nibs and no handle, or two more usual strap handles. Yet another carinated bowl form is that we have called the hole-mouth Saflieni bowl, which continues much as before.

These jars from Tarxien also come in a wide range of sizes, and were probably fo food storage. The term 'amphora' refers t the two tunnel handles in their shoulder. The second here is decorated, but this is unusual.

Then there is an extraordinaril wide range of jar forms, includin ovoid, S-profile, and carinated. Th only one which could be calle standard has a deep swellin bowl-like body surmounted b a long, concave, insloping nec to a restricted mouth. It could b called an amphora since it alway has two tunnel handles in its shou der. In these, the recessed handle of Saflieni have sunk right into th pot. Indeed, the bow of the han dle is no longer a strip attache to the pot wall. Instead, two hole are pierced through the wall an

pouch of clay added inside the r to prevent its contents spilling ırough. While much stronger, nce the 'handle' is now part of ıe pot wall itself, the holes are o small to accommodate fingers, presumably they were meant to old a loop of cord. Similar handles ın be found equispaced around ıe rims of deep bowls or jars, here resumably to attach lids. These are gain tunnel handles, reinvented ter a long interval since the Grey corba ones. A major difference is ıat while the latter were set ver- cally on their pots, the Tarxien ıes are always horizontal. Each pening is also usually surrounded y a slight rib not found earlier. ıterestingly, there is often a small lditional perforation from below, resumably intended to drain any quid caught in the pouch.

The sandy pink ware appears ı two distinct forms. One, the najdra bowl, so-called from the te where it was most frequent, is strange form of unknown func- on. The sides of a broad open dish ırve up to a low vertical wall, the p of which is heavily finger-tip odelled as on piecrusts. A large oop was then cut out of the wall ght down to the level of the base, eaning that it could never have eld liquids.

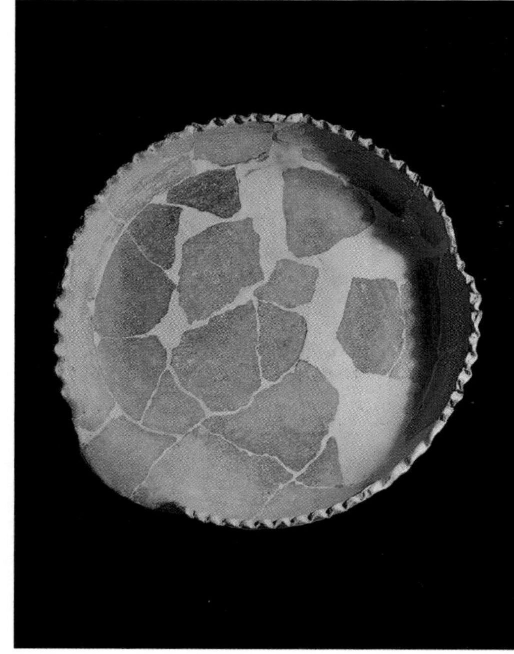

ıis large but shallow bowl from Mnajdra of a coarser and unpolished ware, and always provided with a notched rim. ıe broad scoop lip, lower left, renders its iginal function puzzling.

The second is a more conventional-looking S-profile jar, without handles but bearing four vertical ribs which smooth into the wall below the bulge and stop at an abrupt step on the neck. Between the ribs, incised arcs contain heavily-modelled radiating fluting. This clearly follows on from the Saflieni arco-striates.

Handle forms have been described along with the vessels to which each is appropriate.

Decoration is very varied, and again closely related with vessel shape. On the offering bowls, by far the most frequent (many are not decorated at all) is a double volute pattern of very stereotyped form. It became so conventionalized that on some bowls it was

very lightly grooved, no more than a thin burnished line which can be seen only when light reflects off the polished surface at a certain angle. They thus appear to have been a mere formality. Even the more visible lines were too slight to be of any use for holding ochre incrustation, which hardly mattered as that practice had been completely abandoned by this time. The volutes occasionally end in 'fishtails' or bear projecting 'thorns', closely similar to those we have met in the relief carving on temple blocks.

In a variant to the scratching, strips of clay were gouged out of the surface to be replaced with a different clay, forming volutes alternating vertical bars. This tec nique was applied only to bow with a bright yellow or buff surfac the clay of the inlay having mo iron oxide and so baking to a scarl red. The necks of other bowls be a diagonal lattice pattern. The straight lines betray a marked bre with tradition.

A very different effect is giv by bowls which are covered wi neat, close-spaced vertical striatio though these had already appear more roughly on the pink sandy ja Where the striations on neck ar body meet at the carination, t latter overlap the former to give distinct ripple in relief. Alternative and much less frequently, the stri tions run horizontally, encircli the neck. It is noticeable that the striated vessels are nearly always

The Tarxien volute can be rendered carelessly. The vessel shape of this bowl is unusual too, though its fabric and surface finish are as good as any.

different form from the bowl on p.226, is carinated bowl has the same all-over udded decoration on its neck. n the body, however, an entical technique was nployed to produce fish-iled volutes. It therefore ows an interesting mbination of two quite fferent techniques. was found at Tarxien.

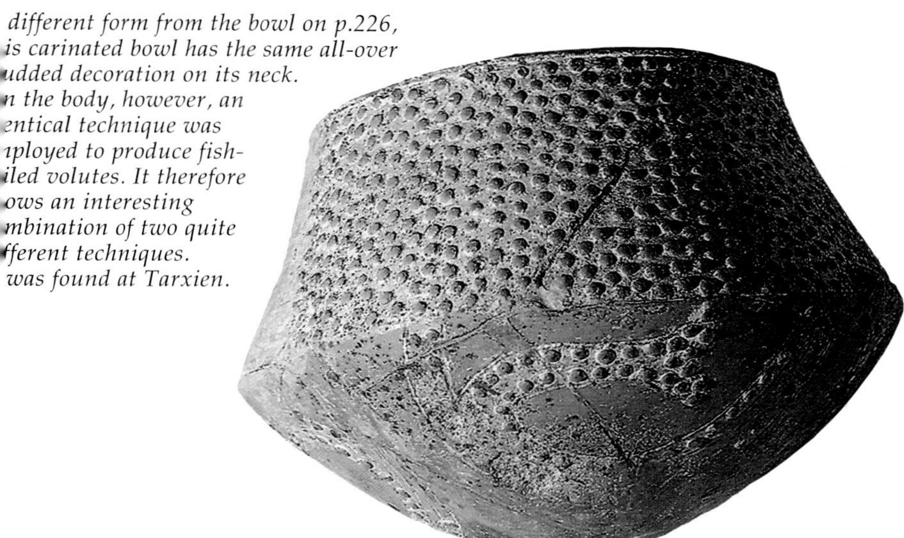

fine light-red ware, quite differ-it from the more usual greys and acks, and nearly all lack handles.

More often found on the straight-alled carinated bowls is yet nother decorative technique, at of applying circular or lentil-aped pellets to the vessel surface. n many sherds, white paste still ings to the surface between the uds, which may have been univer-l at the time, even if it no longer rvives on all. The finished effect ould have been of polished dark rcles or ovals against a white matt ckground. The same was occa-onally, and more expeditiously, hieved by gouging up gobbets of ay from the soft surface, which ould again show through the plied white surface.

The polished surfaces could also be covered with close-spaced impressed dots or shallow round or oval dimples. Though the dimples are too shallow to have held an inlay, the dots may well have done so, particularly where they were used as a background to reserved volute bands.

A variety of rustication techniques was employed on the coarser-ware jars, some of which are grey and polished but most are in the sandy pink ware. Unlike the arco-striate or rosette-fluted jars, the whole exterior surface would be roughened with incisions, finger-tip smearing or poking, or roughly-applied scales. Whether the intention was decorative, or to make the often heavy jars less

A delightful but unique sherd from Ġgantija bears a repeat design, apparent of birds with prominent crests, perhaps hoopoes. It came from the wall of a cup like that on p.227.

likely to slip from the hands, or both, is not clear. Variation on these diverse themes was enormous. Volutes could be worked in studded bands. Ribs could be replaced with applied model animals, probably lizards. Scratched motifs too could include zoomorphic forms such as cattle under trees on one from Tarxien or repeat birds (peacocks? hoopoes?) on one from Ġgantija. Knobs on arco-striate jars could be modelled into little faces.

There is a paradox here. On the one hand, potters seem to have gone for highly competent but unimaginative plain vessels or depressingly slick stereotyped volutes.

On the other, their imaginations ran riot, experimenting with numerous quite new decorative techniques. Interestingly, instratigraphically earlier Tarxien layers that site, lattice-scratching was th only one of these to appear, and th volute design was employed on at its simplest, or even a prototyp form, a curve, concave above, wi two dashes branching inwards ne its tips – a 'boat'. Was the exper mentation a conscious breakin away from the convention-boun rut, an attempt to revivify a failin tradition, or a sign of degeneracy, collapse of accepted norms? Eith way, it developed no further, sin it was cut short, as were the tem ples themselves, and replaced b an utterly different tradition, th of the Bronze Age.

OTHER MATERIALS

Objects of stone, bone, and shell fall into three categories. We have already looked at the first of these, the statuary and other religious paraphernalia.

Secondly, there is a group of what seem to be personal ornaments or the like – axe amulets, perforated shells, or slips of bone, and fascinating tiny carved or modelled birds, animals, and even snails. Some of these, too, may well have had symbolic or religious significance, as with a modern St Christopher medallion, but if so, it will not be possible to recover it now. There are other equally insoluble problems. Who made these trinkets; how were they worn; by whom? They were particularly frequent in Ħal Saflieni, presumably having been placed with the dead; less so in the Xagħra Circle.

Thirdly come purely functional objects. These are frankly uninspiring, though one should hardly be surprised.

Querns and rubbers, bone awls and pins, simple flakes of obsidian, chert, or flint, are too generalized in form and function to change much over time. In Malta they can be dated to phase only by association with the much more diagnostic pottery in discrete levels. The unique multi-quern built into Kordin III temple is of particular note. Little of the flaked stone shows any secondary working, though a few pieces have scraper edges or touches of sickle gloss. Only one or two call for separate comment. The flint knife from the Tarxien altar and the three from the Xagħra hypogeum were presumably used for ceremonial sacrifices.

Unless the few carved sling-stones, if such they are, can be counted, a total of five arrowheads, of which one was barbed-and-tanged and four hollow-based, are the only possible weapons. Even these from Tarxien are not certainly from the temple level. Only two polished stone axes are known from this period, both from the Hypogeum. Another discovered recently at Mistra was a surface find, and so undated. Rather more special is a unique massive axe of local stone from Tarxien, rectangular in section with a hole through each corner large enough to take a hand. It was clearly intended to be wielded by two men, presumably for stone dressing. Not for the first time, we must bewail the dearth of occupation debris for the Ġgantija phase, and the absence of it for Tarxien.

It should be stressed that, with the sole exception of a stone bead from Tarxien inlaid in gold with a motif looking like a set of cricket stumps, no metal has ever been found in a secure Temple Period context in Malta or Gozo. Even that came from a disturbed level so it must be regarded as uncertain. To call the temples Neolithic may be rather misleading, but to attribute them to a Copper Age would be even more so.

SOCIETY

Before turning to the demise of this extraordinary cultural efflorescence, it is time to stand back for a general view. Just how did this society tick?

We have a paradox. On the one hand, we have a simple mixed economy, above but apparently only just above, the subsistence level. It produced a small surplus, to import a modest quantity and variety of raw materials from abroad, and even fewer luxuries, if the stone for miniature axes should be classed as such.

Eight miniature heads, all from Tarxien, show a variety of features and hair styles. Some are broken from their bodies while others, notably the last two, carved on dripstone, were never given any.

In all these it differs in no obvious way from contemporary cultures both around the Mediterranean and further afield. Yet in Malta this society and economy supported complex architecture and art of an entirely different order of magnitude, far in advance of those of its nearer or more distant neighbours. There is no simple explanation for this. Until recently, cultural developments of this sort were explained as the products of chiefdoms, envisaged as a half-way stage between egalitarian societies and states. In these, individuals acquired political power, allowing them to take control of material resources to their own benefit. Religion could be privatised too, the chiefs strengthening their position by becoming the sole intermediaries between the populace and the gods.

'he fine craftsmanship of the temple stone nasons is evident in this view of the nner right apse of Ħagar Qim. The hole hrough the orthostats on the right was 'eliberate, and though less regular than hose in Mnajdra, probably also served for oracles', whatever we understand by that erm.

Three results of this sort of levelopment should be visible in he archaeological record. Most bviously, in chiefdoms burials ended to divide into numerous omparatively poor and simple nes, contrasting with a few in vhich the dead were buried singly vith an often staggering wealth of recious or exotic goods.

The second is those goods themelves, imported deliberately to mphasize the prestige of an elite ver the common people, whose urplus production was tapped, villingly or otherwise, to support it. This leads to competition etween elite, or would-be elite, roups and, as a result, thirdly, lmost inevitably warfare, which oo will become evident in the form of weapons and defensive, or even fortified, sites. This phenomenon is widely spread throughout the world, but simply does not apply in Malta as far as we can see.

Although there is a very modest import of luxury items from abroad, there is no evidence whatsoever for conflict, either within communities in the islands or between them until the next period in the story. Even then, there is little differentiation between poorer and richer burials. Not until the Punic period could any tombs be described as wealthy, and still not as markedly so as in many other places and times.

If there is any hint of social stratification in Temple Period Malta, it lies in a priesthood. Representations of so-called priests and priestesses are possible but not in themselves convincing. However, details of the temple layouts provide a more compelling argument.

While the evidence is admittedly tenuous, it is difficult to picture how the temples could have been planned, and the logistical problems of their construction overcome, without a small body of people organizing the work. And if those people were not chieftains, they were far more likely to have been priests.

The clustering of the temples suggests that there was still a measure of competition betwee the half-dozen communities, wit that above Grand Harbour mar ginally in the lead. However, suc competition seems to have bee sublimated into temple-building and quite probably in other activi ties which have left no trace, lik games, sports, cultural rivalries, o even beauty contests, who knows At least football leagues, eistedd fodds, and the like are preferabl to pitched battles. The alterna tive would be something like th internecine warfare which all bu extinguished the population o Easter Island.

This could be fairly claimed a another major achievement of th early Maltese, a stable, peaceful

Through the porthole slab of its left apse, one sees the porthole of the opposite one across the paved first court of Ħaġar Qim

The standing figure from Tarxien is often called 'the priest', though this is highly speculative. It is 60 cm high and modelled in clay on a straw core.

ı the Hypogeum Holy of Holies, the uncated pilaster lower left suggests an ncompleted enlargement at the time of ɔandonment.

artistic people. It sounds idyllic, even utopian, though whether the inhabitants recognized it as such is another matter. The physical demands of temple-building were great, and we cannot know if they were met willingly or bitterly resented.

Ħal Saflieni, which was still being enlarged when work was cut short, showed that building continued up to the very end. The demands of temple rituals, and the priests who performed them, were clearly a considerable drain too, perhaps crushingly so.

We can certainly admire what these people left behind, but we cannot get into their minds or lifestyles in any meaningful way, more is the pity.

ƆCIAL ORGANIZATION

.H. Morgan in Ancient Society, *1877, divided human social development :to three stages: savagery, the hunter-gatherers – barbarism, the early rmers – and civilization, the city dwellers. Elman Service in* Social rganization, An Evolutionary Perspective, *1962, made a fourfold division: ınds, Morgan's savagery-tribes, segmentary societies of settled farmers chiefdoms, with a centralization of power and a hierarchy of sites – and ates, Morgan's civilization. Marshall Sahlins,* Stone Age Economics, *1972, ıuated the third of these with craft specialization and redistribution systems. !alta was clearly in a state of 'barbarism' by Morgan's definition, but tribe or ıiefdom?*

ıe temple-building programme implies considerable concentration of sources and surely masons and architects as craft specialists. We have gued the same for the potters. But in the absence of evidence for a hierarchy sites, with the Paola group only marginally ahead of the others, it is fficult to argue for a fully-fledged chiefdom society. With that, we should so expect to find evidence of a redistribution system, personal wealth anifested in rich burials, and probably weaponry but we find none of these. ırther, despite its impressive monuments, still less can we talk of civilization Malta at this time, since it was without cities or writing.

After 15 cm of rubbish had accumulated on the floor of Skorba East, its roof burn down, leaving a distinct layer of charcoa Amongst this, experts identified the woo of olive trees.

COLLAPSE OF SOCIETY

If the beginnings of the temples are mysterious and intriguing, their end is equally so, and even more controversial. The facts are not disputed, as far as they go. At a point in time, now thought to lie close to 2500 BC, this extraordinarily sophisticated culture, as shown by their temples and statuary, collapsed.

I avoid the word 'civilization' since there is no sign of cities, writing, or advanced social stratification or craft specialization, all of which one would expect to find in a fully-developed civilization. Monumental building alone is not sufficient.

The end appears to have been quite sudden. Controversy centres on why that collapse occurred and how the succeeding Tarxien Cemetery culture relates to the preceding one. Here one must concentrate on the former problem, postponing tl latter to the next chapter.

The temples collapsed literally well as metaphorically. At Skorl at least it could be seen that gre chips had been knocked out of tl temple structure before new ar rougher walls were botched in the Bronze Age.

Without exception, the templ were abandoned for religious pra tices, though several were adapte to other uses. Tarxien was turne into a cemetery and Skorba and Bo in-Nadur were taken over by squa ters. The others appear to have be

ft to crumble away, perhaps delib-
:ately avoided for superstitious
:asons. The Xagħra hypogeum, for
xample, was sealed off before a sin-
.e Tarxien Cemetery sherd entered
, although there was extensive
ccupation material of that phase
nmediately overlying it.

But how could such a flourish-
ıg culture end so miserably and
ɔruptly? A wide range of sugges-
ons of varying probability has
een advanced, and it is perhaps
keliest that a combination of fac-
rs was involved, since none is
rictly exclusive. A remarkable
ct about the temple culture is the
mplete absence of evidence in any
rm for warfare, whether weapons,
efensive sites, wounds on skel-
ons, or any other. With daggers
rominent in the succeeding Tar-
en Cemetery, and fortifications
impressive size at Borġ in-Nadur
ıd elsewhere, we could suggest
ıat the temple builders were
aughtered by warlike invaders.
ıt populations in the historically
ɔcumented past were very rarely
iped out by war, if often sadly
pleted. Conquerors were more
kely to enslave than massacre
eir victims, once resistance had
een crushed, and of this there is
ɔ sign.

Disease is a tempting solution as most fatal maladies leave no detectable mark on the skeleton to allow diagnosis. Again, even traumatic disease like the plagues of late antiquity or the fourteenth century or, in other organisms, the well-documented recent outbreaks of myxomatosis in rabbits or the fungal disease of elm trees, rarely if ever kills off an entire population. One would expect human survivors to carry over some recognizable elements of their former culture, however debased.

Recent research has shown that the energy demands of temple-building would not, as had been formerly suggested, have put any serious strain on an agricultural economy such as that which supported the Maltese population at the time.

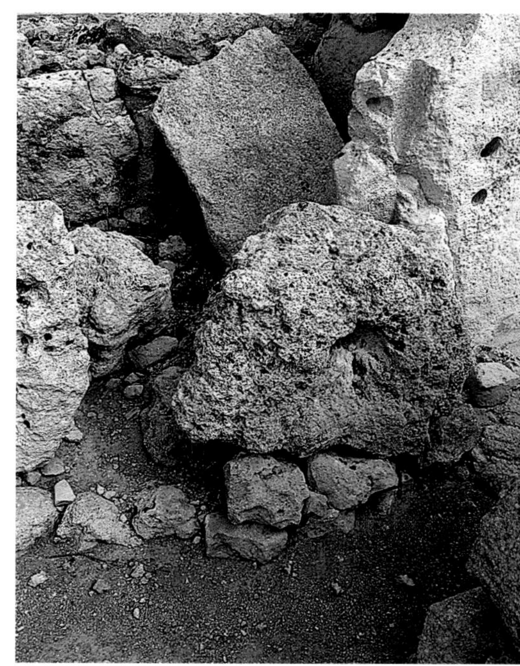

ıe block of the Tarxien Cemetery phase ıll overlaps damage to the door jamb of inner apse at Skorba. This happened er the temple was already partly ined.

What cannot be calculated is the demands of the temple rituals, in food resources or manpower, over and above those needed for constructing the monuments. Those may have been considerable, and could have had adverse effects in two directions.

Firstly, if the large population already implied by the size and number of the temples had to supply these extra demands on its food supply, over-exploitation of the limited agricultural land could lead to soil exhaustion, erosion, and, in turn, famine. Over-felling of timber for temple-building could also have exacerbated tl
problem of soil erosion.

Secondly, with the hints of increa
ing exclusivity of a priesthood w
have deduced from temple plan
particularly the walling off of inn
apses and the presence of the orac
holes, there could have been grov
ing tension between priests makir
increasing demands and a progre
sively more recalcitrant populac
That too could lead to unrest and
turn social collapse.

Conversely, and even mo
unprovably, an increasingly infl
ential priest or priesthood coul
have pointed to any of the earlie
mentioned factors, interpreted the
as signs of divine displeasure, ar
persuaded a gullible people that tl

Soil erosion is painfully obvious in this view, typical of much of highland Malta.

The oracle holes, like this at Mnajdra, imply a priesthood. Were its power and exactions resented by the rest of the population?

he orthostats of the first apses of Tarxien entral were reddened by fire, perhaps ssociated with the fall of the temples.

only course of action left was to abandon the islands, now accursed by the gods, to start again elsewhere. That, however, has taken us far into the realms of wild speculation. At least it cannot be proved wrong.

But by whatever means it passed away, the glory of the temples was gone, to be succeeded by a much lower level of culture, apparently owing nothing to what had gone on before, still interesting but by no means so spectacular.

DATES

We need to put dates on these developments. We saw earlier that the Żebbuġ phase came down to about 3500 BC. We have too few dates from the earlier Temple Period for any assurance on its beginnings. One from the

ORLDWIDE CONTEMPORARIES

hen Malta was first ttled about 5000BC, rming had been tablished in the Near ast for some five ousand years, and had so just spread into uthern and Central urope.

t the time the temples peared at 3500, farming d reached the Atlantic aboard, where megalithic mbs were making their pearance. Egypt and esopotamia, meanwhile, ere on the brink of vilization, with writing d cities already present. y 2500 and the fall of e temples, numerous temples in mudbrick stood all over the Tigris-Euphrates valley, while beside the Nile, pharaohs were about to raise the first pyramids. By now, civilization was dawning along the Indus too. While Malta was way ahead in architecture, it lagged in metallurgy, which all Europe apart from Malta and the far north had already adopted. In the New World, permanent villages had hardly appeared and agriculture contributed only about a third of the food supply.

A portal dolmen at Gaulstown, Eire.

Żebbuġ tomb in the Xagħra Circle at 4600±65 BP (3495-3150 cal BC), 250 years after the Żebbuġ group, must be associated with the latest burial in that chamber, of the Ġgantija phase and so, relevant to our present problem.

One from the Ġgantija Hut of the Querns at Skorba, 4478±56 BP (3337-2943 cal BC) is in close agreement. Two others, at 4640±150 and 4485±150 BP agree well too but are less reliable for two reasons. Their standard deviations are much wider and, even worse, their cultural associations less secure. The first came from the East Temple at Mġarr and could be either Mġarr or Ġgantija phase. The second, from the South Temple at Skorba, was in a layer with material down to Tarxien Cemetery. There is nothing against linking it with the residual Ġgantija sherds, but to use it to date that phase would be a serious example of a circular argument.

Fortunately we now have a very convincing cluster of six analyses for the Tarxien phase, all from the Xagħra Circle, with another from Skorba, though this last with a wide standard deviation. The cluster spans from 4300±60 BP to 4080±65 BP, 3018 to 2504 BC after calibration (at 1 standard deviation). Though it would be pressing the figures rather further than justified to suggest that this bracket represents the precise duration of the Tarxien phase, it probably gives us a quite reasonable approximation. Let us say 300
to 2500 BC. For comparative pu
poses, it is worth noting that th
second is almost exactly the da
at which the pharaohs of Egyp
began building their pyramids.

At much the same time the fir
bronze began to come into use i
northwest Europe, although it ha
reached Sicily and other Centr
Mediterranean regions substan
tially earlier. While the temple
are sometimes attributed to
Copper Age because of this, ther
is no evidence from Malta itse
to support that view. Indeed,
strengthens the argument tha
the terms Stone, Bronze, an
Iron, even more the intermediat
Copper, Ages have outlived the
usefulness.

The opening of the Tarxie
Cemetery phase, and so the en
of the Temple Period, is muc
less securely placed and in co
sequence more controversial. Thi
is unfortunate as the length of an
hiatus between the two migh
throw useful light on the caus
of the latter's collapse. It woul
be better discussed in that conte
later.

*A masterpiece of Temple Period craftsmanship, this shallow plate from H
Saflieni, diameter 25 cm, has a number o
bulls and a goat engraved on one side, an
an abstract design part reserved 'pebbles'
part volutes, on the other. It has had to b
restored from many fragments.*

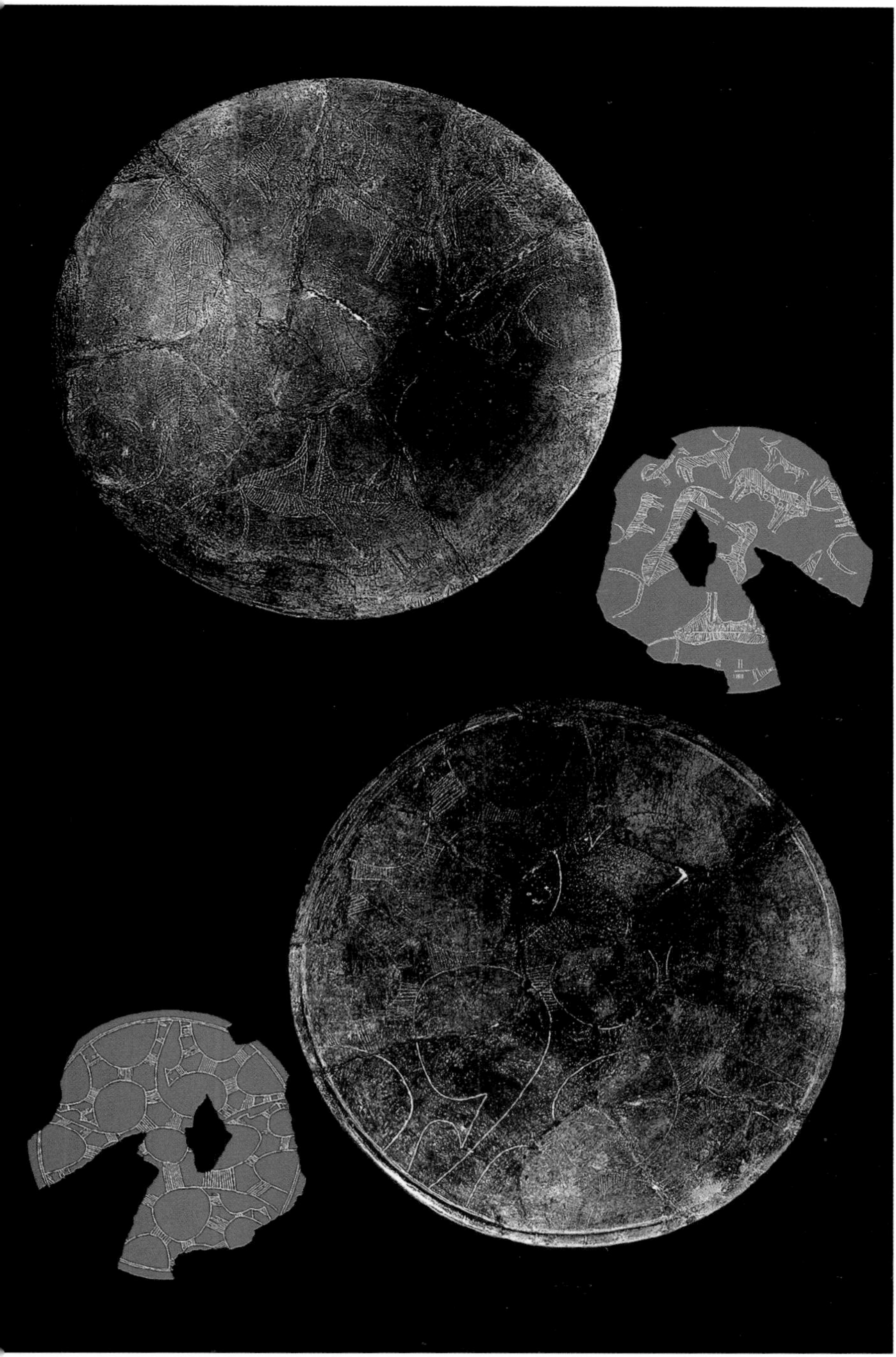

The Bronze Age which succeeded the temples has nothing to compare with their magnificence. However, the period has its own interest. At the least, we must give it full coverage to complete the story of Malta's prehistory.

CHAPTER 5

AFTER THE TEMPLES

The collapse of the temples about 2500 BC is only half of the problem. The other half concerns the people and culture that replaced those responsible for the temples. Despite careful search, no single element of their culture can be traced back to their predecessors in the islands. Improbable though it may seem, it is as if the islands were abandoned utterly, and stood as empty as when the first intrepid seafarers came ashore 2,500 years earlier. Who were the newcomers and where did they come from?

We are still far too far back in prehistory for there to be any chance of recovering the name by which they knew themselves, or were known to their neighbours. Those cannot survive until set down in writing, which was not to reach Malta for at least another millennium-and-a-half. Egypt and Mesopotamia had scribes by this time, but they would have known nothing

The rugged simplicity of the dolmen on Ta' Ċenċ contrasts with the elegance and sophistication of the temples. A different people had a different set of principles and skills.

For the first time, metal came into gener use, copper being imported from abroad. Three of these axes are of the simplest fla form, while one has cast flanges to assist in hafting.

and cared less about peoples way beyond their ken in the far west. We have only archaeological means to guide us.

Firstly, these new peoples brought the knowledge of metal with them. By this date, the use of copper and bronze was quite widespread through the Mediterranean, and had been known for many centuries farther east, in Turkey and the Levant. The tools and weapons of copper which Temi Zammit turned up in the Tarxien Cemetery, however, were of too simple forms – flat axes and daggers – to give any more specific clue as to their origins. In any case, as we shall see, they could have been, indeed must have been, traded over long distances, so where they came from, and where the people with whom they were buried came from, may have been very far apart.

Anthropology is little help he either, since the human remai recovered from the cemetery inser ed into the Tarxien ruins were cr mated, destroying any racial cha acteristics they may once have ha All that one can say is that whe we next have human skeletons study, from the Phoenician tomb of the ninth and later centurie they tend to be round-heade as the average Maltese are toda As explained in the box on sku shapes, the skulls from the Temp Period by contrast had a tendenc to long-headedness. While admi edly physical anthropologists lace much less reliance on this ort of evidence today than at the urn of the last century, this does t least hint at population replacement. Furthermore, round-headedness, if only as a generalization, as held to be characteristic of a entral band of Europe from France the Balkans, the so-called Alpine ace, as opposed to the long 'Mediterranean' heads further south.

If researches into the recovery nd analysis of DNA from ancient ones, which carries the genetic gnature of their original owners, an be applied to skeletons from emple Period Malta, and their esults compared with later material from the island, we might at ast get a clear answer to that all-nportant question – were they the ame people or not? It is a pity hat the practice of cremation in the Tarxien Cemetery will prevent comarisons between before nd immediately after he postulated break. nd if the evidence bears ut that break, further ork would be required see if the newcomers matched up with he genetic pattern of ome other contemporary population in Italy, he Balkans, the Aegean, r elsewhere.

his typically decorated Tarxien emetery jar has two vertical ribs rangely suggesting the legs of the gurines on p.258.

Until that is done, we are left with only two clues, both from traditional archaeology. A second major difference from the temple builders, after the use of copper, has already been touched on. Unlike their predecessors, the newcomers cremated their dead before burying them. Like the copper, however, that is no great help as there are sporadic occurrences of this funerary rite spread widely through space and time.

It is still far too early to be linked in any way with the urnfield cemeteries which spread widely through Central Europe in the later Bronze Age, from the mid-second millennium onwards. There is no area convenient in space and time currently known where cremation was practised, from which the Maltese could have brought the idea. The closest is probably a Hittite cremation cemetery at Boghaz Köy in Central Turkey.

While not impossible that they thought of it for themselves, it seems most unlikely in an environment already severely deforested as we know Malta to have been by this time. It provides, however, yet another illustration of the marked cultural contrast between the populations of Malta before and after the temple collapse.

If these people were immigrant to the islands, their pottery and the monuments offer the most promis ing clues to their earlier homelan Two vessel shapes preponderate i the material from Tarxien Cemeter contexts, both from the cemeter itself and from domestic deposit of the same period. One is the ver general presence of a thickened an sharply-everted lip, whether on globular bowl or deeper jar. Ther is nothing like this from the Templ Period. It can, however, be matche quite closely from Lipari, wher it occurs on bowls of the Earl Bronze Age Capo Graziano war and more widely in Early Helladi Western Greece and Dalmatia, a Evans pointed out in 1956. Th pottery from these areas is by n means identical, as the Għar Dalam Stentinello equation in the Earl

A more open bowl with everted lip was also associated with the burials in the Tarxien Cemetery. Apart from three dimpled knobs on its shoulder, it is undecorated.

'his pedestalled thickened lip owl was found in a Temple Period ontext at Tarxien, though the form s much commoner in the Cemetery hase of the Early Bronze Age. Its ignificance is discussed in he box on p.271.

While the lip and its decoration are ypical, the dotted bands on the pedestal are nuch less common, and the pedestal itself, nd its angled handle, are unique.

Neolithic was, or even as close as he Żebbuġ-San Cono one rather ater. But the family resemblance eems clear.

The second form is more puzzling. In this, an open, straight-sided owl has its lip thickened internally, giving a wide bevel, often lecorated with hatched or dot-filled endant triangles. What is particularly intriguing about this form s that a handful of characteristic xamples turned up in secure Tarien Temple contexts, as has already een noted. One fine complete one ame from Tarxien itself, and sevral more rim sherds from Skorba nd the Xagħra Circle. They are so ew, and so different from the other naterial they were found with, that hey look like imports from abroad. But where from? One is known from Early Bronze Age Castelluccio in Sicily and a number from the Torre d'Ognina, on the coast south of Syracuse. However, they look strange at both these sites, and could be explained, as L. Bernabò Brea, the excavator of the second one, suggested, as exports from Malta. If so, of course, they do not in any way help us to trace where the form started from. Another site providing very close parallels was Thermi on the island of Lesbos, off the Dardanelles in the northern Aegean, with others from the Second City of Troy. The similarities are very close, and the date about right, but it will be immediately obvious that the distances are enormous, though by sea not impossible.

Another dolmen shows that the new-comers could still manoeuvre large blocks of stone. The capstone at Wied Filep is 3.8 m long and was raised 1.5 m above rock level.

If we turn to the monuments of this period, we find that they are rather more specific though not much more helpful, and far less impressive than what had gone before. Malta's dolmens are small chambers consisting of a comparatively large capstone supported on slab walling, usually above a shallow hollow in the rock. Cairns have an even smaller chamber within a stony mound. Both have produced Tarxien Cemetery sherds, and none of any other phase, and both are assumed to have been constructed to house cremation burials which have not survived. The only closely similar monuments are a group of some 30 in a restricted area around Otranto, at the tip of Italy's 'heel'. Unfortunately they are even worse denuded than the Maltese ones, and no material has been recovered from them, though Bronze Age sherds are plentiful in the much larger gallery graves further north in Apulia, also misleadingly called dolmens. Nor is more known of contemporary settlements in the area, to support or confound a suggested connection with those of the Maltese Tarxien Cemetery culture.

In the light of present evidence then, the problem remains unsolved beyond the very general suggestion that the Tarxien Cemetery folk came to Malta from the northeast.

Domestic material of this initial phase of the Maltese Bronze Age

has so far been found on only three sites. At Borġ in-Nadur, two layers were discovered beneath huts of the Borġ in-Nadur phase, the lower with only Tarxien Cemetery sherds, the upper with a mixture of both phases which might imply continuity between the two. A stone setting was also exposed, so rough that it could hardly be claimed as a wall, and certainly gave no hint as to the form of houses of the period. At Skorba we did have a hut, but hardly typical. The inner apse of the earlier temple had been adapted by adding cross walls and a low bench, and there was broken pottery around, one substantial bowl sherd even being wedged into the wall. There is, however, some doubt whether it was actually a dwelling. It was very small and inconvenient, no hearth was found, and the foot of a figurine could suggest that it had a religious rather than a domestic function.

The one fully convincing site is the Xagħra Circle, though even this is much less informative than one might have hoped. In two of the areas excavated, to the north and the east of the hypogeum and still within the stone circle, extensive grey deposits above rock containing plentiful Tarxien Cemetery sherds represent decayed mudbrick. Even here, no actual structure survived, so, as at Borġ in-Nadur, the form of the huts is quite unknown.

Occasional sherds of this type can be found amongst the material from other temple sites, but they are few in number, have no secure contexts, and are therefore unreliable as evidence. They probably represented no more than casual visits – picnic parties, perhaps. One might compare them with the single Tarxien Cemetery bowl fragment recovered from the shipwreck site off the mouth of Xlendi Bay, in that case surely a casual loss from a fishing boat. Nor do sherds turn up as sporadic surface finds. The extensive survey in Gozo found hardly any. The implication seems to be

The cruder walls on the left and in the foreground were added in the inner apse of Skorba West in the Bronze Age, as was the bench round the foot of the walls.

that, in contrast to the succeeding Borġ in-Nadur phase, the population at the time was small.

By that next phase, the situation had altered dramatically. Settlement sites of this period are known from end to end of the islands, and one at least, Borġ in-Nadur itself, produced actual huts. The sites are of at least three clearly distinguishable types.

The most characteristic, and most easily found, are open sites on prominent hilltops, which in the local topography are nearly always flat-topped. Many, like In-Nuffara (Xagħra, Gozo), Il-Qolla above Burmarrad, and Qarraba projecting into the sea betwee[n] Ġnejna and Għajn Tuffieħa bays are completely surrounded by cliffs. That the intention was defensiv[e] is made amply clear by those site[s] where the circuit of cliffs is no[t] complete, lines of easy access bein[g] barred by massive walls. Borġ in-Nadur itself is, of course, the fines[t] example of this by far, but traces o[f] such defences survive at the Wardij[a] ta' San Ġorġ on Dingli cliffs, an[d] at both Qala Hill and Fawwara between Għajn Tuffieħa and Sa[n] Martin. The social significance o[f] this will be discussed later.

Not all settlements were defend-ed in this way. Sherd scatters o[n] level ground near the round towe[r]

Settlements are nearly always located in dramatic, easily defensible sites, none more so than Qarraba, the headland between Ġnejna and Għajn Tuffieħa bays on Malta's northwest coast.

Apart from a scatter of sherds on the surface, silo pits cut into the rock and packed with Borġ in-Nadur phase material are all that is left of the Bronze Age village of In-Nuffara, Gozo.

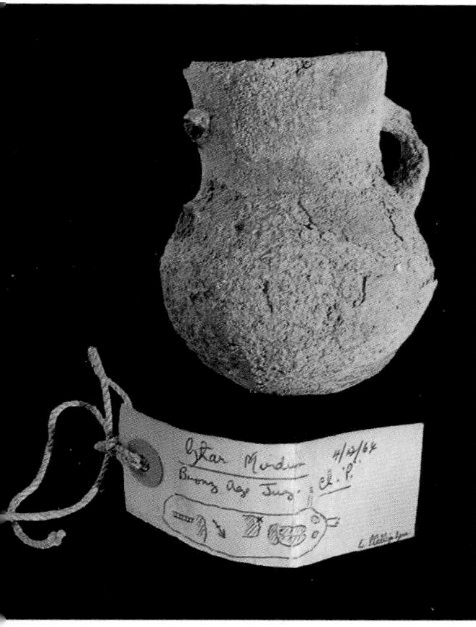

he accompanying label shows that this ttle two-handled jar, though badly ecayed, was found in Għar Mirdum.

of Ta' Ġawhar (Gudja); north of the Temple Period hut on the Mġarr Road (Għajnsielem); on the southern slopes of Tas-Silġ (Marsaxlokk); and elsewhere, must represent open villages. These are naturally less obvious in the landscape, and there may have been many more not yet identified.

Thirdly, cave sites appear to have come back into use, with examples at Għajn Abdul (Santa Luċija, Gozo); below the Baħrija cliffs; and, richest by far, Għar Mirdum (Dingli cliffs). These are often in badly-shattered rock, making their interpretation difficult, and there may once have been more, now swept away by cliff erosion. Were people living in them, making offerings in them, or simply discarding rubbish into them from above? It is rarely easy to tell.

GRICULTURE

he presence of silo pits 1 many Borġ in-Nadur tes (see also p.291) nplies grain production 1 a major scale. At the pe site, there is even suggestion that it was ing grown for export. his example, from the ardija ta' San Ġorġ, has a rebate to hold a lid. Direct evidence, however, is scanty. Carbonized emmer wheat and barley were recovered from the Għar Dalam level at Skorba, confirming crop production from the time of the first settlement Again, wheat, horse beans (a primitive form of the modern broad bean), and peas, preserved by similar charring, were placed with the burials in the Tarxien Cemetery.

Otherwise, the evidence is only circumstantial, notably the frequent occurrence of querns in all periods. In any case, natural resources alone could hardly have supported permanent villages.

Terraced fields also testify to agriculture , but are almost impossible to date.

Two oval huts of the Bronze Age village were exposed at Borġ in-Nadur in 1959. Nothing appeared on the surface beforehand, and even beneath the ploughsoil, only the floors and wall footings survived.

The clearest picture comes from Borġ in-Nadur. In the field immediately inside the great defensive wall, A.A. Caruana excavated huts in 1880, and two more were opened up by the Museum Department in 1959. One of these was 7.5 by 3.5 m; the other at least that, its total area not cleared, and the corner of a third appeared to one side. The hut walls were represented by stone footings, here without the tell-tale grey clay to prove the use of mud brick. They may have used local soil, of course, since there are no exposures of blue clay at this end of the island. On the other hand, the superstructures could equally have been of wattle and daub. Floors were of *torba* and roofs surely of thatch. Each hut was equipped with a hearth, a quern, and a roller. A third hearth, in a double-stone setting, was probably associated with the later hut since blocked the doorway of the earli one. One of the huts had a mort for pounding grain in additio while the other held a 2.9 m-lor stone bench, so neatly cut that had probably been looted from th nearby temple.

The huts, though rather flims appear to have been closely-packe and, since sherds are frequent ov the whole surface of the defende area, some 2.8 ha in all, this impli a village of many hundreds of pe ple. Other sites are of comparab size.

No structures were recovered om the limited trenches at Baħrija, ut with an area nearer 7.5 ha, if the ensity of occupation was the same s at Borġ in-Nadur, its population ould have been twice as great. hat might be an exaggeration as ıe plateau is not level but sloping uite steeply, making it much less ›nvenient. The 1959 excavation, though its upper levels produced xamples of the latest phase of potry, named after this site, showed ıat before the arrival of the latter had already had a long period of ccupation in the Borġ in-Nadur hase.

The dearth of settlement sites f the Tarxien Cemetery phase akes a section on life and econmy difficult. What evidence we ave, particularly from the Xagħra ircle, suggests that there was lite change on this front. As before, mixed economy seems certain, ith the same crops and animals ; in earlier periods. Although not om a domestic site, the bowls of rbonized beans, *Vicia faba*, from e Tarxien Cemetery itself are wory of note. Though ancestors of e modern broad bean, they were uch smaller in size, and best lled 'horse beans' to distinguish em.

We are on firmer ground with the Borġ in-Nadur phase, the villages of which have produced much more evidence. All would have depended primarily on the cultivation of surrounding fields, but Borġ in-Nadur, which had easy access to the sea, like Qarraba but few of the others, probably exploited its advantages for fishing also.

Many of the sites have yielded spindle whorls and loomweights, so also witnessing to a textile industry. The so-called pottery 'anchors', or better, anchor-shaped objects, probably also formed parts of looms, since clear marks of wear can be seen where cords had been looped over their 'flukes'. In classical and later times, Malta had

ɔnical weights of baked clay, with a rforation through the top of each, were ıde to keep the warp threads on an ›right loom taut during the weaving ocess. They are found on all settlement :es of the period.

a reputation for fine weaving. Though we have no way of being sure that it began so early – those whorls, weights, and anchors may have supplied more than an internal market. This might explain how Malta paid for its imports of bronze, scraps of which turn up on domestic sites in this phase, as well as the axes and daggers from the Tarxien cemetery. On the other hand, it is difficult to see what a textile industry could have been based on. The islands hardly look suitable for wool production on a large scale; flax is even less prob able; and cotton, the staple of it textile industry in historical time had yet to be introduced. And th biggest problem is that textile whatever they were made of, deca so rapidly that they have a minima chance of surviving in archaeolog ical contexts. We are reduced t speculation.

By the Tarxien Cemetery phase the knowledge of copper ha been introduced to the islands Among the burials inserted int the ruins of the temples at Tarx ien, Zammit found six axes of tha material. Most were of the sim plest flat form which could be cas in open moulds. One, howeve has high flanges to provide mor secure hafting, implying also more-advanced two-piece mould Not surprisingly, at 324 gm it i the heaviest of the six. All fa between 10 and 12.4 cm in lengt

Possibly also parts of looms, these anchor-shaped pottery objects are equally common. The wear left by a thread can just be made out at the base of the left hand specimen's shank.

hile eight of the burials in the Tarxien ·metery were accompanied by copper es, like the two on the left, seven had t daggers of roughly triangular shape. e two on the right still have some or of the rivets which fixed them to their lts, probably of wood or bone, now ssing. The irregular surfaces of the eces are the result of corrosion of the pper as they lay in the soil.

wo additional smaller and narower ones could be better classed chisels.

Whereas all these, together ith a number of simple awls, ere presumably used as peaceble tools, the seven flat daggers so found are much more conincing as weapons. They too ary in length, from 9 to 13.2 cm, ough some would have been little longer before their tips ere damaged. Five have two vet holes each in the butt, with e rivets themselves surviving one, by means of which they ould have been fastened into eir hilts. The sixth has three vet holes, while the butt of the venth is too decayed to be sure. hese too would have been cast in open moulds. All are thin and on the whole so flimsy that they were probably more for display than for serious combat.

Nothing has yet been found to suggest that they were cast in Malta, though it is perhaps unlikely that a cemetery is the right place to look for evidence of this. They were, then, probably imported as finished articles.

The picture becomes hardly any clearer in the succeeding phase. As has been said, Borġ in-Nadur was well placed on Marsaxlokk Bay for fishing as well as for agriculture; it could also have engaged in overseas trade, the most obvious commodity being bronze. The only piece found in the 1959 excavation was a rivet

from the ploughsoil, and there is no record of any from 1880. Dr Murray in the 1920s unearthed three small and undiagnostic pieces, one of lead and, most interestingly, a limestone mould for casting an ornamental ring, proving that metal was actually worked on the island. But since all were from more or less disturbed levels, which included a Carthaginian coin of the third century BC, there must remain an element of doubt as to which truly belong to the Bronze Age occupation. However, there is no such doubt about the needle, finger ring, fragment of bracelet, and several other small scraps from Baħrija. In the total absence of local sources of either copper or tin, these must represent imports in the Bronze Age.

The cremations were accompanied by strangely stylized ceramic figurines, each representing a seated figure of indeterminate sex. All are decorated in a style identical with that on the pottery. The tallest is 19 cm high.

As regards the exports whic would have been needed to pay fc these, textiles have been mentione as a possibility, and the silo pits o the foreshore of St George's Ba below Borġ in-Nadur (see boxes o silo pits p.291 and Borġ in-Nadu p.289) suggest that they could als have been shipping out grain.

We have no religious building of the period, except possibly th adapted apse of the Skorba templ and possibly the deposits in Għ Mirdum, so our evidence com from only two sources: buri practices and terracotta figurine

Jeither of these is anything like as ıformative as the far fuller record f the Temple Period.

From the cemetery at Tarxien, ,ammit recovered substantial frag-ıents of 16 figurines. One shows a triking female figure 22 cm high, eated on a low stool, the legs clearly ecognizable. Chest and arms are ısed into a plain disc, the breasts eing the only features indicated. he face is circular, flat apart from prominent nose, with mouth, nos-'ils, and eyes marked by impressed ots. Most remarkable is a circular eaddress, folded up at the back.

A second piece has a similar face, 'ith the addition of pierced ears, ut the chest is more naturalistically endered, with stump arms and no reasts. One arm, the lower body, nd hat are broken away. Neither of ıese bears any decoration.

All the others, four virtually com-lete, conform to a uniform type, 18 m or so high, with a large, flat disc ody, featureless knob head, more or ss naturalistic legs, bent at hip and nee, and a flap support to the rear. Vhile the head is plain, all other urfaces are highly decorated in a ectilinear, geometric, style very like ıat of the pottery. The legs make it lear that these too are seated human gures as might otherwise have been in doubt. Plain disc bodies almost identical to the first, though with all other features broken away, were found at both Skorba and the Xagħra Circle. From the former also came a foot, 5.7 cm long, and part of the leg of a much more naturalistic, but tantalizingly incomplete, figurine, again typically decorated. A sherd of a similarly-decorated disc recently came to light in Ġgantija.

What function these figurines served, and how they were regard-ed by their makers, can only be guessed at.

The Bronze Age saw a major break in funerary practices. Whereas all earlier burials on the island that we know of (a necessary qualification when only archaeological evidence is available) were by inhumation in

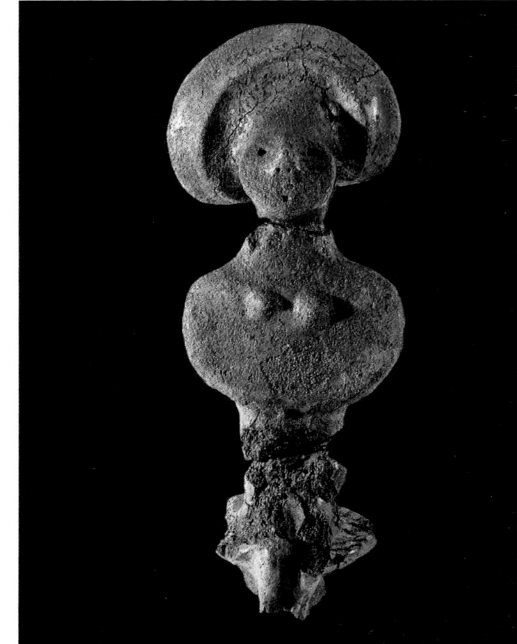

n exception is this more aturalistically rendered one, which is ill quite unlike those of the Temple eriod. It is 22 cm high.

rock-cut chambers, or, more rarely, in caves as at Bur Mgħeż, the universal practice at this period, with the same qualification, was by cremation.

In the best-known case, that of the cemetery established within the ruins of the Tarxien South temple, the bones, burnt but often surviving in quite large pieces, were gathered up and laid to rest in pottery bowls, along with subsidiary vessels and the copper weapons and pottery figurines described above. Personal ornaments were added, including large numbers of discoid beads of faience and fish vertebrae.

Enormous numbers of disc-shaped beads of faience (see also p.293) were found wit the burials in the Tarxien Cemetery.

Fish vertebrae make attractive, if unusual, beads. They were employed in necklaces in the Tarxien Cemetery, and show signs of burning.

In a second burial rite, crema tion can be assumed but not prove A number of dolmens are know across Malta, consisting of a larg capstone supported on low wall When Evans cleared a small on at Ta' Ħammut, inland from Qal Marku on the north coast, he note that it contained a quantity of Tar ien Cemetery sherds but no other and that the chamber beneath th capstone, despite being slightl hollowed into the rock, was hardl large enough to contain a complet corpse. A packet of cremated bon however, would have been no prob lem, though none actually survive in the much eroded site. Whereve evidence of use of dolmens can b found elsewhere, it was as buria

'he capstone of the second dolmen at Ta' Ħammut is so low to the ground that, ssuming it was to house burials, they ould only have been of cremated bone.

chambers, and it is indeed difficult to see what other purpose they could have served here. Thirteen are known (see p.276-9), though only Ta' Ħammut produced anything by way of contents.

To the west of Wied Moqbol, 2.4 km southeast of Żurrieq and 600 m south of the former church at Tal-Bakkari on the road to Ħal Far, three small cairns are known, though not easy to find. From one, Evans recovered more sherds of Tarxien Cemetery pottery in 1952, but no human bone, burnt or otherwise. It seems likely that they also were for cremation burials.

Whereas Borġ in-Nadur settlements are far more numerous, nothing is known for certain of their burial practices. The best evidence comes from Xemxija, where a few

DOLMENS, EUROPEAN DISTRIBUTION

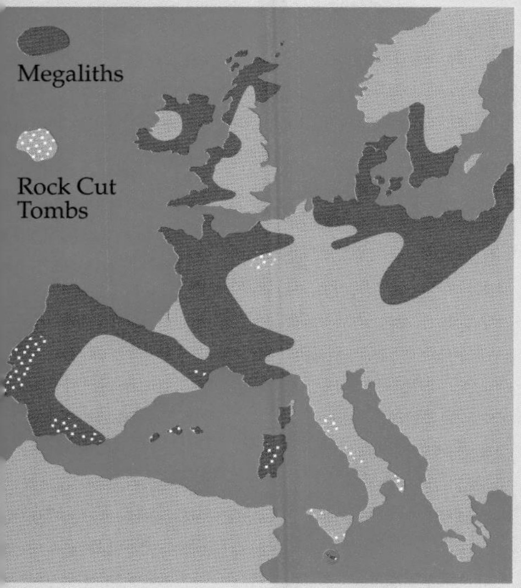

Malta is the southern outpost of a type of monument found widely across Western and Northern Europe. They were constructed of large stones, usually under a massive capstone, and were raised as monuments to house the dead in the Neolithic and Early Bronze Ages.
Two other classes of monument are related. Large stones were erected singly, in circles or in straight rows. Malta has its menhirs and the Xagħra Stone Circle.
Secondly, tomb chambers were cut in the rock, like the dolmens for collective burials, as described on p.44. Rock-cut tombs were more popular in the Mediterranean, and remained in fashion over a much longer period.

Borġ in-Nadur sherds were found in earlier tombs. With the deposits much disturbed, there was no certainty that these accompanied Bronze Age interments, still less, if so, of what form.

At Ta' Vneżja, near Ta' Qali below Mdina, a rock-cut trench 1.5 m long and only 15 cm deep was reported in 1936 as having the poorly-preserved remains of two human skeletons, an adult and a child, together with 'small fragments of Neolithic pottery, tiny lumps of red pigment, and an elongated bead.'

This Punic lamp, with its double pinched lip, was found in a silo pit at Mtarfa with late Borġ in-Nadur pottery.

Evans found a wooden box of Borġ in-Nadur-type sherds labelled 'Ta' Vneżja' in the museum, but it is by no means certain that they came from the same site. Two silo pits were dug by Ward Perkins at Mtarfa in 1939. He considered them tombs though no human remains were found. One contained a quantity of late Borġ in-Nadur pottery, together with a single Punic lamp, the other only Punic. While interesting in suggesting an overlap, to be discussed further in a later section, the presence of animal bone suggests that human bones should have survived too had they ever been present. It therefore remains doubtful if these were tombs at all.

Another site rather more likely as a burial was found beneath a low cairn under Racecourse Street (now Republic Street), Victoria, this time including sherds of Baħrija-type pottery. It was poorly recorded and so, unfortunately, not very informative.

It has to be acknowledged then that we are almost totally ignorant of the funerary rites of the later Maltese Bronze Age.

The contrast we have already noticed between the earlier and later Bronze Age settlements has its implications for our understanding of society at the time. In the Tarxien Cemetery phase known settlements are as scarce as burial sites.

The impression we get is that the population had plummeted since the climax of the Temple Period, with correspondingly little pressure on land ownership. Although the copper daggers of the Tarxien Cemetery hint at warfare, they are few in number, and were probably valued more for the prestige they conferred than for their use in combat, since imported copper would have been far too precious to be available to everyone at the time. The few known sites are in no sense defensive.

By the Borġ in-Nadur phase, the ituation is reversed. Weapons are no onger found, but this is more likely lue to a change in burial practice han to their absence from everyday ife. Indeed, in more troubled times, hey may have become too essential o be disposed of in tombs. What s certain is that of the settlements, early all are on naturally-fortified ites, and where the natural defences vere considered inadequate, massive valls were added to protect them rom hostile attack. Such sites would urely not have been chosen without good reason. Day-to-day living vould have been much easier if one ad set up home on level ground, onvenient to one's fields and water upply, rather than on an uncomfortable hilltop.

The very number and size of ites make the same point, hinting t population pressure and resulting nternal competition for available esources, since there is no sign of hreat from overseas. The one site vhere foreign influence is obvious n its pottery, Il-Qliegħa at Baħrija, is ery puzzling, being about as remote rom an 'invasion beach' as it is posible to get in Malta.

No extensive excavation has been arried out on any of these settlenents, most of which in any case now consist of only a scatter of potsherds on a rock surface eroded bare of any deposits. Nor have we discovered any cemetery; so we have no evidence on the make-up of society within any one settlement, or the relationship of settlements to each other. It is probable that each would have needed a leader with military abilities – warfare strongly encourages communities to accept strong leadership – and in other parts of the world, the introduction of what must always have been expensive metal is almost invariably accompanied by the appearance of sharp divisions within society, between an upper level with access to copper or bronze and a more or less subject population whose surplus production is required to pay for it.

he promontory of Wardija ta' San Ġorġ, t the eastern end of Dingli cliffs which urround it on three sides, supported Middle Bronze Age village. This is onfirmed by sherds and silo pits. There re traces of a wall closing in the fourth ide.

But, as with so many other aspects of life in the past, evidence from Malta is still lacking for the details.

CART-RUTS

One of the most intriguing problems, or series of interrelated problems, in Maltese archaeology is that of the cart-ruts. These are paired grooves found widely across Malta and Gozo wherever bare rock is exposed. Outside Malta, similar worn grooves in rock have occasionally been noticed in Sicily, Italy, Provence, and Cyrenaica, usually associated with quarrying and of widely varied dates. There they are assumed to have been produced by wagons heavily laden with stone. None elsewhere form such extensive systems, and they help little in explaining the Maltese ones.

For a start, there is considerable controversy over their date. Some authorities argue that they must go back to the Temple Period, others that they come right down to the Christian era under the Romans. More popular is to attribute them to the Phoenicians.

While only a personal point of view, my preference is for the later Bronze Age, for which the evidence, while far from watertight, seems appreciably stronger than for earlier or later periods. It is for that reason I include them here. They certainly have to be described somewhere.

One of the most significant pairs is this one, approaching the wall of Borġ in-Nadur. The grooves are picked out in pink Sedum flowers.

Two pairs of ruts intersect on bare rock heading for the valley down to Binġemma and Mġarr.

lore ruts at San Ġwann fork
wilderingly out of each other. The
regularity of depth of wear is clearly
pparent.

The facts on dating are few. In several places, ruts are cut by Punic tomb shafts, which can be dated roughly to the later centuries BC. Though these ruts must be ealier than that, it does not necessarily follow that all of them are. At Marsaxlokk and Mellieħa bays, ruts are covered by seawater. A rise of sea level of a mere couple of metres would be enough to explain these – and we simply do not know how far back that took place. Even less well dated are the rock falls which truncate ruts along the western cliffs, at Ras il-Pellegrin and Għar Żerrieq, for example. While their use for transporting building stone to the temples is plausible, no ruts are known leading to any temple site. One pair on Ras il-Pellegrin runs to the site of a Roman villa, but

OREIGN CART-RUTS

There are scattered records of ruts similar to those of Malta elsewhere. The most convincing are shown here. Unlike the Maltese ones, their date and purpose are known. They were worn by wagons carrying building stone from the quarries at the Anse de St Croix to the water's edge. From there it was shipped across the bay to build the walls of the Greek city of Massalia, modern Marseilles in Provence, within a few years of 600 BC. How relevant these are to the Maltese ruts is debatable, and discussed in the text here.

continues blithely beyond, and so is no more convincing than another at San Martin tal-Baħrija which did the same to a modern bar until it was recently covered with tarmac.

Contrary to some interpretations, their varied distribution does not suggest to me deliberate planning, and so some central authority.

The only reasonably secure associations are at Borġ in-Nadur, Qala Hill, and Fawwara, the last two both on the Wardija ridge, where ruts can be seen running out to fortified Bronze Age villages, with slopes too steep for them to continue beyond. Their multiplicity and depth argue for heavy use over a long period. We can show that the Borġ in-Nadur phase lasted for many centuries, with a dense population. Until secure evidence is found pointing in some other direction, I hold to my view

It is clear how the name Clapham Junction came to be applied to this multiplicity of ruts on bare rock south of Buskett.
Note how several pairs cut across others.

that the Bronze Age looks the likel est historical context for them.

The gauge between the ruts i not exactly uniform but varies littl around 1.41 m, or almost exactly feet 7 inches (very close to the late standard railway gauge of 4′ 8″ the depth much more, up to 60 cn Ruts can occur as single pairs but ar often duplicated, sometimes man times over, so much so that the 2 or 30 fanning out over a slope sout of the Buskett Gardens are popu larly known as Clapham Junctio However, where ruts do fork, th two branches can frequently b

hown to be successive rather than ontemporary, one pair being more eeply worn than the other. The esemblance to a railway marshal-ng yard or passing places is, there-ore, misleading.

It is generally accepted that they arried some form of vehicle, the few ases where they tapped rain run-off fill water cisterns being clearly a econdary use, but consensus goes o further. Sledges, slide-cars or avois and wheeled carts are pro-osed heatedly, or dismissed as npossible, and it is true that there re arguments for and against each. ledges would have had difficulty turning some of the sharp corners bserved, or bumping over marked regularities in the rock. Slide-cars re recorded from the American reat Plains, the Philippines, and the ish peatbogs, but nowhere nearer. ince the gauge of individual pairs f ruts has been shown to vary by everal centimetres, there would ave had to be considerable flexibil-y in the attachment of cartwheels they were not to lock in the ruts r be wrenched off, and they would ave to be large to give clearance here ruts are worn deep in the ock. Wheeled vehicles, however, o seem to attract the least serious bjections.

What loads were carried in these vehicles, whatever they were? Stone would produce the heavy wear observed, and it has been noted that ruts are frequently found in localities where there are signs of former quarrying.

But some ruts run for kilometres, uphill and down, and one does not need to travel that far to find stone in Malta. Since both ruts and quarries will be visible only where rock is exposed, it is hardly surprising that they are often found in proximity to each other, though never in direct association. That is not quite true, since there are a few cases where later quarrymen have taken advantage of ruts to make their extraction of stone easier. Here manifestly it was the ruts which

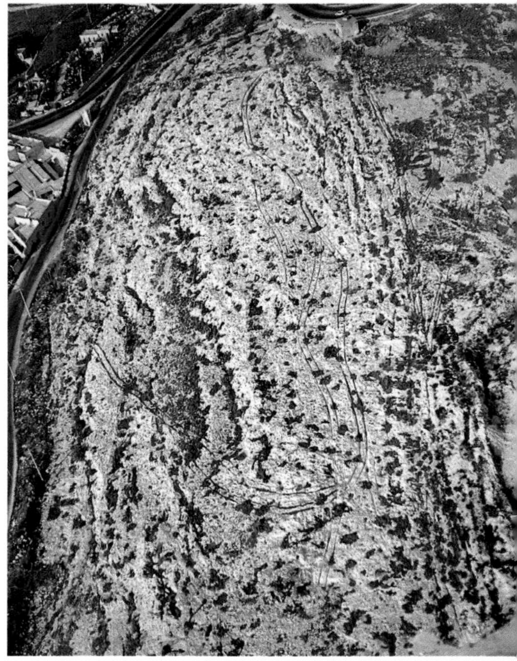

ne pair of ruts hairpins down the scarp San Pawl tat-Tarġa, Naxxar, while hers continue more or less straight to e bottom of the picture. Though less umerous than at Buskett, this group has any interesting features.

came first and the quarrying after, probably long after.

Much of Malta's cultivated soil has been moved around to increase the area of crop production, but again the distribution of ruts does not agree with any sensible pattern in this context. The suggestion that soil was moved from the level tops to build up terraces on the slopes is surely highly unconvincing, since unlike the former, the latter would have needed far more effort in both construction and maintenance.

The ruts at Għar Żerrieq appear to take off into space over the Mtaħleb valley. The crack in the rock to the right serves to explain how this came about.

Water for crop irrigation woul also increase productivity, but it transport in waterskins would nc be easy, and no association of ru with water sources has been demon strated.

The transport of general agricu tural, and marine, produce avoid all these difficulties, but would it b sufficient to cause the depth of wea observed, even allowing many centu ries of activity?

Whereas the ruts can be wor very deep, there is no sign of wea between them, which one woul have expected from whateve animal pulled these vehicles. Eve bare human feet would over tim have polished or smoothed the roc We shall offer a possible explanatio shortly. The problem is exacerbate in cases where both ruts, or eve more remarkably one only, climb

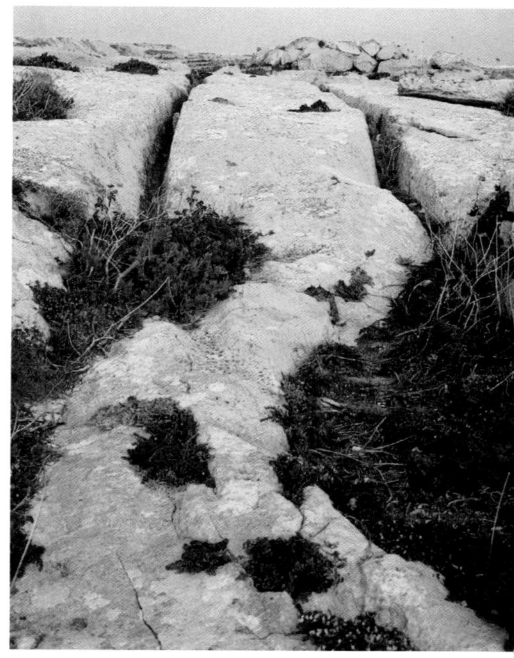

A deeply incised pair above Dwejra, San Lawrenz, Gozo, drops over almost a step, a puzzling feature noticed at several other sites.
Like most Maltese stone, the rock here has taken on a golden glow in evening light.

tep at an angle of as much as 45°. These vehicles cannot always have been travelling downhill.

Ruts, though rarely strictly continuous, can be traced over distances up o 3 km, as at San Martin tal-Baħrija, but almost invariably disappear under ater fields, walls, or roads, over cliffs or under the sea, or simply fade out on bare rock. All these have their significance, the last in particular. This an only be the result of a former soil cover, since stripped off by erosion. This would also explain the bsence of hoof wear between them, nd more obviously the cases where uts lurched in and out of dissolution ollows, which 'drivers' could, and ertainly would, have avoided quite asily had they been aware of them. There are good examples of the latter t San Pawl tat-Tarġa, Naxxar, much he best site to study the ruts. A thin ayer of soil would also have provided brasive grit, greatly speeding up the rocess of wear.

While making the ruts easier to nderstand, this does not help in their ating, since we no more know when ny particular area of soil was lost than we do of when sea level rose or fell.

POTTERY STYLES

TARXIEN CEMETERY

It has already been stressed that there is a complete break between the pottery-making traditions of the Tarxien Temple and Cemetery phases in every respect. It is impossible to believe that the same potters could be responsible for both. The latter ware is generally thicker, coarser, usually with a thick slip of the same clay. The core is always black but the surface is very variable in colour. Vessel shapes have nothing in common with what went before.

A variety of bowls includes round and flat bases, sometimes on pedestals. They occasionally have a slightly oval mouth raised into two

peaks – the so-called 'helmet vase'. All have a single rather lumpy vertical handle on the shoulder and a sharply out-turned lip.

Deeper jars are even more varied, pear-shaped or globular, some with separate short swelling necks. The sharply out-turned lip is again almost universal but handles are more varied: high ones joining lip and shoulder, smaller ones on the latter, sometimes two or three, sometimes one of each type.

A few more unusual forms include Siamese-twin bowls and jars, a jar with multiple spouts and asymmetric, duck-shaped, vases, the askos form.

Two juglets, also from the Cemetery, hav their bodies and handles strangely fused into a double vessel.

While the cross-hatched triangles and multiple chevrons are typical, as on the next two vessels, the stamps on the neck of this one are not.

Decoration is quite commo occurring on about one vessel i five or six in the Cemetery itsel Even the smallest piece is immediately distinguishable fro Temple Period wares. For a star this decoration is now strictl rectilinear, with bands of parall heavily-incised lines, horizontal or forming deep zigzags Resulting triangles are hatche or divided into diagonal plai and hatched chequers.

The hatching may be eithe lighter incised lines or b impressing with a seashell o fossil shark's tooth, producing punctuated effect. Some otherwis undecorated vessels bear singl or paired knobs, and one or tw

nother unusual vessel is this duck-
aped vessel or askos, a form found rarely
Italy, more frequently in the Aegean
ea.

have a V-cordon above, providing 'eyebrows' to two knob 'eyes'.

A rather different ware occurred only as scattered sherds in the Cemetery, but was common at both Skorba and the Xagħra Circle. It comes in the form of an open straight-sided bowl, its lip thickened on the inner side. The bevel thus formed often bears standing or pendant dot-filled or diagonally hatched triangles, and there may also be similarly filled zigzag bands or rows of triangles on the outer wall. There too may be found a single vertical handle. These bowls occur in grey or black only.

The foreign parallels for these, crucial evidence for the origins of these people, were discussed on p.213 above and in the box below.

HERMI' BOWLS

his distinctive form surprisingly widely stributed. The cross-ctions of the rim show e thickened, or internally velled, lip. This can plain or decorated ith triangular motifs, ese dotted or variously atched.

he three on the top w were recovered om deposits at Skorba, arxien and the Xagħra ircle, where they were und rarely in Temple eriod contexts, and much ore commonly in Tarxien emetery deposits. The wer three are from astelluccio, an Early

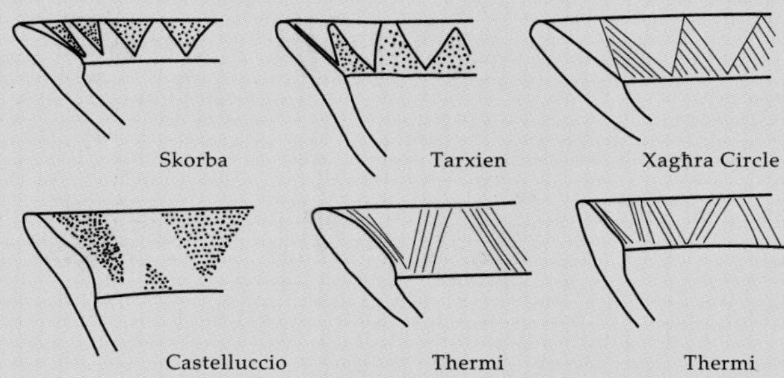

Bronze Age site in Sicily, those at bottom right from Thermi on Lesbos, at the northern end of the Aegean. Identical ones were found in the First and the Second Cities at Troy.

Despite the distances between them, the similarity of form and decoration strongly suggest that all these must somehow be closely related.

A bowl from a silo pit at In-Nuffara (see p.252) has typical Borġ in-Nadur phase red slip. The potter has amused him/herself by adding dots of paint to the unslipped interior.

BORĠ IN-NADUR

The change to the Borġ in-Nadur phase is almost as strongly marked, and would seem to imply further immigration, or at least foreign influence.

The fabric is even thicker and coarser but now nearly always fired in an oxidizing atmosphere to give an orange-buff surface, though the core remains black, a sandwich effect. Most striking, pots are now given a bright red slip. This, and the distinctive core, make it easily recognizable, even among red-slipped sherds from other periods. At Borġ in-Nadur itself, three sub-phases were separated stratigraphically. In the first, the red slip was lightly burnished and slightly shiny. In the second this was no longer done, leaving the surface matt, and the slip often shows a crackle effect. In the third, the firing was less strictly controlled and the colour more variable, often grey, brown or black.

In vessel shapes, the most noticeable difference is that the thickened and everted lips vanish completely. Open bowls are now large, with simple lips, curved walls, and two opposed handles which are simple, vertical, and markedly splayed. Bowls are often set on tall straight pedestals. Simple cups have handles on the rim to which are added

ıll projecting axe-shaped crest, ıe upper corners of which can be rawn out into a T- or Y-shape. ɔme cups have a separate collar. variety of jar forms is known. ʼne strange vessel is a rectangu-ır trough, divided internally by septal wall. This is the one form ʼhich has been noted in Tarxien emetery contexts too.

Four sorts of decoration occur. ommonest and most character-tic are simple bands of three or ɔur closely-spaced heavy lines, ɔllowing a rim or forming chev-ɔns on the wall below. The lines re occasionally interrupted by single cross bar with a dot at ther end. The second also relies n bands and zigzags, now thinly ıcised. These, possibly the thick-r ones too, held a white paste ılay. Thirdly, on the unslipped ıteriors of red-slipped bowls, ıe slip was dribbled over the uff surface or applied in casual ots and lines, a technique particularly employed at In-Nuffara. And fourthly, some coarser vessels, and particularly the handle projections, have applied bars or pellets of clay, occasionally a row of them stuck into an incised line to ensure adherence.

Some Borġ in-Nadur ware was exported to appear in Sicily, in tombs at Thapsos, 11 km north of Syracuse, and on a settlement site about the same distance east of Agrigento. There are also marked similarities of shape in the local pottery in that area which, however, is always grey and usually undecorated. There is certainly a family resemblance here, extending to the Milazzese ware of northern Sicily and Lipari.

fine pedestalled bowl from Borġ in-ıdur is slipped in red, though here ɔroduced in black and white. The rallel lines and chevrons 'stitched' ɡether are characteristic, as are the ʼayed handles.

BAĦRIJA

Since it has been shown to overlap with the latest Borġ in-Nadur at Il-Qliegħa, Baħrija, is better described as a ware or style than a phase. Much of its pottery continues Borġ in-Nadur traditions, now always in grey or, where slipped, black. Dove-tail zigzags become popular. Rather rough-and-ready painted designs appear rarely, red on cream, on external surfaces, and could be derived from the earlier ones inside bowls. Sherds of these are too small to show the vessel shape.

More striking are large shallow cups with rounded or carinated pro file and single high loop handle. is these which closely imitate Calab rian forms. Horizontal corrugation covering the necks of some also loo foreign, but most characteristic o both areas are intricate meande patterns including bands of fals relief zigzags, where two rows o inward-pointing cut-out triangle interlock.

DATING

The opening of the Maltese Bronz Age is reasonably roughly fixed a around 2563-2051 CalBC. The crucia date of 1930 ± 150 BC comes from sample of carbonized horse bean from the Tarxien Cemetery itself.

There can have been little laps of time between their harvesting an their burial, whereas wood charco

The two outer handles, bearing horned pillars, and the axe-shaped central one, all have close parallels in the Apennine Culture of Italy. Their decoration and red slip, however, are typically Maltese.

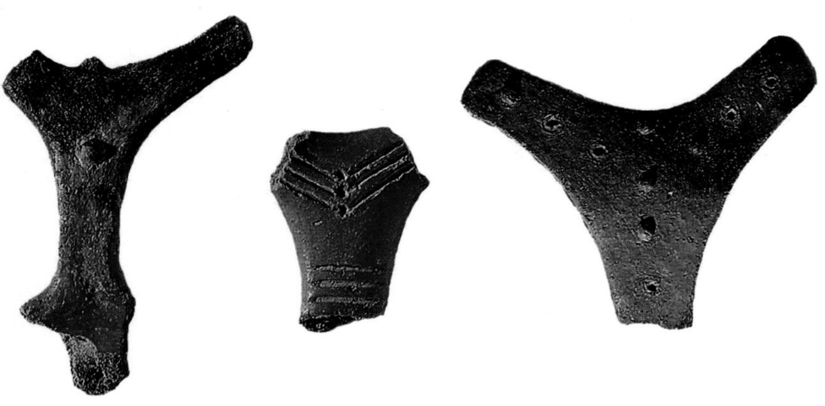

his magnificent hemispheric bowl was und almost intact at Baħrija. It bears ı intricate design of running square eanders which, with its polished ack slip, mark it off from the receding Borġ in-Nadur ware. oth these features, however, re well matched in Calabria the latter's Iron Age, and ust represent some form cultural influence from e Italian mainland at this eriod.

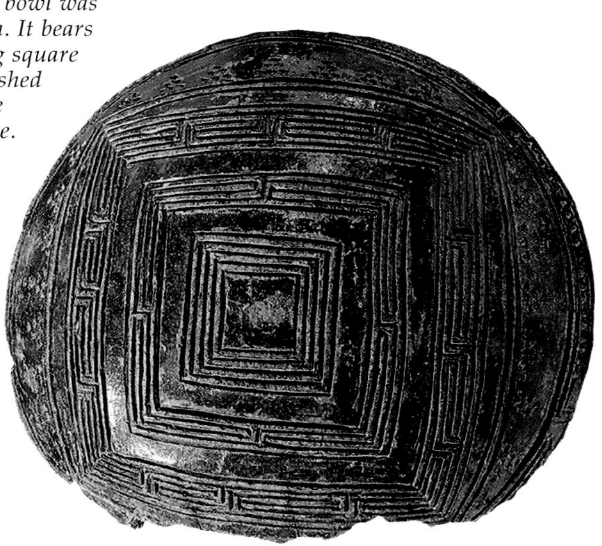

ould easily come from old timer. On the other hand, the large tandard deviation (see the box n radiocarbon p.309) means that his date has to be used with some aution. In particular, we have no irect evidence on the crucial queson, the significance of which is iscussed elsewhere, of whether here was a hiatus between the emple Period and the Bronze Age, nd if so, how long it was.

A few more dates, both radioarbon and archaeological, come rom succeeding centuries. The ransition from Tarxien Cemetery o Borġ in-Nadur is poorly fixed, hough we can say that the latter was well developed in time to be ssociated with Mycenaean IIIB jars t Thapsos. These were imported from southern Greece and can be placed in the thirteenth century thanks to their appearing in historically dated contexts in Pharaonic Egypt.

At Baħrija, the latest Borġ in-Nadur and Baħrija wares appeared to be in use at the same time, and, indeed, there are strong hints that a somewhat debased variety of the former was still current when the Phoenicians began to settle in the islands, probably in the ninth century or later. This will be considered further in the next section. Additionally it can be noted that the close similarities of the 'foreign' ware at Baħrija are with the Fossa Grave Culture of Calabria, which is also dated to the ninth century.

DOLMENS

VARIOUS LOCATIONS

Dolmens are simple chambers consisting of a large flat capstone supported on uprights or built walling. Since they are usually standing on bare eroded rock, archaeological deposits are rarely found within them, and if they were once covered in mounds of earth or stone, they too have long since been swept away. Their original function is assumed to be for burial of the dead, thus relating them to the megalithic tombs of Western Europe.

Several of those found in Malta merit fuller description:

WIED FILEP

Two at Wied Filep standing 1 km north of Mosta beside the road to Għargħur, overlooking Wied il-Għasel, are the most accessibl The larger and better-preserve consists of a slab of rock 3.8 1.6 m propped up on several larg ish blocks at a height of 1.5 m.

WIED ŻNUBER

In the limits of Birżebbuġa, it i sited to the west of the head of th rocky valley of that name, sout of the former airfield of Ħal Fa It is of very similar size.

MISRAĦ SINJURA

Though prominently visible fro the Siġġiewi road 1 km west c Qrendi on a pinnacle left by quar rying, it is for that reason not easil approached. It is further marked b having a small field hut built on to of it. Its capstone is appreciabl

The larger of the two dolmens above Wied Filep, Mosta, has one of the biggest capstones, 3.8 m from end to end.

At the extreme southern end of the islan the Wied Żnuber monument is a typical dolmen.

)olmens are dotted across the two islands, ·ut their present distribution has little ignificance since there were probably more originally, though how many we have no way of knowing.

Aisraħ Sinjura, is heavily disguised y modern walling, now serving as a asement beneath a field hut. It is further solated by quarrying, not apparent in his photograph.

Though one of the smallest, Ta' Ħammut, towards top right in this photo, is the only one to have yielded crucial dating evidence. The water-filled hollow in front may have been covered by another dolmen.

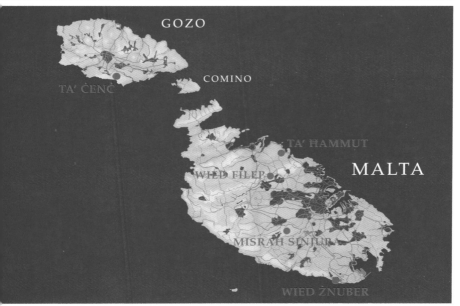

larger, 4.4 x 3.8 m, supported on irregular walling which may, however, be of more recent date. A notable feature is a groove cut round its perimeter, interrupted at one point by a hole piercing the slab.

TA' ĦAMMUT

This is in some ways the most important since its excavation by Evans in 1955 yielded a quantity of sherds of typical Tarxien Cemetery form. It is one of three small ones on the hill slope some 200 m inland from the head of Qalet Marku near Baħar iċ-Ċagħaq.

TA' ĊENĊ

An intriguing group of monuments stands on the lip of the Ta' Ċenċ plateau, a little over a kilometre east of Sannat and 400 m north-east of Ta' Ċenċ Hotel. The first consists of two rows of slabs on edge, which might be the remains of a megalithic gallery grave. Close to its east end is a more typical though small dolmen, 1.75 x 1.1 m with another built into a field wall 600 m further east.

OTHERS

Some nine others are known in eastern Malta, the exact number difficult to be sure of as it is not always clear whether an isolated block of stone was once a dolmen or not, and there may well have been yet more which have been utterly destroyed. With the exception of Ta' Ħammut, referred to above and in the main text, none has produced archaeological finds, so the Tarxien Cemetery date suggested there, though likely, cannot be confirmed for the others.

There is no doubt about this one, on the northern edge of the Ta' Ċenċ plateau, overlooking the fault scarp, Wied Ħanzira, and Xewkija.

One of several probable dolmens at Bidni, west of Marsascala, this is the most convincing one. It lies in fields south of the calvary.

Both the adjacent dolmens at Wied Filep appear in this photograph. It is obvious at a glance that it would have required considerable effort to raise the capstones onto their supports.

On the northern edge of Xagħra, Gozo, this huge block, known as the Ġebla ta' Sansuna, is propped up at a strange angle. Despite a passing resemblance, there is uncertainty as to whether it is really another dolmen.

Cairns at Wied Moqbol, west of Ħal Far, also produced a few sherds of the same phase when excavated by Evans in 1953. They are slight structures, not easily found.

THE CART-RUTS
VARIOUS LOCATIONS

CLAPHAM JUNCTION

This is the popular name for the bewildering complex of cart-ruts which cross a bare rocky ridge 300 m south of Buskett Gardens. They emerge from fields in the valley containing the gardens, fan out to cross the ridge to the south, then disappear beneath fields again. While it is difficult to estimate their exact numbers, there must be at least 30 pairs. In contrast, a single one follows the ridge from east to west, cutting across all the others.

One rut is demonstrably older than the shaft of a Punic tomb which cuts through it. The transverse rut is clipped by a huge rock cavity, Għar il-Kbir, but this could be merely the result of a comparatively recent rock fall. In any case, though we know when occupation of the cave ceased (1835), we have no idea when it started, possibly as early as prehistoric times but possibly not until long after.

NAXXAR, SAN PAWL TAT-TARĠA

The Naxxar-Salina road descends the scarp of Malta's Great Fault, connecting the Naxxar-Għargħur plateau with the lower ground below by means of a hairpin bend on a bare rocky slope. To the west of the road, behind the restored pill-box, a fine set of cart-ruts can be followed doing much the same. At least, one pair doubles back as does the modern road, while a second continues straight to the fields at the foot of the slope,

This is the fork, centre right, in the air photo of Clapham Junction on p.266. If there were ever 'points' to direct vehicles onto the right 'track', they have long since gone.

The multiplicity of ruts at Clapham Junction is here obvious on the ground, though only from the air, as on p.266, can their full extent be appreciated. Why should so many have been needed? The mind boggles.

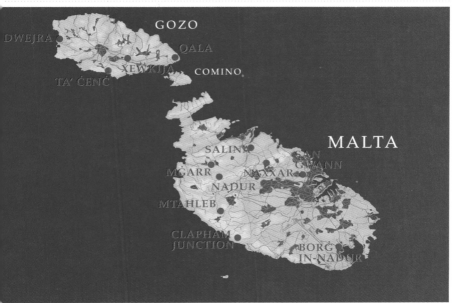

uts are widely distributed across both lands. Only the more important groups re marked here or there would not be space on this map to name them all. Probably many more await discovery and recording.

any pairs criss-cross the Binġemma idge (see also p.264), like this pair near e Nadur Tower.

A fine example of a fork is in the San Pawl tat-Tarġa group, shown from the air on p.267. Readers may like to try to identify which particular junction this is. The patches of vegetation give the best clue.

where it swings northeast to follow the edge of the Burmarrad plain towards the head of Salina Bay.

Within the group can be found good examples of most of the puzzling phenomena associated with the ruts – a sharp bend; ruts up to 60 cm deep; others lurching in and out of dissolution hollows or over harder ridges of rock; and even one used to tap rainwater run-off into a cistern. While less numerous than the Clapham Junction group, these at San Pawl tat-Tarġa are a particularly fascinating set to study on the ground.

OTHERS

Whereas Clapham Junction and San Pawl tat-Tarġa are undoubtedly the most significant groups, a number of others are mentioned in the main text or illustrated here. Besides these, many more occu throughout Malta, and they shoul be looked for on country walk over any rock exposure.

For example, there are goo sets beside the road along Dingl Cliffs, both near the Wardija ta San Ġorġ and just east of Madl iena chapel. A pair appears to tak off into space south of the ridg beside the Żebbiegħ-Pwales roa at San Martin, with several mor crossing Bajda Ridge on the nort side of Pwales.

On Gozo there are fewer, th groups above Ta' Ċenċ cliffs; a Xewkija close to the Heliport some pairs at Qala point; and hairpinning pair down the slop towards the Azure Window, a Dwejra, being the most interest ing.

A small area of rock surface at San Ġwann has been preserved from housing development in order to protect these two pairs of ruts, the one forking out of the other.

A close-up photograph of the same group shows how complex they can be in detail.

'his very clear pair runs along the scarp f Xemxija Hill, with Mistra valley below. It has recently been cleared of vegetation, soil, and stones.

. pair of ruts on the foreshore of St ;eorge's Bay, Birżebbuġa, below the ronze Age site of Borġ in-Nadur, now uns into the sea. The silo pits of p.291 re a few metres off to the right.

The deeper parts of some of the ruts at Ta' Ċenċ hold water after a recent shower of rain. This can cause slow dissolution of the rock round the lips of the puddles, but not linear erosion.

The two main alternatives for what ground out the cart-ruts appear in this artist's reconstruction. Both show ox-drawn vehicles carrying agricultural produce, though other loads are of course possible. On the left, a cart with large solid disc wheels trundles along. On the right a slide car or travois skids in the ruts. The stone runners are purely speculative, but would make the wear easier to understand.

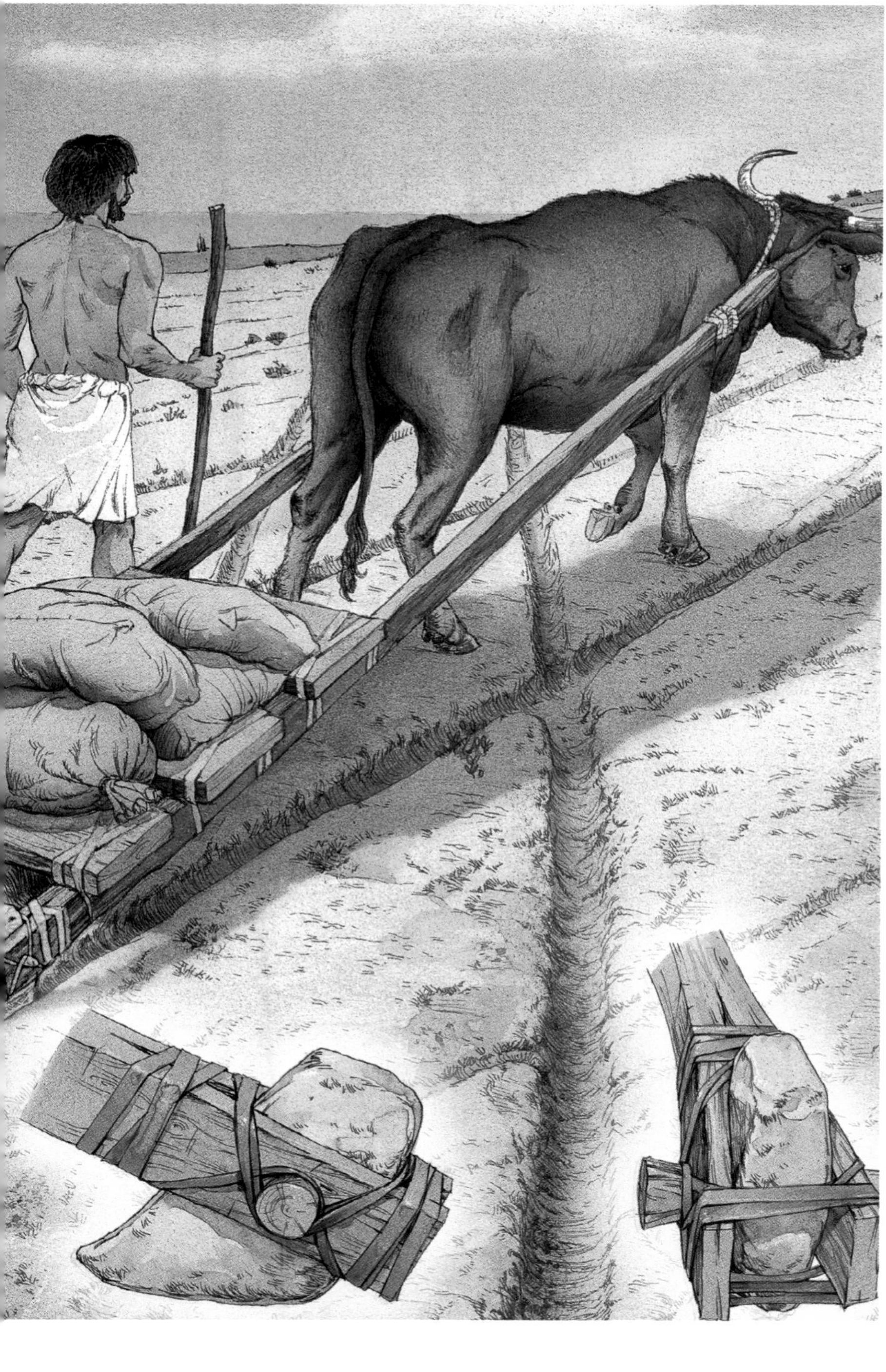

TARXIEN CEMETERY

TARXIEN

The Bronze Age cremation cemetery occupied nearly all of the centre of the southern temple at Tarxien, with parts of the adjacent apses and central niche.

The Temple Period deposit on the floor was covered by 50 cm of sterile silt, on top of which were laid the cremations and associated pottery, later to be covered by further soil, rubble, and ploughsoil. None of this is visible today, having been dug away by Zammit in 1915-16.

The silt layer was taken to imply a long period of abandonment, but this should not be pressed too far since Malta's short, heavy rainstorms are capable of shifting large quantities of soil quite rapidly.

The burials themselves consisted of cremated bone placed in jars and accompanied by subsidiary vessels, personal ornaments like faience beads and fish vertebrae, striking figurines, and a number of flat axes and daggers of copper or bronze. A feature which might belong to this phase is visible only when sunlight falls at the right angle quite early in the morning. On smooth standing blocks on the right of the entrance to the first apse left, one can just make out scratched figures interpreted as rough drawings of boats (see p.214). The dating, however, is quite uncertain.

A fascinating photograph of Temi Zammit's shows three of his workmen clearing the entrance of Tarxien South in 1916. The cemetery layer had already been removed, but would have extended across the central courtyard to the right of the picture.
The battered giant statue of the goddess at left centre is barely recognizable from this angle.

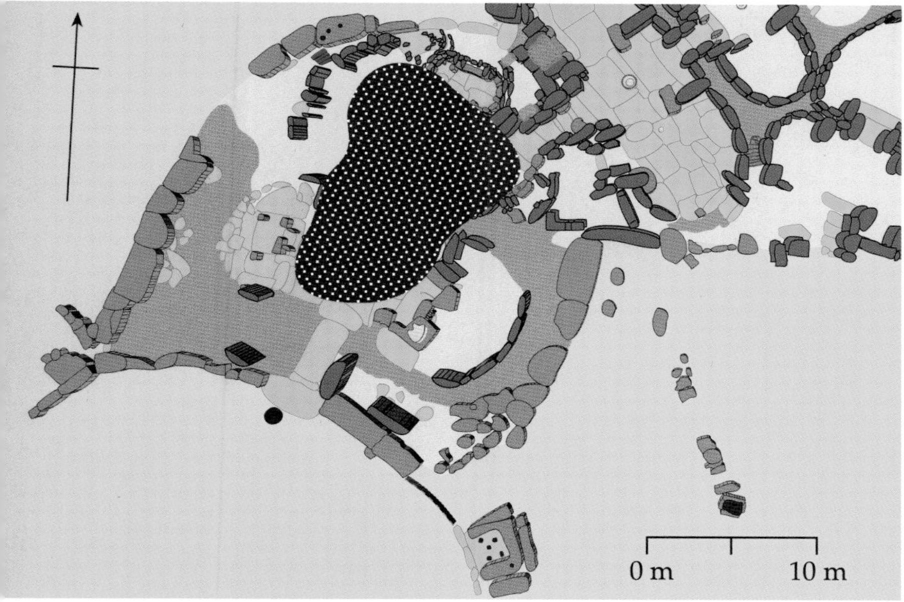

The Tarxien Temples were already in ruins and covered in a layer of silt before the site was adopted for a cemetery by the Bronze Age immigrants. The grey patch marks the extent of their burials.

Under later disturbed deposits (see the schematic section on p.308) the cemetery was represented by a dense scatter of pots, some intact but many broken. Larger vessels still contained cremated human bone. Associated were copper tools and many personal ornaments. Three large spindle whorls can be seen right of centre. Much ash was present, so cremation may have taken place on the spot, but most of the ornaments were added to the interments unburnt afterwards.

BORĠ IN-NADUR
BIRŻEBBUĠA

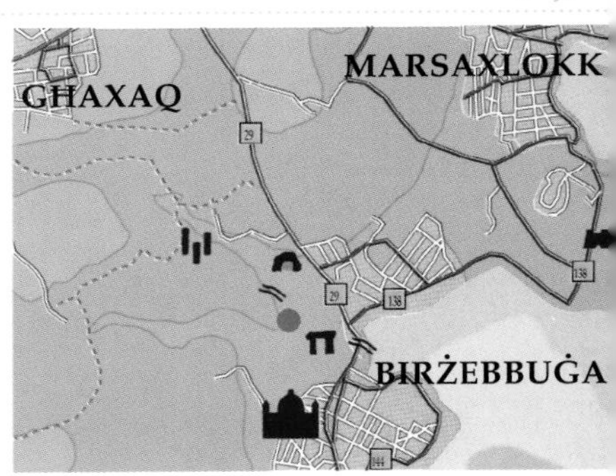

The site is situated in open fields. Drive toward Birżebbuġa along Triq iż-Żejtun until you arrive a St George's Bay. Turn to the right (next to the Bu Stop) up Triq A.M. Galea and then right into Sqa in-Nadur. Then walk along the path at the edge o the field, along the east side of the site. The bes viewpoint is from the top of the mound of earth i front of the megalithic wall.

This important site on the western outskirts of Birżebbuġa, above the head of St George's Bay, has three areas of interest. The Tarxien Period temple site near the tip of the promontory has already been dealt with.

Then, in the Bronze Age, the whole tip of the rocky spur supported a flourishing village, as demonstrated by numerous sherds scattered over the whole area. The most spectacular feature is a massive wall, still standing as much as 4.5 m high and originally barring access along the ridge to the northwest. At its centre is a D-shaped bastion, the outer face of which is original though the cross wall at the back is mostly modern reconstruction. The mound outside the wall is misleading, being simply the spoil A.A. Caruana's diggers pulled back in 1880.

The original entrance, now obscured by loose rubble, was probably beside this on the north

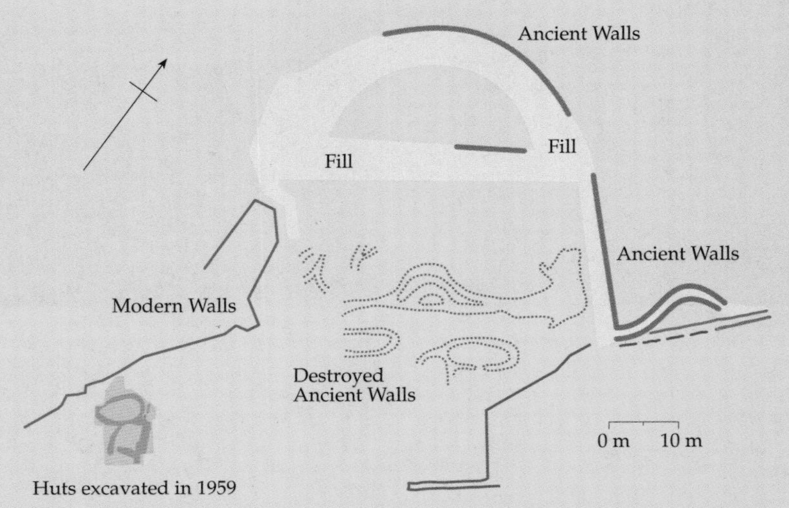

ince the wall beyond can be seen o curve back. On the further side f the field wall beyond the modern ath and oil pipeline, a pair of ruts an be seen heading towards this oint, see p.264.

In the field behind the bastion, uts were exposed in excavations in 880 and 1959 but the trenches were efilled. A little Tarxien Cemetery naterial was found here too. There nust be many more huts beneath he present-day fields. While umerous sherds of this date were ecovered from the temple site, it s not clear whether those earlier emains were in any way reoccu-ied, or simply used as a rubbish umping area.

In 1999 a further stretch of efensive wall was discovered o the southeast, protecting the entler slope up the tip of the romontory.

Thirdly, on the rocky foreshore below, where the road swings round the point, another pair of ruts and a large number of bell-shaped cavities are cut into the rock. A rise in sea level means that several are now flooded, some are plugged for safety reasons, some partly cut away by quarrying, and some reddened by fire. All these activities are quite recent, and the original date and function of the complex is still a matter of controversy, as discussed in the box on silos/cisterns. Visitors must make their own choice between grain or water storage, or cloth-dyeing vats. Though by no means proven, my preference is for the first, probably in connection with overseas trade using the bay as a harbour, which would explain their position beside the sea rather than within the defences.

he D-shaped bastion is here seen om the west, with the defensive wall unning from top left to mid-right. he village lay under the fields in the top ght corner of the photo.

The impresive bastion wall still stands to 4.5 m. All larger blocks are original, but the smaller rubble is modern restoration. The blue waters of Marsaxlokk Bay can be seen in the distance.

IL-QLIEGĦA TAL-BAĦRIJA

BAĦRIJA

This is surely the most dramatic site on the islands. It is an almost entirely cliff-girt plateau of Upper Coralline Limestone at the northern end of Malta's western cliffs, 1 km across the valley from the road-head at San Martin tal-Baħrija.

The views to the north over further headlands and bays, with Gozo in the distance, are superb. Unlike other plateaux, however, it dips steeply to the east, towards Wied il-Baħrija, one of Malta's very few permanent streams. The only easy access is by a neck of rock to the south, which may once have had a length of defensive wall spanning it. The ridge continues with two more Upper Coralline caps, of which the second was also large enough to support a Bronze Age settlement.

Il-Qliegħa is freely sprinkle with sherds of the second an third Bronze Age phases, th last named after this site. Ther are other features too. Two ston mortars for pounding grain ca be seen built into field walls, an there are said to be about 40 rock cut bell-shaped cavities, a numbe of which are still open. Most o these now serve as water cistern though, as discussed on the oppo site page; grain storage is also distinct possibility.

Ashby and Peet dug here fo three days in 1911, and the Muse um Department for a fortnight i 1959. While rich cultural deposit were found in the deeper level behind the terraces, neither di discovered actual huts.

This is the most extensive of the Bronze Age village sites, sherds of the Borġ in-Nadur and Baħrija phases being found over its entire surface. Gozo appears on the distant skyline.

There are two options to get to the site. Either driv through Baħrija through Triq Ġnien tan-Noqra an down into the Baħrija valley where you have t park the car and walk across the valley. Or driv along the cliffs of Rdum tas-Sarġ on road 126 fro Imtaħleb, until the road becomes quite rough. Par the car and do the last part on foot.

;ILOS AND CISTERNS

/ARIOUS LOCATIONS

)n many Borġ in-Nadur sites, bell-haped cavities up to 4 m deep are ound cut in the rock. Some have rebate to hold a lid. Many are till used by farmers cultivating he fields around for the storage)f water. Other pits, however, are in uch fissured rock that they could ıever have held water unless thick-y coated with plaster or clay, of vhich there is no sign. These then nay have served to hold grain, for :onsumption or for sowing the next eason. Over 40 occur at Baħrija. The settlement to which a group ıt Tal-Mejtin (Luqa) belonged has ıot been found, but most lie within :nown Bronze Age villages.

A remarkable exception is he group on the foreshore at St George's Bay, Birżebbuġa, below the Bronze Age site of Borġ in-Nadur. These are now mostly flooded with seawater, but that is surely due only to a rise in sea level, which has also submerged a cart-rut nearby. Could these be for an import/export trade in grain? A case has been made recently for their being dyeing vats, but that can hardly be so on dry hilltops like In-Nuffara, Xagħra, or Baħrija. Water or grain storage, though of course not both at the same time, seem much more likely for all of them.

)ark openings of silos lie along the rocky oreshore below Borġ in-Nadur and :re lapped by the waters of Marsaxlokk 3ay. Some are indeed flooded and others eddened by recent fires. These were urely for grain.

One silo pit has been cut in half by later quarrying, showing clearly its typical bell-shaped section.

OTHER TOPICS

COPPER

Through most of prehistory the principal tools were made of stone, particularly flint or other fine-grained stone like jasper, obsidian, and chert which could be similarly flaked. Later it was discovered that metal could be extracted from rocks, with certain advantages. The earliest was copper, less hard than stone, but unlike that it could be resharpened, or recycled by melting down and recasting, without wastage. Bronze, an alloy of copper with other metals, most commonly tin, was harder, melted at a lower temperature, and could be cast without flaws more readily.

The main disadvantage was that metals are much less widely distributed than stone. Malta, for example, had none, so would be dependant on supplies fro abroad, the nearest sources bein Sardinia, Etruria, and Cyprus. It scarcity must have given it hig prestige value. It is noticeable i the Tarxien Cemetery as elsewhe that weapons figure prominentl amongst the early products o metal. The flat daggers and axe found there are of very simpl forms, too simple to be identifie as to their source. However, chemi cal and physical analyses are no available to trace where a give metal sample came from, even i they have not yet been applied t the Maltese finds.

MYCENAEANS

One sherd from Borġ in-Nadur wa recognized by Evans as belongin to a drinking cup with an octopu painted on it in red. It is totall unlike anything being produce

The copper axes accompanying the Tarxien Cemetery burials were the first metal to be imported to Malta, though in 2500BC at a comparatively late date. Their forms are of the simplest, all but the flanged axe being cast in open moulds.

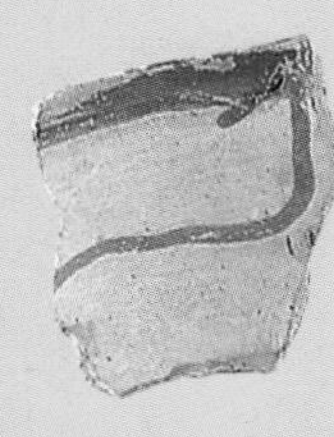

This small painted sherd, less than 4 cm across, is from a wheel-made Mycenaean 'octopus' cup. It is quite unlike any Maltese pottery, and highly significant for overseas contacts, by way of trade or otherwise. It was found at Bor in-Nadur.

on Malta but can be matched closely in Mycenaean Greece in its IIIB phase, dating to the thirteenth century BC. Tombs at Thapsos on the Sicilian coast yielded complete pots of both Borġ in-Nadur and Mycenaean type, as well as local Sicilian products.

They suggest that Mycenaean sea-faring traders, in the course of their voyages to Apulia, Etruria, Sardinia, and even southern Spain, primarily in search of metal supplies, were in contact with the Maltese. There was probably little to interest them in Malta itself, but that one sherd shows that Malta was not completely cut off from the outside world.

FAIENCE

This is an artificial substance related to glass, produced by heating a sand/clay mixture to a temperature where its surface begins to fuse. It was popular in Greece, Egypt, and elsewhere in the Near East to make beads, scarab seals, figurines, etc. Frequently copper compounds were added to give it a bright blue colour, in imitation of the semi-precious stone lapis lazuli. Several hundred disc beads found inside the Tarxien Cemetery funerary urns were of this material. It is most unlikely that the Maltese could have discovered it for themselves. The fact that one of the beads was of the so-called segmented form, resembling several globular beads run in together, as found also in the Near East and, even more remarkably, in Britain, strengthens the argument that the beads themselves, or at least the know-how for making them, were introduced to Malta from the east.

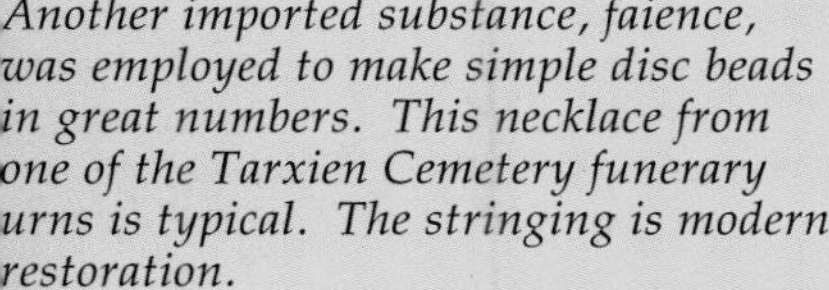

Another imported substance, faience, was employed to make simple disc beads in great numbers. This necklace from one of the Tarxien Cemetery funerary urns is typical. The stringing is modern restoration.

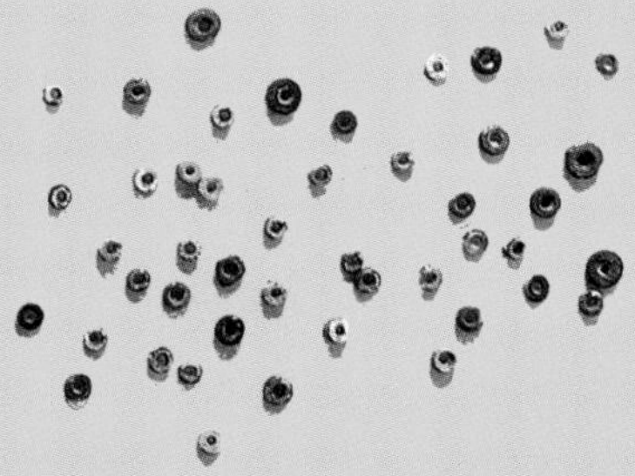

It is inconceivable that faience could have been independently invented in Malta. It was being produced widely in the Eastern Mediterranean at the time, and the beads were probably imported, or if made locally, using imported skills.

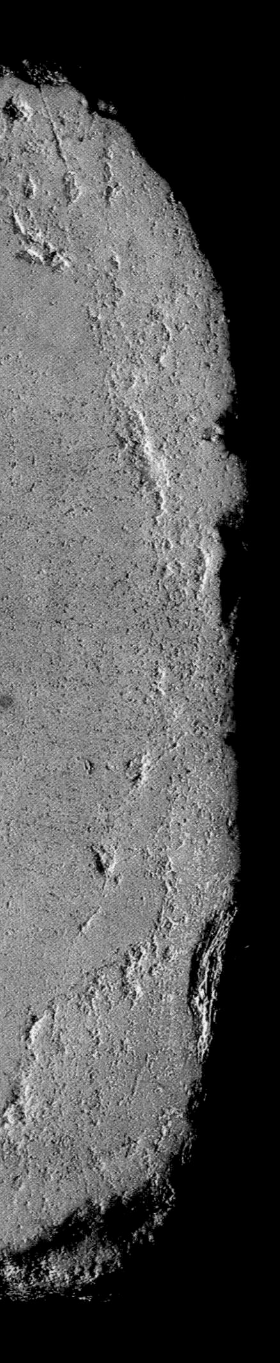

With the coming of the Phoenicians, Malta for the first time joins the mainstream of Mediterranean history. While archaeology still has much to tell us of local activities, the major outlines of its story now come from written sources outside the islands.

CHAPTER 6

THE END OF PREHISTORY

Writing, allowing the compilation and preservation of historical records, appeared first in Mesopotamia around 3500 BC, and was employed in Egypt by 3000. It is found again in Crete around 1700 and in Greece soon after, though it progressed no further west until much later. It was the peoples of the Levant who devised a script based on the alphabet, much simpler and more versatile than the complex and vastly more difficult earlier ones. When the Phoenicians began their ventures round, and across the middle of, the Mediterranean around 1000 BC, they carried the technique with them as an invaluable aid to their trading enterprises. They made little use of it, however, for writing history, which hardly affected Malta before the arrival of the Romans in 218 BC. Effectively, then, prehistory continues down to that date or later, but Professor Anthony Bonanno is far

This beautifully inscribed text was found in Gozo. It is a commemorative stele of the second century BC, and so, soon after the Roman conquest.

more competent than I to tell that part of the story. However, we can show that the native inhabitants of the islands neither simply vanished nor abandoned their local culture immediately the Phoenicians first appeared, in favour of that new and more advanced one.

The end of the Bronze Age was less dramatic than its beginning. The first Phoenician sailors would have explored the coasts and rapidly recognized the strategic value of Grand Harbour, and, probably, Marsaxlokk also. They would soon have established bases at both, and cultivated the goodwill of those already in occupation, probably with their equivalent of glass beads, gin bottles, and umbrellas.

A rut, diagonally from the left, cuts across a tomb shaft near Clapham Junction.

They would have had little interest in the hinterland: the Phoenicians were not normally colonisers. If they could secure peaceful control, and the profits of trade, they were content.

The Phoenicians' discovery of Malta's harbours coincided with the Greeks taking over the eastern Sicilian coast, thereby forcing the Phoenicians to risk a detour farther away from the sheltered southern coast. Their cultural influence, though, would surely have spread rapidly through the islands, strengthening all the while, but whether the earliest known Phoenician tombs were of Maltese who had adopted the new ideas of Phoenicians who had settled in the island, perhaps taking local wives, is not clear. Once more, future DNA studies may be able to tell us. Either way, in a quite short space of time, Phoenician culture prevailed utterly.

The rock-cut tomb, presumably a reintroduction in the absence of examples from the local Bronze Age, became standard, and wheel-made pottery, with its antecedents in the Levant, took over completely as the potters turned their domestic craft into an industry. Architecture too, as exemplified above all by the temple of Astarte at Tas-Silġ, owed far more to the Near East than to earlier Malta. The Neolithic temple incorporated into the last is unlikely to have retained any flavour of sanctity after 1,500 years of abandonment.

However, despite the oriental veneer, the population of the island probably continued with very little change. There are hints of overlap in the archaeological record, though none is unambiguous. A

silo pit at Mtarfa dug in 1939 contained poor late Borġ in-Nadur pottery, but also a typical Phoenician two-spouted lamp, apparently securely associated since it was found right at the bottom. This looks like native activity after the arrival of the first foreign influences. Puzzlingly, a second silo nearby had only Phoenician contents – a slightly later date by which time the cultural takeover was complete? Or merely a later emptying for reuse? More significantly, a number of early Phoenician tombs in the island include coarser hand-made jars beside the more typical wheel-made vessels. These appear to be a surviving native tradition, though it did not continue for very long. It has even been suggested that the red slip employed at this period derived from Borġ in-Nadur rather than from Lebanon or Palestine.

There is considerable debate as to when the Phoenician period began in the islands, with arguments swaying between the tenth century BC and the seventh. I lay no claims to be an expert in this period, so must leave it to those who are. With the evidence on the latest phase of prehistory so scanty, that gives us no help. Indeed, this may in some sense be a meaningless question if, as we have suggested, there was a good deal of overlap, as is supported by new evidence from deposits beneath the medieval and modern Mdina now coming to light. The first Phoenician visitor probably landed in the islands long before a permanent trading settlement was established beside the Grand Harbour, and several centuries before the last native gave up making recognizable Borġ in-Nadur or Baħrija pottery back in the hinterland. More detailed study of the changeover is obviously required, but already there is enough to suggest that the meeting of natives and orientals was peaceful and, though there was overlap, the culture of the latter soon prevailed.

From now on, Malta, even if geographically central in the Mediterranean, culturally occupied an outlying position in a much wider world. Its highly individual contribution, peaking so dramatically back in the Temple Period, then declining through the Bronze Age, was finally over.

A ceramic coffin, found in the 18th century in a tomb at Għar Barka, Rabat, shows the strong influence of Egypt on Phoenician culture. It is clearly based on an Egyptian mummy-case.

Our interest in prehistory is based on curiosity. Scholars wish to find out more about our ancestors and their way of life. The general public shares that interest, and has the right to have the results made available in an understandable form.

CHAPTER 7

MALTA'S PREHISTORY PAST, PRESENT, AND FUTURE

Prehistory, of course, belongs way back in the distant past, but attitudes to it are very much of the present, and as the present is constantly moving through time, so those attitudes can and do change.

We saw in the first chapter how traditional folklore was replaced by antiquarianism in the seventeenth and eighteenth centuries, lasting well into the nineteenth. By 1900 that was turning into true archaeology, antiquities now regarded not as objects of wonder but as sources of historical information, exemplified by the researches of people like Thomas Ashby.

Sir Temi Zammit, with his scientific mind, adopted this readily, and added a new factor, the realization that exposing the sites by excavation rendered them liable to attack from the elements. His decision to protect the reliefs in

A team of excavators work on the funerary deposits within the Xagħra Circle. Trowels, paintbrushes, sieves, hand shovels, and buckets are all in use here to extract the evidence and remove the spoil. Pens, rulers, and notebooks stand ready to record the findings.

the Tarxien Temples by facing them with thin slabs of stone deserves high praise for its forethought. Yet he was well aware of what this was denying visitors, as shown by his decision to use stone for the facing, and even more importantly to have it carved into replicas of the decoration it masked, where cement casts would have been much simpler and cheaper. His writing of *Prehistoric Malta, the Tarxien Temples* showed equal sensitivity, by making the new discoveries available to the general public in a popular work they could well understand, rather than in obscure articles in learned journals. Both are needed of course, and John Evans also provided both in the 1950s, a tradition I have mysel tried to maintain.

There are indeed three group of people with at least a potentia interest, deserving of every encouragement, in Maltese prehistory and its antiquities. I use that rathe old-fashioned word as it covers adequately both the monuments and the smaller finds.

The first group are the scholars who wish to understand bette the people and events of the pas and the processes by which they were shaped. By recovering further remains, carrying out eve more varied and detailed analyses and by devising and testing nev

Here the first apse left of Tarxien South is as Zammit found it. Only the row of conical stone objects on the altar to the right have been re-arranged.

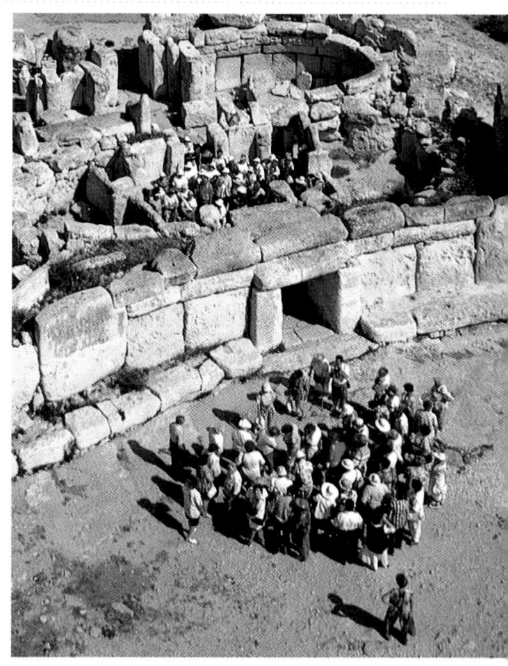

Groups of visitors, from many parts of the world as well as from Malta itself, have the wonders of Ħaġar Qim explained to them.
The Maltese temples fully merit their being included on the list of World Heritage Sites.
But visitor numbers themselves pose a threat to their survivial, and this must be carefully monitored, and remedial action taken where necessary.

hypotheses and interpretations, as well as re-examining old ones, it is confidently hoped that we will appreciate better the achievements, failures as well as successes, of our distant forebears.

That brings us to the second group, the present-day Maltese. While it seems probable, though by no means certain, that because of that break in the sequence between the cultures of the temples and the cemetery at Tarxien, they are not the direct descendants of the temple-builders, yet they can certainly recognize them as forebears. They have every justification for pride in those early achievements.

The English are no more closely-related to the builders of Stonehenge, or the French to the painters of the Upper Palaeolithic caves, and both rightly show a similar respect. The practice of welcoming school parties to the museums and monuments, and the popularization of those scholarly researches, are excellent ways of encouraging this.

The third group are the foreign visitors. Just as Stonehenge and Lascaux are felt to be part of the common heritage of mankind, so are the Maltese temples, as has been recognized by their also being given World Heritage Site status, a point we shall return to. Malta should certainly stress in its tourist literature its outstanding historical monuments, not only the temples but also the military and religious architecture of the Order of St John, rather than its sandy beaches.

As well as an honourable role as guardians of World Heritage Sites, there is of course practical pecuniary advantage in a flourishing tourist industry. But with those three groups, each more than the one before, there is a flip side. Over and above the natural forces of decay, the higher the number of visitors, the greater the wear and tear on the monuments themselves.

The responsible authorities have to bear in mind the needs and wishes of those groups not only today but also off into the future. World Heritage status, although encouraging financial support from international sources, involves heavy responsibilities too. Malta, with its disproportionate number of sites for its small size and wealth carries a greater burden than perhaps any other country. Even Easter Island, with its colossal heads, though much smaller and poorer, is politically part of Chile, with the resources of the whole of that country behind it. There is a serious conflict of interest here, for which there is no perfect compromise solution.

On the one hand, the benefits of access to the sites should be made available to the greatest number of people possible, in each and all of those three categories. On the other, the future of the monuments themselves must be safeguarded, since they are quite irreplaceable. Various methods have been applied, like higher entrance fees (except to school parties), by fencing round, restriction of access to parts of sites, by adding modern flooring, and by concrete capping of the Tarxien uprights amongst others, all of which to some extent detract from the appeal of the sites.

The Hypogeum of Ħal Saflieni is an extreme example, it being particularly vulnerable to excessive visitors, if immune from wind and rain. Here there has to be even more severe limitation on both numbers and duration of visit. At least visitors are not yet restricted to a modern replica, as has been found necessary at the cave of Lascaux, or worse still, to a computer simulation. In the long term, the alternative of open access, with the slow but inevitable damage this would cause, first to the paintings but then to the stone floors and surfaces, is unthinkable. The monuments and small finds that have come down to us, recovered by the unremitting efforts of successive researchers and now in the assiduous care of the Heritage Malta and the Superintendence of Cultural Heritage, fill us with wonder, admiration, and curiosity in equal measure.

Long may they do so.

The contrast could hardly be more stark between the ultra-modern display area within the refurbished Hypogeum of Ħal Saflieni, and the five-thousand-year-old chambers in the rock beneath. It illustrates admirably the often contradictory requirements of conservation and accessibility, both physical and intellectual.

THEMISTOCLES ZAMMIT

Sir Themistocles (Temi) Zammit, had at least three distinguished careers. As an administrator, he played a major role as rector of the University of Malta. As a medical man, he contributed significantly to the study, and conquest, of brucellosis, the dreaded undulant or Malta fever.

As an archaeologist, he far outshone his predecessors. He was appointed director of the Valletta Museum, as it was then known, in 1904. He salvaged what he could from the Hypogeum of Ħal Saflieni in 1910 and, largely self-taught, produced brilliant results from his excavation of Tarxien (1915-19).

It was this which not only brought Maltese prehistory fully to the attention of scholars world-wide (he published his results in *Prehistoric Malta, The Tarxien Temples*, 1930) but set the islands' archaeology on a firm basis. As noted elsewhere, his estimates of date, 3000 BC for the temples, 2000 BC for the Bronze Age, 1000 BC for the Phoenicians, which he would have been the first to admit were little more than guesses, are much closer to those now accepted than those of most of his successors.

Amongst his later excavations, of many Punic and Roman tombs for example, the most important was at Ta' Ħaġrat, Mġarr. His interpretations have not all stood the test of time, but few archaeologists' do.

For example, Zammit believed that the broad cut-out bands on pottery recovered from Mġarr

After his excavation, Zammit had the wall at the back of this apse rebuilt, and replaced the relief decorated blocks with replicas. This was a far-sighted move to protect the recently exposed blocks from weathering.

The back of the giant statue, with the adjacent altar and niche, as found by Zammit in 1915. A small heap of sherds still lies on the block to the right.

represented a late and degenerate phase of the temple culture, whereas Evans demonstrated that in fact they came from a settlement which pre-dated the temple.

On his death in 1935, laden with well-deserved academic honours as well as a knighthood, his son Capt. C. G. Zammit was already curator of archaeology at the Museum, and later its director.

Sir Themistocles Zammit.

A general view of the 1915-17 excavations at Tarxien. Contrast this with the view on p.127, both for the tidying up of the temples themselves, and for the building up of the neighbourhood.

A cache of jars (compare p.228) as found at Tarxien, nestling at the foot of the temple walls. An enormous amount of pottery and other material was recovered from the site.

JEAN HOUEL

Jean Houel, engraver to Louis XVI, king of France, visited Malta in the late eighteenth-century.

In 1787 he published his *Voyages pittoresque des isles de Sicile, de Malte et de Lipari*, volume IV of which contains descriptions and engravings of Maltese and Gozitan sites. While earlier travellers mention the monuments, his are the best accounts down to his date, and the first detailed illustrations. As such, they are invaluable for showing us the state they were in before the commencement of excavation or modern destruction – the terms unfortunately often mean the same thing.

CHARLES BROCHTORFF

An artist of German extraction, Charles Brochtorff or Brockdorff, settled in Malta in the 1820s and produced a number of charming sketches and watercolours, now in the National Library of Malta, of archaeological sites in Gozo. As well as being invaluable for showing the state of preservation of Ġgantija soon after its clearance, they are the only record we have of Otto Bayer's excavations in the Xagħra Circle, which is often in consequence, if rather misleadingly, referred to as the Brochtorff Circle. They were refilled soon after and lost for the next 140 years until re-identified by Joseph Attard Tabone and re-excavated in 1986-94. Brochtorff's descendants maintain the family name in the island down to the present.

Ħagar Qim appears here in one of Houel's engravings, before any excavation had been carried out. While the local figures and cloud effects are artistic additions, the details of the structure make it also a useful historical document.

The charming watercolours of Gozitan monuments, Ġgantija here and on p.6, show us what they were like at the time of Brochtorff's visit around 1825. The contemporary scale figures add a welcome touch of human interest and colour.

THE FUTURE

Having looked at past developments in Maltese prehistory in the Prologue, and again in the last three pages, we might attempt to look ahead into the future.

It is of course impossible to predict chance discoveries, though doubtless there will be many. The continuing analysis of the Xagħra Circle finds could well throw up points of interest, and the imminent publication of the site is eagerly awaited. It is also coming to be felt that a reconsideration of the Bronze Age is overdue.

A new analytical technique with enormous promise is DNA studies.These have already been applied, for example, to tracing the impact of Viking settlement around northern Britain back in the 9th to 11th centuries. A similar study of the Maltese could hardly fail to produce results.

More difficult, but more directly relevant to our problems in prehistory, would be the recovery of DNA, however fragmentary, from ancient bones. This has at least on occasion been done successfully elsewhere. Here it might be a scientific way of resolving the controversy over the break between the population of the Temple and Cemetery phases at Tarxien.

It seems highly likely that in the near future, DNA could have as big an impact on our interpretations of prehistory, in Malta as elsewhere, as ^{14}C did 50 years ago.

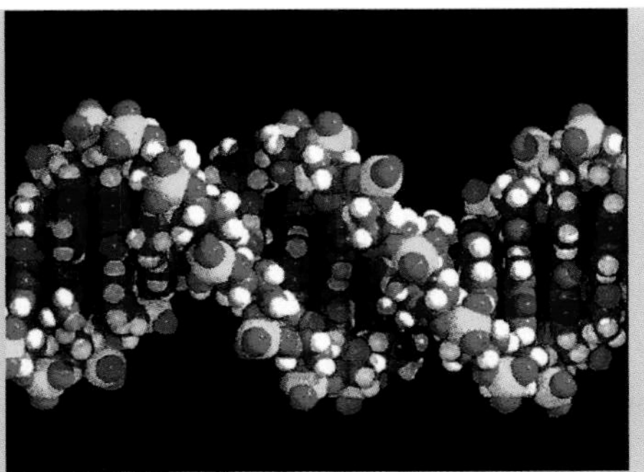

The double helix of DNA is the means by which genetic information is passed from generation to generation. Some identifiable groups of genes are characteristic of particular human populations, which could throw invaluable light on the relationships of the early Maltese.

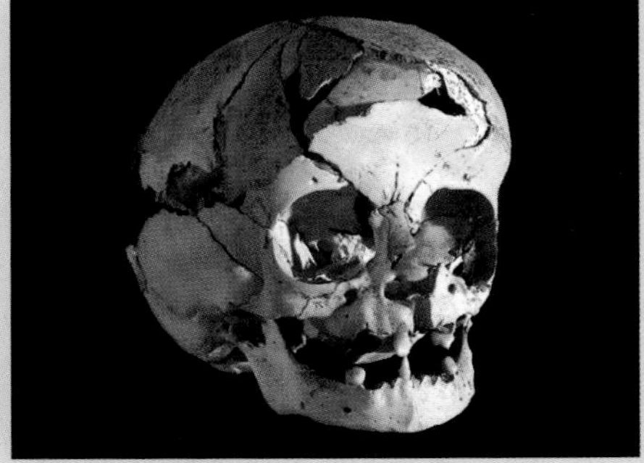

DNA can be preserved in the traces of collagen surviving in ancient bones (as this baby skull from Għar Mirdum). Even if only in a fragmentary state, useful results can be obtained, but it requires very careful treatment to avoid contamination from modern sources.

RELATIVE DATING

Sherds recovered from beneath torba *floors provide relative dating.*

While radiocarbon can give us absolute dates, three principles developed by geologists were equally applicable to archaeological material, providing relative dates – association, stratigraphy, and typology. Of these, the most important is stratigraphy.

If one undisturbed layer lies on top of another, it must be of more recent date. It may contain earlier material brought in from elsewhere, but again, repeated observations will probably prevent mistakes. Best of all is a series of superimposed layers, as found at Skorba, which provided confirmation, with minor correction, of Evans's sequence, based on typology.

While stratigraphy is invaluable for sorting phases into order, it is also very helpful in extending the information given by the often very few carbon dates.

Simpler than the multi-phase sequence at Skorba (p.58) was the stratigraphy Zammit found at Tarxien, illustrated schematically below. As early as 1915, this established clearly the two major periods of Maltese prehistory.

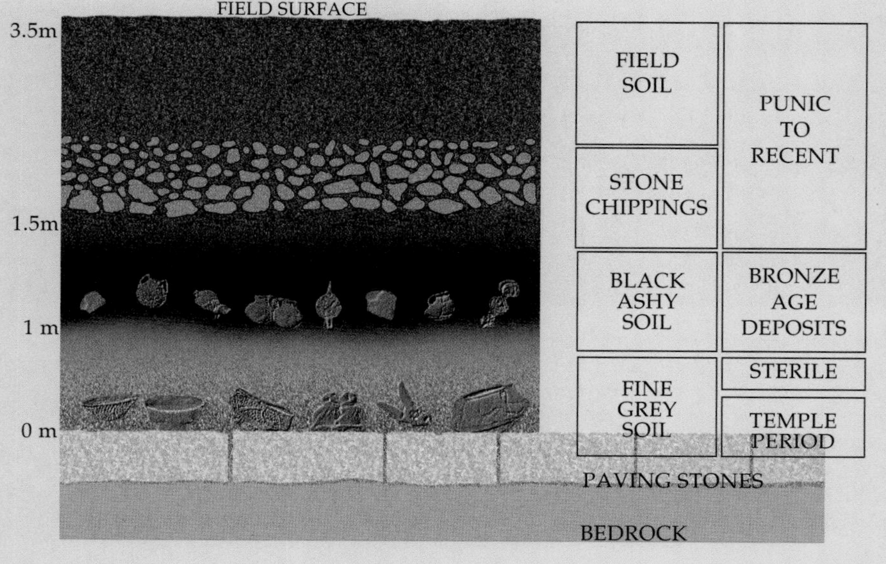

RADIOCARBON DATING

^{14}C, the radioactive isotope of ^{12}C, is produced in the atmosphere by cosmic radiation and is taken up by all living organisms.

On death, however, ^{14}C decays at a known, fixed rate, and by measuring the proportions of the two isotopes on samples recovered by archaeology, the lapse of time since death can be calculated. When samples of wood dated by counting the tree-rings were analysed, a serious discrepancy was discovered but could be corrected by comparing the readings from the samples under test against those of known age.

By this calibration, accurate dates can now be obtained. On the one hand, these are only in the form of statistical probabilities, as shown by the ± figure which accompanies each. The true date has a 67 per cent chance of lying within that bracket, or a 95 per cent chance of falling within twice that limit. On the other hand, if the sample is uncontaminated and correctly associated with the archaeological material, the date is a strictly objective one, immune from archaeological fashion.

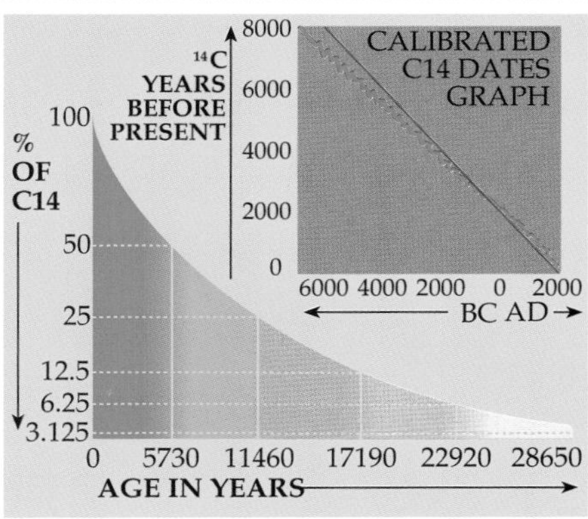

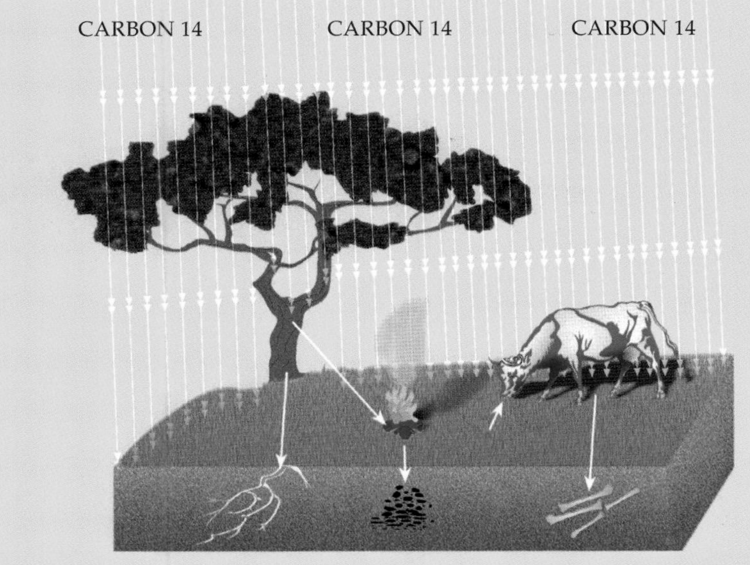

THE NATIONAL MUSEUM OF ARCHAEOLOGY

The Auberge de Provence, built by the Knights of Malta on the north side of what is now Republic Street in Valletta, became the home of the National Museum in 1958. The entrance hall and, even more, the elaborately frescoed dining hall on the first floor, give a good idea of the building's original magnificence. Now it houses the islands' principal archaeological collections, together with offices of Heritage Malta, stores, a library, workrooms, and the like.

After turning right from the ticket desk, the room on the left sets the scene and recounts the story, as retold in chapter 1 here, down to the appearance of the temples. Note the careful reconstruction of a rock-cut tomb, the obsidian cores, and the Red Skorba figurines, forerunners of the Temple Period statuary.

A passageway beyond this has photographs of the Hypogeum of Ħal Saflieni and models of temples.

The main hall on this floor is devoted to temple carvings, particularly the giant statue and altar blocks from Tarxien. These are the originals, brought indoors to protect them from the weather. They give a startling impression of the artistic skill and sophistication of the temple builders.

In the next room are representations of animals and the temple models, with the next two rooms housing the remarkable human statuary, in an extraordinary range of scales. Of particular note are the 'Sleeping Lady' of Saflieni and the Venus of Ħaġar Qim and other 'fat ladies' from the same site.

The Tarxien Room includes most of the decorated blocks from that site, together with photographs of their discovery in Zammit's excavations of 1915-17.

The first Human Figure Room displays most of the temple 'fat lady' statues. These two cases have the seated and standing figures from Ħaġar Qim (see also p.98).

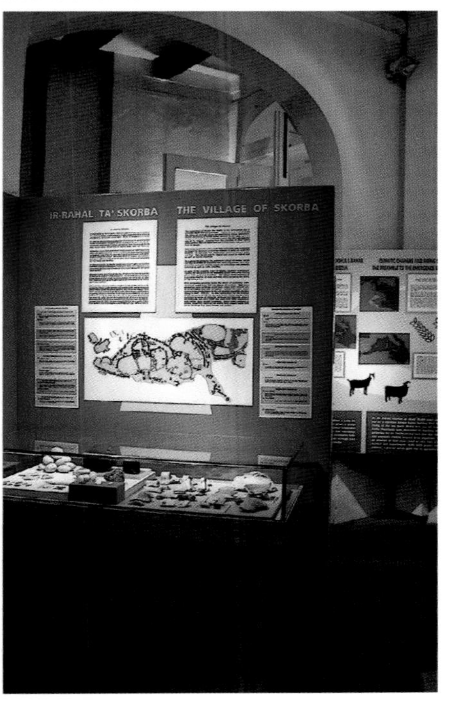

The last room in this wing has a case of Temple Period pottery, which does scant justice to the remarkable skills of the Maltese prehistoric potters. Also displayed are tools of flint and obsidian, beads, and other ornaments.

Rooms upstairs are planned to house the Museum's collections from the Bronze Age, Phoenician-Punic, Roman-Paleochristian, medieval and early modern (till the 16th century) material.

While the temples can be appreciated only in visits to the sites themselves, the personal possessions and ritual paraphernalia housed here bring us closer to the men and women who built and worshipped in them.

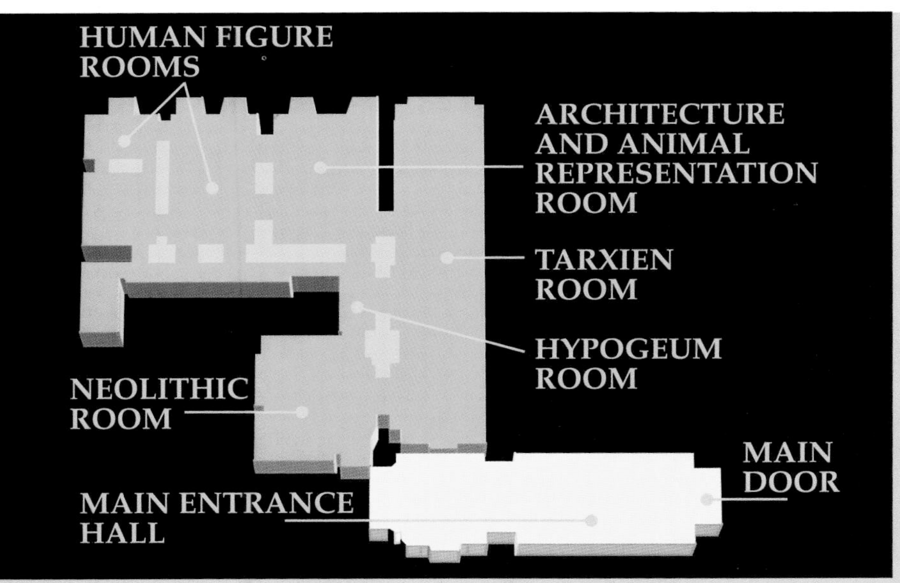

GLOSSARY

Betyl: A small free-standing stone, usually of circular section, assumed on the evidence of better documented examples common in the Near East to be an aniconic (non-representational) image of a deity.

Bronze Age: That period of the past when the extraction and working of copper and its alloy bronze had been mastered, these replacing stone for the making of tools and, more dramatically, weapons. In Malta, it covers the Tarxien Cemetery, Borġ in-Nadur, and Baħrija phases, though by the time of the last, some iron may already have been entering the islands.

Carination: A sharp break in angle in the profile of a pot, leaving a projecting ridge.

Chert: Chemically and geologically very similar to flint, but having a rather coarser structure, it is inferior to flint and obsidian for flaking. It is, however, locally available.

Collective burial: The practice of placing the dead within a re-openable chamber, successive burials joining earlier ones, often after the bones of the latter had been pushed to the back or thrown out altogether.

Corbel: A block of stone projecting further from the face of a wall than the one in the course beneath. A single such block could support an arch or timber beam. A whole row of corbel blocks would constitute a string course. Where successive courses of corbel blocks gradually and increasingly encroach on and finally close over a circular space, it is called a corbel, or beehive, vault.

Cremation: The practice of burning the dead and burying only their ashes.

Emmer: A primitive variety of wheat, amongst the first cultivated and still grown in some remote areas of the world. Botanically *Triticum dicoccum*.

Flint: A siliceous stone forming in chalk or in limestone. Its hardness and lack of grain make it very suitable for flaking into tools. Not being found locally, it had to be imported. See also p.53.

Libation hole: A vertical hole piercing a paving slab, assumed to be to allow liquid offerings (libations), to pass through, to soak away to underworld gods or ancestors.

Megalith: A block of stone used in building requiring at least two, and often many more, men to move it into position.

Menhir: An isolated standing stone, usually of large size.

Necropolis: Complex or extensive cemetery, literally 'city of the dead'.

Neolithic: That period of the past when societies depended primarily on raising crops and domesticated stock for their subsistence, using some ground stone tools in addition to flaked ones.

Ochre: An iron oxide occurring naturally, though not in Malta, employed as pigment for its bright red colour, with an added significance as symbolic of blood and life. A yellow variety was also used although less highly prized.

Offering bowl: A common shape of pot in the Tarxien phase having a markedly concave, vertical neck, a sharp carination, a shallow open body, and a small flat base. It usually has a single vertical nose-bridge handle with a D-shaped nib opposite, both set above the carination. That it was used for making offerings is suggested by its frequency within the temples, but remains unproven. (p.53).

Oracle hole: A horizontal hole through a temple wall slab. Its use, albeit uncertain, is discussed on p.111.

Orthostat: A slab of stone set with its longest axis vertical, usually with its face, i.e. its second longest dimension, exposed in the line of the wall.

Palaeolithic: That period of the past when societies were dependent on hunting and food-gathering for their subsistence, and used only flaked stone or bone for their tools. Not yet securely attested for Malta.

Potsherd, sherd, or shard: A broken fragment of pottery.

Quern: A slab of hard stone, commonly oval or rectangular and usually slightly concave, on which grain was ground to flour with the help of a smaller hard stone or rubber.

Slingstone: A biconical carved stone or natural oval pebble hurled as a missile with the help of a cord or thong sling. Actually some stones of this form found in the temples are too large to have been thrown in this way and may have had some other function.

Stele, pl. stelae: Standing stone slab or pillar, often with carved decoration or inscription, usually set above a grave.

Trilithon: Three large stones, a horizontal one supported at its ends by two vertical ones.

V-perforation: Two holes drilled obliquely into a flat surface, meeting at their tips. Large examples are found in temple door jambs to hold screens, smaller ones in shell buttons to allow them to be attached to a cloth or garment.

Other topics are discussed in detail elsewhere:

RECOMMENDED READING:

T. Zammit, *Prehistoric Malta, The Tarxien Temples* (Oxford, 1930).

J.D. Evans, The Prehistoric Culture-Sequence in the Maltese Archipelago, *Proceedings of the Prehistoric Society* (1953), 41-95.

J.D. Evans, The "Dolmens" of Malta and the Origins of the Tarxien Cemetery Culture, *PPS* (1956), 85-101.

J.D. Evans, *Malta* (London, 1959).

J.D. Evans, *The Prehistoric Antiquities of the Maltese Islands* (London, 1971).

D.H. Trump, The Later Prehistory of Malta *PPS* (1961), 253-62.

D.H. Trump, *Skorba*. Reports of the Research Committee of the Society of Antiquaries of London, XXII (Oxford, 1966).

D.H. Trump, *Malta: an Archaeological Guide* (London, 1972; third edition, Malta, 2000).

D.H. Trump, *Radiocarbon dates from Malta* Accordia Research Papers, vi (1995-6), p.173-7.

C. Renfrew, *Before Civilization* (London, 1973), 147-66.

A. Bonanno, The Archaeology of Gozo from Prehistoric to Arab Times (chapter from *Gozo, The Roots of an Island*, Malta, 1990).

A. Bonanno, *Malta, An Archaeological Paradise*, (Malta 1991; 1997).

C. Malone, S. Stoddart, A. Bonanno, T. Gouder, D. Trump, Mortuary ritual of 4th millennium BC Malta: the Żebbuġ period chambered tomb from the Brochtorff Circle at Xagħra (Gozo), *PPS* (1995) 303-46.

ACKNOWLEDGMENTS:

Dr Louis Galea
Minister of Education
Mr Anthony Pace
Director of Museums
Mr Nathaniel Cutajar
Curator
National Museum of Archaeology
Mrs Suzannah Depasquale
Assistant Curator
National Museum of Archaeology
Mr Mark Anthony Mifsud
Assistant Curator
National Museum of Archaeology
Mr Pierre Bonello
Graphic Designer
National Museum of Archaeology
Mrs Josian Bonello
Graphic Designer
National Museum of Archaeology
Mr Mario Coleiro
National Museum of Archaeology
Mr Charles Borg, Museum Officer,
National Museum of Archaeology

The 'Discover Road Map of Malta and Gozo' (maltamap.com) was used as reference to the site maps.

PHOTO CREDITS:

David Trump:
Pg. 10 bottom far left; Pg.29; Pg.32; Pg.59; Pg.60 bottom; Pg.61 right; Pg.77 bottom; Pg.87; Pg.117 top; Pg.206; Pg.238; Pg.241 bottom; Pg.254; Pg.265 bottom; Pg.308 top.

Midsea Books/Inklink:
Pg.53 bottom: Pg.64 left; Pg.65 right; Pg.84; Pg.96; Pg.99 bottom; Pg.117 bottom; Pg.134-135; Pgs.180-1; Pgs.284-5;

National Museum of Archaeology:
Pg.164 right; Pg.286; Pg.287 bottom; Pg.273; Pg.300; Pg.304, Pg.305, Pg.306 all; Pg.307 all;

National Library:
Pg.4; Pg.176 both, Pg.306

A

B

C

D

E

F

G

H

I

J

K

L

M

T

U

V

W

X

Z

Malta's Living Heritage Series is produced by
Midsea Books Ltd in collaboration with;

and with the support of:

The Ministry of Finance

Malta's Living Heritage
Edited by Louis J. Scerri

MALTA: PREHISTORY AND TEMPLES
First Published in Malta in 2002
Second Edition Published in 2004

Midsea Books Ltd

ISBN 99909-93-93-9 Hardback
ISBN 99909-93-94-7 Paperback

Text D.H. Trump

Illustrations by Inklink, Firenze

Scanning: Scancraft (Malta) Ltd

Printed and bound by Poligrafici Calderara S.p.A., Bologna, Italy